THE GIFTS OF CHRIST

By

Derek R Aylward

For the broken in spirit
who are still searching for the goodness...

May you discover
that love was closer than you ever imagined.

Why This Book Exists...

There's a quiet question most people carry, even if
they don't say it out loud:

Is this really it... or is there more?

We build, we strive, we search.
We reach for success, for peace, for meaning—
hoping that somewhere along the way, life will
finally feel... full.

If you've ever felt like there's more to life than what
you've been shown—
you're not wrong.

And you're not alone.

This is an invitation
to discover what has been there all along...

The Gifts Of Christ

By Derek R. Aylward

Published by Body of Christ Creative
bodyofchrist.online

Printed and distributed by IngramSpark.

First published in Australia, 2026

For more resources, teachings, and related works, visit bodyofchrist.online

THE GIFTS OF CHRIST

INTRODUCTION

Why This Book Was Written and the Journey Ahead

There are few subjects in the modern church that stir more hunger, hope, confusion, argument, and caution than spiritual gifts.

Some believers have been taught to avoid them. Others have been taught to chase them. Some have been strengthened by genuine grace carried beautifully. Others have been bruised by real gifts carried through immature vessels. Some have watched titles become heavier than love. Others have quietly carried grace for years without being recognized, because their part did not fit the visible mold.

This book was written to help bring clarity, safety, maturity, and beauty back to that conversation.

It is not written to create suspicion around the gifts.
It is not written to flatten every grace into sameness.
It is not written to build another ladder of spiritual status.

It is written because the gifts of Christ are real, the Body still needs them, and grace must be carried in the nature of the One who gave it.

The aim of this book is not merely to help the reader identify categories.

The deeper aim is to understand the source, purpose, stewardship, and safe environment of spiritual grace in the Body. This is not simply a book about gifts. It is a book about how grace functions under Christ.

This book also belongs inside a larger building project.

Living the Very Good Life helps us build the house.

The Book of Christ helps us see the life.

The Doctrine of Christ helps us lay the foundation.

The Body of Christ shows how that house becomes a living spiritual home filled with shared life under Christ.

The Gifts of Christ helps us understand how the house is furnished, governed, and made livable by grace.
That is the line of the build.

Because gifts do not exist in isolation. They must be understood in the light of Christ as Head, governed by God's love, stabilized by the doctrine of Christ, discerned within the spiritual landscape, and carried for the strengthening of the Body.

The church does not merely need more gifted people.
It needs safer people.
Truer people.
Mature people.
Humble people.
People who understand that grace is not a performance, but a trust.

This book was written to address one of the great tensions in the modern church: real gifts carried by immature vessels.

It also speaks into platform without formation, fear of the Spirit, confusion around leadership, neglect of hidden parts, misuse of power, lack of discernment, and the absence of love as the governing environment of grace.

Many believers have either been wounded by spiritual dysfunction or starved by spiritual neglect.

Some have reacted to excess by shutting down. Others have reacted to dryness by chasing anything that feels alive. But both paths can miss the deeper way.

The answer is not to despise the gifts.
The answer is not to idolize the gifts.
The answer is not to fear the Spirit.
The answer is not to abandon discernment.

The answer is to bring the whole conversation back under Christ, under truth, under love, and inside the life of a healthy Body.

What This Book Is Addressing

This book addresses spiritual gifts as part of a larger living reality.

It asks:

Who gives the gifts?
What is grace?
What nature makes grace safe?
How does fruit protect function?
Why does inner formation matter before visible ministry?
How do the major New Testament gift frameworks fit together?
Why do visible and hidden graces both matter?
How should grace be stewarded?
And why must every gift remain under the government of love?

This is why the book moves carefully.

Before we talk about visible expressions, we establish the ground.
Before we identify function, we examine fruit.
Before we celebrate gifting, we strengthen formation.
Before we discuss leadership, we understand equipping.
Before we admire visibility, we honor hidden supply.
And before we end with knowledge, we return to stewardship, integration, and flow.

The Objective of This Book

The objective is to help the reader understand that spiritual gifts begin with Christ the Giver, not the ego of the receiver.

Grace is not merely a label. It is the divine influence on the heart and the reflection in the life. That influence must be carried with fruit, character, discernment, humility, doctrine, faithfulness, and love.

This book aims to help the reader distinguish the major New Testament gift frameworks without turning them into theological soup. It also aims to restore honor to the quieter graces that often carry the Body when no one is clapping.

The goal is not to make the reader more impressed with gifting.

It is to make the reader more grounded in God's love, In Christ.

The Desired Outcome

By the end of this book, the hope is not simply that the reader can name more categories.

The hope is that the reader becomes less drawn to hype, less intimidated by spiritual language, less impressed by title alone, and more anchored in Christ as Head.

The hope is that the reader becomes more discerning without becoming suspicious, more humble about their own measure, more honoring of the measure in others, and more faithful with what has been placed in their hands.

In simple terms, the desired outcome is this:

that the reader would stop asking only, "What gift do I have?" and begin asking, "How can what Christ has given me become safe, fruitful, and beautiful in His Body?"

That is a better question.

And it leads to a healthier church.

The Journey Through This Book

This book unfolds in eight chapters. Each chapter builds on the one before it, moving from worldview, to safety, to formation, to function, to stewardship, and finally back into integration under Christ.

1. THE GROUND THE GIFTS GROW IN

God's love, In Christ, the doctrine, the Body, the spiritual landscape

This opening chapter establishes the spiritual environment in which true gifting makes sense. Before discussing categories, the reader must understand the soil: God's love, Christ as Head, the doctrine of Christ, the Body of Christ, and the wider spiritual landscape. This is the worldview chapter.

2. THE FRUIT REVEALS THE ROOT

The fruit of the Spirit as the trustworthy evidence of true connection

Before outward gifting is identified, inward evidence must be examined. Fruit reveals whether the root is healthy. This is the safety chapter, keeping the reader from chasing power without nature.

3. THE FOUNDATIONAL GRACES OF THE SPIRIT

The inner building blocks of spiritual maturity that prepare a believer to carry all other gifts well

Using 2 Peter 1:5–7, this chapter explores faith, virtue, knowledge, temperance, patience, godliness, brotherly kindness, and charity as inner graces that help stabilize the believer. This is the formation chapter—the sapling growing into a tree strong enough to shelter others.

4. THE GIFTS SET IN THE CHURCH

1 Corinthians 12:28 gifts explained and distinguished

This chapter explores the gifts Paul says God has "set in the church": apostles, prophets, teachers, miracles, healings, helps, governments, and tongues. This is the first major function chapter, giving a clear Pauline framework without turning the subject into theological soup.

5. THE ASCENSION GIFTS OF CHRIST

Ephesians 4 gifts explained as equipping grace

This chapter clarifies apostles, prophets, evangelists, pastors, and teachers as equipping graces given by Christ for the maturing of the saints and the building of the Body. These are not titles of spiritual rank, but graces of responsibility and service.

6. THE OTHER GRACES OF THE BODY

Romans 12 and broader gifts, practical capacities, hidden strengths

This chapter broadens the reader's vision beyond the most visible gifts, exploring service, exhortation, giving, mercy, leadership, hospitality, intercession, creativity, music, and other practical capacities. This is the hidden supply chapter, where we honor the people who quietly carry tables, tears, and truth.

7. THE GIFTS ARE GIVEN TO BE USED

Stewardship, faithfulness, heart, eternal reward, overcomer mindset

This chapter brings the gifts into personal responsibility. What God gives must be stewarded. This is the activation chapter: use it, grow it, steward it, do not bury it, do not compare it, do not idolize it, and do not neglect it.

8. THE GIVER, THE HEAD, AND THE FLOW

Summary, re-anchor, integration, next steps into BOC

The final chapter gathers the whole book back into God's love, Christ as Head, the ministry of the Holy Spirit, and the believer's place in the living flow of the Body. It does not end with categories. It ends with the Giver, the Head, and the Flow.

Closing Invitation

If this book does its job well, it will not simply help you admire spiritual gifting from a distance. It will help you see that grace is meant to be carried well.

So before we begin naming gifts, we begin where all healthy spiritual life begins: with the ground.

Because before we ask what the gift is,
we must understand the soil it is growing in.

CHAPTER 1. THE GROUND THE GIFTS GROW IN

God's love, In Christ, the doctrine, the Body, the spiritual landscape

Before we discuss gifts, we must understand the ground they grow in.

Core Scripture

Ephesians 4:7 (KJV)
"But unto every one of us is given grace according to the measure of the gift of Christ."

Introduction

This opening chapter establishes the spiritual environment in which all true gifting makes sense.

Before we begin naming categories, distinguishing functions, or exploring how grace moves through the Body, we must first understand the soil: God's love, Christ as Head, the doctrine of Christ, the life of the Body, and the broader spiritual landscape in which grace must be discerned and carried.

This is the worldview chapter.

Before discussing gifts, the reader must understand the ground.
Before examining function, the reader must understand nature.
Before identifying grace, the reader must understand the Giver.

This chapter puts **God's love** and **In Christ** first—exactly where they belong.

Because if the ground is wrong, even real grace can be misunderstood.
But if the ground is right, what grows from it can be carried with clarity, humility, and trust.

In This Chapter

1. GIFTS BEGIN WITH THE GIVER, NOT THE RECEIVER

Grace is not self-generated. Every true gift begins in Christ, not in human ambition, personality, or spiritual performance.

2. GOD'S LOVE IS THE SOIL TRUE GIFTS GROW IN

A real gift may be present, but only God's love creates the kind of environment where grace matures safely and reflects the nature of Christ.

3. THE DOCTRINE OF CHRIST GIVES GIFTS THEIR FRAME

Without sound foundation, spiritual function can become sincere but unstable. The doctrine of Christ gives grace direction, order, and maturity.

4. GIFTS ONLY MAKE FULL SENSE INSIDE THE BODY

No gift exists for isolated self-expression. Grace is given to supply, strengthen, and build the living Body of Christ.

5. THE SPIRITUAL LANDSCAPE MUST BE READ RIGHTLY

Not everything spiritual is the Spirit. Gifts must be understood within the wider reality of spiritual influence, discernment, and life in the Spirit.

Chapter Anchor

The gift is not the beginning—Christ is.
The goal is not visibility—it is faithful supply.
And the safest place to begin is where all true grace begins:

with the Giver, under God's love, In Christ.

Bridge

So before we ask what the gifts are, we must first ask where they begin. Because grace is never self-made.
It is received. And that means the first thing this book must settle is simple, but foundational:

The gift is not the beginning—Christ is.

SECTION 1
GIFTS BEGIN WITH THE GIVER, NOT THE RECEIVER

Before a gift can be understood, the Giver must be seen.

Core Scripture

"But unto every one of us is given grace according to the measure of the gift of Christ." Ephesians 4:7 (KJV)

Section Introduction

The first thing this book must settle is simple, but it changes everything:

the gift is not the beginning — Christ is.

If that truth is missed, the rest of the conversation will drift almost immediately.
The church has often spent enormous energy trying to identify gifts, define gifts, rank gifts, desire gifts, imitate gifts, platform gifts, protect gifts, and sometimes even fear gifts—while quietly forgetting the Person from whom all true grace comes.

That is where confusion begins.

Because once the gift becomes the starting point, the soul naturally moves toward comparison, ambition, insecurity, performance, self-importance, and spiritual vanity.

But when Christ remains the starting point, the entire atmosphere changes. What was once a competition becomes stewardship. What was once ego becomes gratitude. What was once pressure becomes peace. What was once fascination with power becomes reverence for the One who gives it.

This matters because **spiritual gifts are not random spiritual accessories.**
They are not decorations hung on impressive personalities.
They are not badges of superiority.
They are not proof that someone is more loved, more chosen, or more valuable than someone else.

They are **measures of grace**—distributed by Christ, for the good of His Body.

And that means the first question is never merely:

"What is my gift?"

The first question is:

"What kind of Christ gives gifts like this, and why?"

That is the beam we must set first.

Because if the foundation is wrong, the whole structure leans.

1. EVERY TRUE GIFT BEGINS IN CHRIST

Paul does not say that grace begins in personal desire, temperament, natural charisma, or spiritual hunger.
He says:

"Unto every one of us is given grace according to the measure of the gift of Christ."

That one sentence is weight-bearing.

It tells us several things immediately.

First, **grace is given.**
It is not self-generated.
It is not manufactured by discipline alone.
It is not earned by intensity.
It is not secured by personality strength.

Second, **the measure belongs to Christ.**
The distribution is His.
The wisdom is His.
The timing is His.
The purpose is His.

Third, **what is given is not detached from Him.**
It is "the gift **of** Christ."
Not merely a gift *from* Christ in a casual sense, but a grace that still carries the mark, intention, and nature of the One who gave it.

This is why spiritual gifting can never be understood correctly if Christ is treated like the doorway we passed through instead of the living Head we remain joined to.

The gift does not make sense outside the Giver.

A branch may carry fruit, but the fruit only exists because the branch remains connected to the life of the vine. In the same way, a believer may function in grace, but that grace is only healthy, trustworthy, and fruitful when it remains consciously rooted in Christ Himself.

This is why Paul says elsewhere:

"Having then gifts differing according to the grace that is given to us..." (Romans 12:6)

Notice the order again.

Grace first.
Gift second.

That is not accidental.
The gift is not the source.
The grace is not the servant of the gift.
The grace is the life-flow that makes the gift possible.

And grace itself is not an abstract force floating in the air.
In the New Testament, grace is deeply personal.
It is the generous, active, empowering outflow of Christ toward His people.

So before we ever discuss manifestations, ministries, functions, offices, hidden helps, visible leadership, or the mature order of the Body, we must anchor the heart here:

Every true gift begins in Christ because every true gift is an expression of His grace.

If that remains clear, the soul stays smaller.
The gratitude stays larger.
And the gift remains safer in the hands of the one carrying it.

2. WHAT YOU RECEIVED WAS NEVER MEANT TO BECOME YOUR IDENTITY

One of the quietest dangers in any conversation about gifting is this:

People begin to mistake what they have **received** for who they **are**.

This is where subtle distortion often begins.

A person receives a grace, and over time that grace can become tangled with self-image.

The teacher begins to need being seen as wise.
The prophetic person begins to need being seen as spiritually sharp.
The leader begins to need being needed.
The helper begins to quietly build identity around indispensability.
The one who carries visible grace begins to fear obscurity.
The one who carries hidden grace begins to resent invisibility.

And all of that can happen while the gift itself is still real.

That is why Paul asks a devastatingly simple question:

"...what hast thou that thou didst not receive?" (1 Corinthians 4:7)

That verse cuts clean across the grain of human pride.

What do you have that you did not receive?

Not your breath.
Not your mind.

Not your opportunities.
Not your open doors.
Not your spiritual capacity.
Not your grace.
Not your measure.
Not your timing.
Not even your hunger for God, if we are honest, is fully self-originating.

At every level, we are receivers before we are stewards.

And that means the right posture toward gifting is **never possession.**

It is **humble stewardship.**

This is not a small correction.
It is a foundational one.

Because once a gift becomes identity, it becomes emotionally dangerous.
Anything that threatens the gift now feels like it threatens the self.
Correction feels like rejection.
Silence feels like neglect.
Another person's grace feels like competition.
Seasons of hiddenness feel like death.
Loss of platform feels like loss of worth.

But if the gift is received—not owned—then the soul can breathe.

You are not the source of what you carry. You are the vessel. And vessels are safest when they remember what fills them.

This is one reason the healthiest people in the Body are often the ones who can carry real grace without constantly needing it to be recognized.

They know the gift matters, but they also know **Christ matters more.**

That is freedom.

And that freedom protects both the vessel and the Body.

3. THE FATHER IS STILL THE SOURCE OF EVERY GOOD THING

James gives us another framing line that keeps the whole structure honest:

"Every good gift and every perfect gift is from above, and cometh down from the Father of lights..." (James 1:17)

That means gifting must never be discussed in a way that makes heaven feel mechanical.

The source is not "the system."
The source is not "the flow" in an impersonal sense.
The source is not "the gift realm."

The source is **the Father**.

This matters because when people become fascinated with gifts while losing sight of the Father's nature, the conversation can become strangely cold, technical, or sensational. The focus shifts from love to power, from relationship to function, from trust to display.

But the New Testament never allows us to separate grace from the character of God.

The Father is the source.
Christ is the giver and distributor within the Body.
The Spirit is the one who manifests and empowers according to divine wisdom.

It is relational at its core.

It comes from love.
It moves through Christ.
It is carried by the Spirit of Truth.
And it is meant to bless people, not inflate personalities.

That is why the nature of the Giver matters as much as the
reality of the gift.

If the Father is generous, then gifts are expressions of
generosity.
If Christos is self-giving, then gifts are meant to serve.
If the Spirit glorifies Christ, then true manifestation will not
ultimately glorify man.

This is one reason why the spiritual life can become
distorted when people talk constantly about power but
rarely about the nature of God.

Power detached from nature becomes dangerous.
Grace detached from character becomes unstable.
Function detached from love becomes mechanical.
Revelation detached from humility becomes brittle.

So before we ever move deeper into categories of gifting, we
need to hear this clearly:

**Every true gift carries the fingerprint of the
Father's goodness.**

If what is being carried is moving people away from trust,
humility, safety, truth, and the likeness of Christ, then
something in the carrying—or perhaps even in the claim
itself—must be examined.

Because the source of what is truly from above is not
confusion.

The source is GOOD.

4. CHRIST GIVES DIFFERENT MEASURES ON PURPOSE

One of the quickest ways the soul gets bruised in conversations about gifting is through comparison.

Why do they carry that and I do not?
Why are they more visible?
Why does their grace seem stronger?
Why does their role seem weightier?
Why does their impact look larger?
Why does my part seem small?

But Scripture gives us a stabilizing truth:

Christ distributes different measures intentionally.

Paul does not say everyone receives the same expression.
He says grace is given ***according to the measure of the gift of Christ.***

That means difference is not a design flaw.

It is part of the design.

And Jesus Himself illustrates this in the parable of the talents:

"...who called his own servants, and delivered unto them his goods... and unto one he gave five talents, to another two, and to another one; to every man according to his several ability..." (Matthew 25:14–15)

Notice what was delivered:

his goods.

Not theirs.

And notice the distribution:

different measures.

Not because one mattered and another did not, but because the Master knew what He was doing.

This is where many believers need inner healing.

Because the soul often reads difference as inequality of worth.

But heaven does not.

Difference of measure is not difference of value.

The eye is not superior because it is visible.
The hand is not more loved because it is active.
The heart is not less important because it is hidden.
The ligament is not less glorious because nobody applauds it.

The question is never:

"Do I have what they have?"

The question is:

"Am I faithfully carrying what Christ has placed in my hands?"

That question heals comparison.

It also restores peace.

Because the kingdom is not built by everyone trying to become the same thing.
It is built by each part receiving, honoring, and faithfully stewarding what has been given.

This is one reason comparison is so destructive in the Body. It does not merely create emotional pain—it blinds people to their own assignment. A person obsessed with another person's measure often becomes negligent with their own.

And that is how grace gets buried.

Not because it was absent.

But because it was dishonored through comparison.

So we must say it plainly:

Christ does not mis-measure His Body.

He does not accidentally overbuild one part and forget another.
He does not distribute grace randomly.
He does not create a Body where only the visible parts matter.

He gives differently because the Body needs diversity.
He gives wisely because the Body needs function.
He gives purposefully because the Body is meant to grow.

And that means peace begins when comparison ends.

5. THE FIRST WORK OF MATURITY IS GRATITUDE, NOT SELF-IMPORTANCE

If all true gifting begins in Christ...
If every good gift comes from above...
If what we have was received...
If different measures are intentional...

...then the first right response to gifting is not excitement alone.

It is **gratitude.**

Not false humility.
Not gift denial.
Not pretending grace is unimportant.
Not shrinking back from what God has truly placed in you.

But gratitude.

Deep, stable, reverent gratitude.

Because gratitude keeps the heart soft.

It allows a person to carry real grace without becoming swollen by it.
It allows a person to serve visibly without needing worship.
It allows a person to remain hidden without becoming bitter.
It allows a person to grow in grace without turning growth into status.

Gratitude is often the first sign that a gift is still resting in the right atmosphere.

This is why the mature believer does not merely ask:

"What can I do?"

They ask:

"What has Christ entrusted to me, and how can I carry it in a way that honors Him and strengthens His people?"

That is a different spirit entirely.

It shifts the whole conversation away from self-display and toward stewardship.

And that is where this book must begin.

Not with spiritual ambition.
Not with fascination.
Not with title.
Not with hierarchy.
Not with speculation.

But with reverence.

Because the moment we forget the Giver, the gift becomes vulnerable to misuse.
The moment we remember the Giver, the gift begins to find its proper place.

And that proper place is never self-exaltation.

It is **edification in love.**

That is where the whole book is headed.

But before we speak of how gifts function, we must understand the atmosphere they were always meant to live in.

Because Christ does not merely give gifts.

He gives them inside the logic of His own nature.

And that means the next beam must be laid carefully:

not only do gifts begin with the Giver—

they only remain healthy in the environment of His love.

Guided Discovery

1. **When you think about spiritual gifts, do you instinctively begin with the gift—or with Christ as the Giver?**
   If your first instinct is function, role, or visibility, what might that reveal about where your attention has been trained?
2. **Have you ever subtly tied your worth to what you carry, what you do well, or how others respond to your grace?**
   Where might Christ be inviting you to separate identity from assignment so your soul can breathe again?
3. **Are there places where comparison has made you overlook, minimize, or bury what Christ has actually entrusted to you?**
   What would gratitude look like if you fully honored your measure instead of measuring yourself against someone else's?

Bridge Into Section 2

If the first truth is that **every true gift begins with Christ**, then the second truth must follow close behind:

Christ never gives gifts outside the nature of God's love.

Grace does not grow in ambition.
It does not mature in ego.
It does not become trustworthy in comparison, pressure, or spiritual vanity.

It grows in the atmosphere of the One who gave it.

Which means before we explore the gifts themselves any further, we must establish the deeper environment they were always meant to live in:

SECTION 2
GOD'S LOVE IS THE SOIL TRUE GIFTS GROW IN

A real gift may be present, but only God's love creates the kind of environment where grace matures safely and reflects the nature of Christ.

Core Scripture

Exodus 34:6 (KJV)
"And the Lord passed by before him, and proclaimed, The Lord, The Lord God, merciful and gracious, longsuffering, and abundant in goodness and truth."

Section Introduction

A gift may be real and still not yet be safe.

That may sound strong this early in the book, but it must be said now, because if it is not said now, the rest of the conversation can drift toward fascination with function while quietly neglecting the nature that makes function trustworthy.

The church has often learned how to identify gifts before it has learned how to measure the spirit in which those gifts are being carried.

We notice power.
We notice confidence.
We notice accuracy.
We notice movement.
We notice outcomes.

But heaven does not first ask, **"Was something impressive present?"**
Heaven asks, **"What kind of nature is carrying it?"**

This is why the soil matters.

A seed may be alive, but the soil determines what kind of growth it can sustain.
A gift may be genuine, but the environment around that gift determines whether it matures into something beautiful, stable, and life-giving—or whether it becomes distorted by ego, pressure, insecurity, performance, or spiritual immaturity.

And the soil true gifts grow in is not hype.
Not intensity.
Not charisma.
Not platform.
Not spiritual vocabulary.

The soil true gifts grow in is God's love.

Not love as sentiment.
Not love as softness.
Not love as vague kindness without truth.

God's love.
The kind revealed in the nature of God Himself.

When the Lord declared His own nature before Moses, He
did not begin with power.
He did not begin with thunder.
He did not begin with display.

He began with character.

Merciful.
Gracious.
Longsuffering.
Abundant in goodness and truth.

That is not a side note in Scripture.
That is the plumb line.

That is the line in the sand.

If we are going to talk about gifts, ministries,
manifestations, discernment, order, maturity, and the life of
the Body, then we must establish from the beginning that
everything must be measured **in God's love, In Christ**—
that is, in the anointed presence and flow of God's love like
Jesus.

If a gift is being carried, we must ask:

- Is it **merciful**, or is it harsh?
- Is it **gracious**, or is it demanding?
- Is it **longsuffering**, or is it impatient and pressuring
  people?
- Is it abundant in **goodness**, or does it leave people
  bruised?
- Is it anchored in **truth**, or does it depend on
  manipulation, exaggeration, or fog?

And as the fuller witness of Scripture unfolds, the same measuring rod continues:

- Does it release **forgiveness**, or does it weaponize offense?
- Does it show **good judgment**, or does it confuse reaction for discernment?

This is not perfectionism.
This is direction.

None of us carry this perfectly yet.
But the pendulum cannot be swinging in the opposite direction while we still call it maturity.

Because gifts do not merely need authenticity.
They need atmosphere.

And the atmosphere where grace matures safely is the nature of God.

1. GOD REVEALS HIS NATURE BEFORE HE REVEALS HIS POWER

One of the great mistakes in spiritual culture is to treat God's power as though it can be understood apart from God's nature.

But Scripture does not allow that.

Before the gifts are explained, before ministries are listed, before the church is taught how to function together, the Bible repeatedly reveals something deeper:

Who God is...

This matters because gifts are not independent energies floating around for human use.

They are expressions of grace flowing from Christ into His
Body.

And if the source is Christ, then the nature of the source
must define the shape of the expression.

A river may flow through many channels, but the water still
carries the character of its source.

That is why Exodus 34:6 matters so deeply in a book like
this.

When God describes Himself, He gives us the climate of
heaven:

- mercy
- grace
- patience
- goodness
- truth

This is not just theology.
This is how the Kingdom feels when it touches people
rightly.

Where God is moving rightly, people may be convicted, but
they are not crushed.
They may be corrected, but they are not humiliated.
They may be stretched, but they are not manipulated.
They may be called higher, but they are not driven by fear.

This is a vital distinction.

Because many believers have encountered something called
"spiritual" that was forceful, intense, controlling, or
emotionally unsafe—and because it wore religious language,
they assumed it must have been God.

But the nature of Christ says otherwise.

The Spirit of God does not need corruption to accomplish His will.
He does not need intimidation to produce reverence.
He does not need pressure to produce surrender.

He is fully capable of being both holy **and** merciful.
Strong **and** gracious.
True **and** patient.

That is the nature of Christ.

And if the gift being carried cannot live under that nature, then even if something real is present, something is already out of alignment.

Power that cannot remain inside love is not yet safe power.

That line will matter more as this book unfolds.

2. GIFTS GROW BEST WHERE THE NATURE OF CHRIST IS HONORED

A seed can survive in poor soil for a while.

It may even sprout.

It may show signs of life.

But whether it becomes healthy, fruitful, stable, and able to endure is another matter altogether.

So it is with spiritual grace.

A person may begin to move in something genuine from God—discernment, prophecy, helps, leadership, teaching, healing, exhortation, wisdom, mercy, administration, intercession, hospitality, faith—and yet if that grace is carried in an atmosphere dominated by ego, insecurity, competition, suspicion, or performance, the growth becomes uneven.

The gift may still function.
But it will not mature cleanly.

This is where many believers become confused.

They assume that because a gift appears to work, the environment must therefore be healthy.

But fruitfulness and health are not always the same thing.

Something can still be active while already being warped.

A plant can be alive and still be stunted.
A limb can be growing and still be twisted.
A ministry can be fruitful in moments and still be relationally unsafe over time.

That is why the church must stop asking only, **"Is there a gift?"**

It must also ask, **"What kind of soil is this gift growing in?"**

Is it growing in:

- humility, or self-importance?
- mercy, or harshness?
- patience, or urgency-driven pressure?
- truth, or image management?
- forgiveness, or stored offense?
- peace, or constant emotional instability?

This is not cynicism.
This is stewardship.

God's love is not just the moral wrapper around gifts.
It is the growth medium.

It is the soil.

It is the environment in which grace becomes beautiful
instead of dangerous.

A church may admire gifted people.
But heaven is building something deeper than admiration.

Heaven is forming a Body that looks like Jesus.

And Jesus does not merely do powerful things.
He reveals the Father.

That means true gifting is never meant to merely
demonstrate ability.

It is meant to carry **the nature of Christ into human experience**.

That is the standard.

Not just manifestation.
Representation.

Not just function.
Nature.

Not just "Did something happen?"
But "Did it look and feel like the heart of God?"

3. LOVE IS NOT AN OPTIONAL VIRTUE ADDED TO GIFTS—IT IS THE SAFETY OF THE GIFTS

Many believers unconsciously treat love as though it is the "nice" chapter.

The soft chapter.
The warm chapter.
The part we get to after the real power discussion.

But Scripture does not frame it that way.

Love is not the decorative trim around spiritual life.

Love is the structural integrity.

Without it, the whole thing may still stand for a while, but it will not remain sound under weight.

This is why the church has sometimes produced gifted environments that were spiritually exciting but emotionally exhausting.

People were moved.
But not always cared for.

Impressed.
But not always shepherded.

Activated.
But not always formed.

Seen in moments.
But not always made safe enough to stay.

And when that happens, believers often become confused because they think, "But God was moving."

Perhaps He was.

But that does not automatically mean the vessel was mature, the environment was healthy, or the culture was aligned.

A gift can be present in an environment that is still under formation.

That is why love must not be treated as an optional add-on.

Love is what makes the gift safe enough to trust.

Love is what keeps discernment from becoming suspicion.
Love is what keeps prophecy from becoming performance.
Love is what keeps teaching from becoming control.
Love is what keeps leadership from becoming dependency-building.
Love is what keeps helps from becoming resentment.
Love is what keeps truth from becoming a weapon.

In other words:

**Love does not weaken spiritual function.
Love rightly governs it.**

That is a major beam in this whole book.

The more real a gift is, the more important love becomes.
Because the more influence a grace carries, the more damage it can do if carried outside the nature of Christ.

This is why immature power can wound.
This is why visible gifting can confuse people.
This is why the church needs both celebration **and** discernment.

Not because we are trying to reduce expectancy.
But because we are trying to preserve beauty.

The goal is not merely gifted people.

The goal is a trustworthy Body.

And trust grows where God's love is consistently present.

4. JESUS IS THE PERFECT PICTURE OF POWER REMAINING INSIDE LOVE

If we want to understand what safe gifting looks like, we do not begin with personalities.

We begin with Jesus.

Because in Him, power never outran nature.

He carried authority without self-exaltation.
He carried discernment without paranoia.
He carried correction without cruelty.
He carried truth without posturing.
He carried miracles without self-advertisement.
He carried holiness without losing tenderness.

He could confront Pharisees and comfort children.
He could rebuke Peter and restore Peter.
He could cleanse the temple and still weep over Jerusalem.
He could speak with authority and still wash feet.

This is what spiritual maturity looks like.

Not weakness.
Not softness without spine.
Not tolerance without truth.

But power fully governed by the nature of God.

That is what it means to live **In Christ**.

Not merely to believe certain truths about Him, but **to increasingly flow in the anointed presence of God's love** like He did.

That is why Jesus is not only the giver of gifts.
He is the pattern for how gifts are meant to be carried.

The church often studies what Jesus did.
It must also study **how He did it**.

Not just the miracle, but the manner.
Not just the authority, but the atmosphere.
Not just the outcome, but the nature.

Because the nature is the witness.

A miracle may get attention.
But the nature of Christ is what tells people heaven is truly near.

And this is the burden of this section:

If the church learns to pursue gifting without equally pursuing the nature of Christ, it may still produce activity—but it will not produce the kind of mature beauty the Father desires.

But when grace grows in the soil of God's love, something different happens.

The gift does not merely impress.

It nourishes.

It steadies.

It builds.

It protects.

It heals.

It reveals.

It begins to feel less like performance and more like home.

And that is what the Body of Christ was always meant to become.

5. THE BODY MUST LEARN TO MEASURE EVERYTHING BY THE NATURE OF GOD

If this book is going to help the church, it cannot simply teach people how to identify categories of gifting.

It must give them a measuring rod.

Because discernment without a measuring rod quickly becomes preference.
And preference dressed in spiritual language can do enormous damage.

Some people call intensity "anointing."
Some call confidence "authority."
Some call pressure "conviction."
Some call control "covering."
Some call reaction "discernment."
Some call emotional force "the Spirit."

But what if the real question is simpler and deeper?

Does it agree with the revealed nature of God?

That question has teeth.

Does this expression carry mercy?
Does it show compassion to the suffering?

Does it carry patience, or does it create pressure?
Is it rooted in loving-kindness?
Is it dependable in truth?
Does it release forgiveness?
Does it show good judgment?

This is not a formula.

It is a plumb line.

And like any plumb line, it is not there to shame the builder.
It is there to keep the wall straight.

The pendulum does not have to be perfect, but it cannot be swinging in the other direction.

That is mature discernment.

Not perfectionism.
Not suspicion.
Not idealism detached from reality.

But a sober, loving commitment to keep measuring spiritual life by the nature of Christ.

Because in the end, every grace will be accountable to the Kingdom that endures forever.

And the Kingdom that endures forever is not built on charisma.
It is not built on gifted personalities.
It is not built on moments of power divorced from character.

It is built on the nature of God.

Mercy.
Grace.
Patience.
Goodness.
Truth.

And through the wider witness of Scripture, we see the same kingdom pattern continue:

Forgiveness.
Righteous judgment.

This is the kind of environment where gifts become trustworthy.
This is the kind of environment where people can breathe.
This is the kind of environment where growth can endure.
This is the kind of environment where the Body begins to look like Jesus again.

And that is why God's love is not merely a theme in this chapter.

It is the soil everything else in this book must grow in.

Guided Discovery

1. Do you notice Power first or nature first?
If you notice power first, that does not make you wrong—it just means you may have been trained to equate visible impact with spiritual maturity. The healthier pattern is to appreciate the gift **while immediately asking what kind of spirit is carrying it**.

2. What warning signs are often missed?
Common early warning signs are pressure, self-focus, impatience, emotional instability, lack of humility, inability to receive correction, or a repeated pattern where people feel impressed in public but unsettled in private. Often the gift was real—but the soil was poor.

3. What needs re-evaluating?
Look for places where something appears spiritually effective, but does not consistently reflect mercy, patience, truth, peace, forgiveness, and good judgment. The goal is

not to become cynical. The goal is to become **lovingly accurate**.

Bridge to Section 3

If God's love is the soil true gifts grow in, then the next question becomes unavoidable:

How do we know when that soil is actually healthy?

Because it is possible to talk about love in vague language while still carrying a life that does not truly reflect Christ.

That is why the next foundation must be laid carefully.

Before we move into outward expressions of grace, we must establish the inward evidence that tells us whether the root system is sound.

Because in the Kingdom of God, **the fruit always tells the truth about the root.**

SECTION 3
THE DOCTRINE OF CHRIST GIVES GIFTS THEIR FRAME

Without sound foundation, spiritual function can become sincere but unstable. The doctrine of Christ gives grace direction, order, and maturity.

Core Scripture

Hebrews 6:1–2 (KJV)
"Therefore leaving the principles of the doctrine of Christ, let us go on unto perfection; not laying again the foundation of repentance from dead works, and of faith toward God,
Of the doctrine of baptisms, and of laying on of hands, and of resurrection of the dead, and of eternal judgment."

Section Introduction

If **Section 1** settled that gifts begin with **the Giver,** and **Section 2** settled that gifts must grow in the **soil of God's love,** then this section must now settle the next great necessity:

true grace also needs a frame.

A seed may be real.
A seed may be good.
A seed may even be alive.

But if there is no right environment...
and no right support...
and no right structure...

it can still grow crooked.

The same is true in spiritual life.

A person may carry a real measure of grace.
A person may have encountered the Spirit.
A person may even move in something that genuinely
touches others.

But if that grace is not held inside the **Doctrine of Christ**,
it can become **sincere but unstable**.

This is where much of the modern church has quietly
drifted.

Many have pursued experience without foundation.
Many have chased manifestation without formation.
Many have emphasized power without process.
Many have celebrated gifts while neglecting the very
doctrine that was meant to mature the vessel carrying them.

But the New Testament never separates these things.

Christ does not merely **give gifts**.
Christ also **forms people**.
And He forms them through truth.

The Doctrine of Christ is not dry theology for scholars.
It is not a dusty shelf of religious information.
It is not a technical category for seminary classrooms.

It is **the living framework of maturity**.

It is the spiritual architecture that keeps grace from
collapsing under its own weight.

Because a gift may attract attention...

but only sound doctrine teaches a life how to **stand**.

And if this whole chapter is about **the ground the gifts grow in**, then here we must say it plainly:

God's love is the soil.
The Doctrine of Christ is the frame.
And together, they create a life where grace can grow safely In Christ.

1. FOUNDATION IS NOT OPTIONAL

Before anything rises, something must be settled underneath it.

That is the language of Hebrews 6.

The writer does not dismiss the Doctrine of Christ as elementary because it is unimportant.
He calls it foundational because **everything built after it depends on it**.

A builder never insults the slab.

He may not stand there admiring concrete all day, but he knows this much: if the foundation is wrong, the whole house pays for it later.

The church often admires what is visible.

Gifts are visible.
Power is visible.
Influence is visible.
Words are visible.
Platforms are visible.

But foundations are usually hidden.

Repentance is hidden.
Faithfulness is hidden.
Baptismal reality is hidden.
Submission to Christ is hidden.
Resurrection hope is hidden.
Eternal accountability is hidden.

Yet hidden things carry visible things.

And when hidden things are weak, visible things eventually begin to crack.

That is why Hebrews does not say, *Skip the foundation and chase the spectacular*.

It says, in effect:

settle the foundation so maturity can actually hold.

This matters deeply for gifts.

Because gifting without foundation can produce:

- zeal without stability
- boldness without wisdom
- language without understanding
- movement without direction
- confidence without accountability
- sincerity without maturity

A person may mean well and still be structurally unsound.

That is not condemnation.

That is construction language.

And construction language is mercy when used early enough.

The Doctrine of Christ tells us that the goal is not merely to have **activity**.

The goal is to become the kind of person who can **carry grace well**.

Because heaven does not only care whether something is real.

Heaven also cares whether it is **safe to build on**.

A real gift may begin a moment.
A real foundation can sustain a life.

2. THE DOCTRINE OF CHRIST TRAINS THE INNER MAN

Many believers think doctrine means information.

But in Scripture, true doctrine is not merely meant to fill the mind.

It is meant to **shape the person**.

The Doctrine of Christ is not just a list to memorize.
It is a pattern that trains the inner life toward maturity.

Hebrews 6 gives us six foundational movements:

- repentance from dead works
- faith toward God
- the doctrine of baptisms
- laying on of hands
- resurrection of the dead
- eternal judgment

These are not random religious topics.

They are structural beams.

They form how a believer thinks, turns, trusts, receives, hopes, and lives under accountability.

Take the first one:

repentance from dead works.

That is not merely feeling sorry.

That is learning to stop building life on what cannot produce life.

That alone changes how gifts are carried.

A person who has not learned repentance may still minister, but they will often protect image over truth.

A person trained in repentance can be corrected without collapsing.

That is maturity.

Then:

faith toward God.

Not faith in self.
Not faith in gifting.
Not faith in charisma.
Not faith in atmosphere.
Not faith in emotional intensity.

Faith **toward God**.

That means the center of gravity is not the vessel—it is the Father.

That changes everything.

It keeps the soul from trying to become the source.

It keeps the gift from becoming identity.

It keeps ministry from becoming self-importance with a Bible verse attached.

Then:

the doctrine of baptisms and **laying on of hands**.

These teach that spiritual life is both personal and participatory.

There is cleansing.
There is identification.
There is impartation.
There is recognition.
There is shared life in the Body.

But these things are never meant to become mystical shortcuts around character.

And finally:

resurrection of the dead and **eternal judgment**.

Now the horizon widens.

The believer is trained to live in light of what outlasts this age.

That changes motive.

That purifies urgency.

That steadies ambition.

That humbles pride.

A person who truly lives in the light of resurrection and eternal judgment cannot casually turn grace into performance forever.

Sooner or later, eternity sobers the room.

This is why the Doctrine of Christ matters so much to gifts.

Because it does not merely tell you **what you can do**.

It teaches you **who you are becoming**.

And in the Kingdom, that is always the more important question.

**A gift may express grace in a moment.
Doctrine teaches the vessel how to live under grace over time.**

3. GIFTS NEED DIRECTION, NOT JUST ACTIVATION

There has been much emphasis in modern church culture on activation.

Activate the gift.
Stir the gift.
Impart the gift.
Release the gift.
Step out in the gift.

And there is truth in that.

Scripture absolutely speaks of stirring what God has given.
Paul told Timothy not to neglect the gift in him.
He told him to stir it up.
Grace is not meant to remain buried in fear.

But activation without direction can create movement without maturity.

A man can start a chainsaw.

That does not mean you hand him the framing plan and leave him alone near the load-bearing wall.

That, my friend, is how churches end up with a skylight where the roof used to be.

The issue is not whether something can move.

The issue is whether it knows **what it is for**.

That is what doctrine gives.

Doctrine gives:

- **context** for spiritual function
- **purpose** for spiritual expression
- **boundaries** for healthy use
- **order** for shared life
- **language** for discernment
- **process** for growth and correction

Without that, gifts can become detached from their intended aim.

Prophecy can drift into personality projection.
Teaching can drift into intellectual pride.
Leadership can drift into control.
Helps can drift into resentment.
Discernment can drift into suspicion.
Mercy can drift into enablement.
Faith can drift into presumption.

The gift may still be operating.

But the frame is warping.

That is why the Doctrine of Christ does not quench gifts.

It **protects their purpose**.

It keeps the grace connected to the Head.

It keeps the Body from mistaking intensity for maturity.

It keeps people from building entire spiritual identities around one function while neglecting the larger work of becoming like Christ.

And that is the real point:

**The goal of the gift is not merely expression.
The goal of the gift is edification under the nature of Christ.**

The Doctrine of Christ teaches a believer how to ask better questions:

Not just:

Is something happening?

But:

- Is this aligned with Christ?
- Does this reflect the nature of God's love?
- Is this producing maturity or dependency?
- Is this strengthening the Body or centralizing a personality?
- Is this helping people grow up into Christ, or merely admire the vessel?

Those are Doctrine of Christ questions.

And the church desperately needs them again.

A gift can be activated quickly.
A life is framed slowly.
The wise do not confuse the two.

4. THE MEASURING ROD IS STILL GOD'S NATURE

If gifts begin with Christ...
and if gifts must grow in God's love...
then the Doctrine of Christ must never be treated as a cold system disconnected from the nature of God.

The frame is not mechanical.

The frame is moral.

The frame is relational.

The frame is Christ-shaped.

This is where your plumb line must be driven into the ground again.

Exodus 34:6 (KJV)
"And the Lord passed by before him, and proclaimed, The Lord, The Lord God, merciful and gracious, longsuffering, and abundant in goodness and truth..."

This is not just an Old Testament description.

This is the revealed nature of the God who gives the gifts.

And because Christ is the exact image of the Father, this remains one of the clearest measuring rods in all of Scripture.

So if someone claims spiritual function...
if someone claims authority...

if someone claims revelation…
if someone claims power…

we must still ask:

- Is it **merciful**?
- Is it **compassionate toward the suffering**?
- Is it **patient**, or is it applying pressure?
- Is it rooted in **loving-kindness**?
- Is it **dependable truth**?
- Is it releasing **forgiveness**, or storing offense?
- Is it showing **good judgment** under God?

This is not softness.

This is discernment.

And this gives the church something far better than suspicion:

it gives the church a **Christ-shaped standard**.

Not every expression will be perfect.

Not every vessel will be fully mature.

We are all in process.

But the pendulum cannot be swinging in the opposite direction while still demanding to be called spiritual.

That is one of the most dangerous confusions in church culture.

Intensity is not the same as Christlikeness.
Boldness is not the same as purity.
Certainty is not the same as truth.
Influence is not the same as authority.
Manifestation is not the same as maturity.

Exodus 34;6 helps the believer keep asking:

Does this feel like the Kingdom that will endure forever?

Because we will all be measured by the nature of God in the end.

Not by how dramatic we were.
Not by how followed we were.
Not by how impressive we appeared.
Not by how gifted we sounded.

But by what kind of life we built under His name.

That is sobering.

And strangely, it is also freeing.

Because it means the aim is not to become spectacular.

The aim is to become **true**.

The measuring rod is not hype.
The measuring rod is the nature of God revealed in Christ.

5. SOUND DOCTRINE DOES NOT COMPETE WITH THE SPIRIT

One of the great errors of immature spirituality is assuming that doctrine and the Spirit are enemies.

As though structure kills life.
As though truth restrains grace.
As though testing something is automatically unbelief.
As though order is a threat to movement.

But the Spirit of Truth is not offended by truth.

He wrote the Book.

The Holy Spirit is not in competition with the Doctrine of Christ.

He is the One who **illumines it**, **applies it**, and **forms Christ through it**.

So when believers say things like:

- "Don't put God in a box."
- "You're overthinking it."
- "Just flow."
- "Doctrine divides."
- "We don't need teaching, we need fire."

...they may sound spiritual, but often what they are actually doing is resisting the very framework that protects genuine life.

A river without banks becomes a floodplain.

Water is still real.

Movement is still real.

But life becomes damage when it loses form. The Spirit is like living water. Doctrine gives the banks.

Love gives the nature. Christ gives the Headship.

And the Body becomes the place where that life can flow without destroying what it was sent to nourish.

This is why Paul never separated spiritual life from instruction.

He taught.
He corrected.
He established.

He reminded.
He warned.
He framed.
He fathered.

Not because he loved control.

Because he loved the church.

And that is the real heart of this section:

Sound doctrine is not there to make the church less alive.
It is there to make life sustainable.

It keeps grace from becoming confusion.
It keeps freedom from becoming disorder.
It keeps sincerity from becoming instability.
It keeps power from outrunning love.
It keeps gifts from forgetting their purpose.

And the more a person truly understands the Doctrine of Christ, the more they should become:

- humbler, not harder
- clearer, not colder
- steadier, not stiffer
- more teachable, not more defensive
- more alive, not less

Because true doctrine is not dead information.

It is truth that forms a life **In Christ**.

The Spirit does not fear the frame.
The Spirit fills what Christ has built.

Guided Discovery

Take a moment before moving forward—the key is found in the reflection.

This section is not asking whether you believe in gifts.

It is asking whether your understanding of gifts is sitting on a strong enough foundation to carry them safely.

1. When you think about spiritual gifts, what has been emphasized most in your experience: activation, experience, doctrine, maturity, or character?

Many believers were first taught how to recognize or pursue gifts before they were ever taught how gifts fit into the larger journey of becoming mature **In Christ**. This question helps expose where your spiritual framework may be strong—and where it may still need reinforcing.

2. Which part of the Doctrine of Christ in Hebrews 6:1–2 feels most neglected in today's church culture —and why?

For many, it is repentance, eternal judgment, or even resurrection hope. These doctrines stabilize motive, humility, and accountability. When they are neglected, gifts can become disconnected from reverence, and spiritual life can quietly drift toward performance or imbalance.

3. Have you ever seen a real gift carried in a way that felt structurally weak, confusing, or unsafe? What made it feel that way?

Often the issue is not whether the gift seemed real, but whether the life around it felt trustworthy. Pressure, pride, confusion, defensiveness, lack of accountability, or a drift away from God's nature are often signs that grace is operating in a vessel that still needs stronger framing.

4. Using Exodus 34:6 as a measuring rod, how would you test a spiritual expression in real time?

Ask simple but powerful questions: Is this merciful? Compassionate? Patient? Rooted in loving-kindness? Dependable in truth? Releasing forgiveness? Showing good judgment? This does not require cynicism. It gives discernment a relational, Christ-shaped standard.

5. What would become safer, stronger, or clearer in your own life if your gifts were more consciously framed by the Doctrine of Christ?

For some, it would bring humility. For others, courage. For others, peace, clarity, or steadiness. The goal is not to become less available to God—it is to become more deeply formed, so what He entrusts to you can remain fruitful, trustworthy, and life-giving over time.

Bridge to Section 4

So now the frame is starting to show itself.

Gifts begin with Christ.
Gifts grow safely in God's love.
Gifts are stabilized by the Doctrine of Christ.

But there is still one more essential widening that must happen before this chapter is complete.

Because gifts were never given to isolated individuals as private trophies.

They were given to a **Body**.

And until the believer sees that grace was designed to function **in relationship, under Headship**, and **for shared edification**, even sound doctrine can still be misunderstood as something merely personal.

Which means the next beam-line is ready to lay:

Grace becomes most beautiful when it finds its place in the Body.

SECTION 4
GIFTS ONLY MAKE FULL SENSE INSIDE THE BODY

Grace is never given merely for personal expression. Every true gift is designed to supply, strengthen, and build the living Body of Christ.

Core Scripture (KJV)

1 Corinthians 12:7
"But the manifestation of the Spirit is given to every man to profit withal."

Section Introduction

One of the clearest ways gifts become distorted is when they are removed from the reason they were given.

A person may have something real.
A person may carry a measure of grace.
A person may even be accurate, powerful, insightful, or unusually effective.

But if that grace is understood mainly as **personal identity**, **private significance**, or **spiritual self-expression**, something essential has already been lost.

Because in scripture, gifts are not first presented as badges.
They are not trophies.
They are not private possessions.
They are not spiritual accessories added to help a person feel special.

They are presented as **supply**.

The New Testament does not introduce gifts so believers can build private ministries detached from shared life. It introduces gifts so the **Body of Christ** can function as a living organism under one Head.

That means this truth must be nailed down early:

A gift may appear in a person, but it only makes full sense in the Body.

This matters more than many realize.

Because once gifts are separated from Body life, they often drift in predictable directions:

- gifting becomes identity instead of stewardship
- grace becomes platform instead of supply
- spiritual function becomes performance instead of participation
- visibility becomes more important than edification
- independence begins to masquerade as maturity

But Christ did not distribute grace to create spiritual celebrities.
He distributed grace so that **His Body would grow.**

And that changes how everything must be read.

A hand makes sense on a body.
An eye makes sense on a body.
A foot makes sense on a body.
A mouth makes sense on a body.

Lift any one of them out of the organism, and what once looked powerful becomes tragic.

That is not because the part was false.
It is because the part was never meant to live by itself.

So this section restores a foundational lens:

Grace is personal in its placement, but corporate in its purpose.

Christ gives to individuals.
But He gives through individuals **for the sake of the whole.**

And once that truth is seen, many modern distortions become easier to discern.

1. A GIFT MAY BE IN YOU, BUT IT WAS NEVER GIVEN ONLY FOR YOU

A grace can be genuinely present in a person and still be badly misunderstood if the person assumes the grace exists primarily for personal fulfillment.

That is one of the subtle dangers of modern spiritual culture.

People often ask:

- *What is my gift?*
- *What is my calling?*
- *What am I anointed to do?*
- *How do I step into my assignment?*

Those questions are not automatically wrong.

But if they are asked apart from the life of the Body, they can quietly train the soul to think in the wrong direction.

Because scripture does not first ask:

What makes you feel most significant?

It asks:

What has Christ placed in you that helps the Body live?

That is a very different question.

Romans 12 does not frame gifts as self-discovery for the sake of self-fulfillment. It frames them as differing graces that must be used rightly in service, proportion, humility, and function within the larger life of the Body.

1 Corinthians 12 does the same.

Paul does not say, *"Each has a gift, so now each should build a private lane around that gift."*
He says the manifestation is given **"to profit withal"**—for the common good, the shared gain, the mutual strengthening of the whole.

That means the first mature response to grace is not excitement alone.

It is responsibility.

Not:

"How do I become known for this?"

But:

"Who is meant to be helped by this?"

That single shift protects the heart from a thousand spiritual vanity traps.

Because once a gift is seen as supply, humility has room to breathe.

And humility is not pretending the grace is small.
Humility is remembering **who the grace belongs to.**

It came from Christ.
It remains under Christ.
And it was given for Christ's Body.

2. THE BODY IS NOT A METAPHOR ONLY — IT IS THE GOVERNING LOGIC

The phrase **"the Body of Christ"** is not decorative church language.

It is governing language.

Paul does not use the body image because it sounds warm, poetic, or communal. He uses it because it explains how grace actually works.

A body is not a collection of unrelated talents.

A body is a living, coordinated organism where:

- many parts exist
- no part is self-sufficient
- no part carries the whole
- each part has a real function
- hidden parts matter as much as visible ones
- supply must move relationally
- life comes from one head

That last point is critical.

A body is not governed by its most visible member. It is governed by the head.

So when Paul speaks of the Body of Christ, he is not merely saying believers should be nice to one another.

He is saying this:

All grace must remain ordered under Christ as Head if the organism is to function rightly.

That means gifts are not random spiritual events.

They are part of a living architecture.

A word of wisdom may protect.
A word of knowledge may reveal.
Mercy may soften.
Teaching may establish.
Helps may support.
Leadership may organize.
Discernment may guard.
Prophecy may strengthen, exhort, and comfort.
Administration may keep life from leaking through disorder.
Giving may provide what the rest of the Body cannot yet supply.

Each measure matters.

But none of them were meant to operate as independent kingdoms.

When a part starts behaving as though it is the whole, distortion begins.

This is why the church becomes unhealthy whenever one expression of grace is over-celebrated while others are neglected.

If only the visible platform gifts are honored, the hidden parts begin to starve.
If only public ministry is celebrated, quiet supply is undervalued.
If only spectacular manifestations are pursued, stabilizing graces are treated as lesser.

But in a real body, the quiet systems often keep the visible parts alive.

The lungs do not perform.
The liver does not seek applause.
The joints do not trend.

But remove them, and the whole structure collapses.

So the Body language is not sentimental.

It is structural.

It is Christ teaching us how to read grace.

3. ISOLATION DISTORTS WHAT RELATIONSHIP WOULD HAVE STABILIZED

One of the most dangerous environments for spiritual gifting is **prolonged isolation without meaningful Body connection**.

A gift can remain real in isolation.
But it often becomes harder to read accurately.

Why?

Because many things that help stabilize grace are found in relationship:

- feedback
- correction
- confirmation
- accountability
- perspective
- patience
- shared burden-bearing
- testing over time
- the friction that reveals motive
- the humility of being one part among many

Isolation often removes those things.

And when those stabilizers are removed, the soul can begin interpreting spiritual experiences without enough checks and balances.

That is where drift begins.

A person may start sincere.
A person may begin with real hunger.
A person may have genuinely encountered God.

But without Body life, several distortions often creep in:

- impressions become unquestionable
- private revelation becomes private authority
- correction begins to feel like persecution
- disagreement feels like resistance to God
- loneliness can masquerade as special separation
- pain can disguise itself as prophetic intensity
- independence can wear the costume of spiritual strength

This is not because all solitude is wrong.

There is holy solitude.
There is hiddenness.
There is wilderness.
There is waiting.
There are seasons where God forms a person away from noise.

Jesus Himself withdrew.
Paul had seasons of preparation.
The prophets knew isolation.

But holy solitude is not the same as **detached self-governed spirituality**.

One is a season under God.
The other can become a pattern under the soul.

And the difference is enormous.

Healthy solitude returns to the Body cleaner, clearer,
humbler, and more usable.
Unhealthy isolation returns with private certainty that
cannot be tested.

That is why gifts only make full sense inside the Body.

Not because God cannot meet a person alone.
He can.

But because grace was not designed to remain **unread,
untested, and unshared**.

It was designed to become **edifying supply in living
relationship**.

4. HIDDEN GRACE IS NOT LESSER GRACE

One of the most healing truths in Body life is this:

visibility is not the measure of value.

This must be said plainly because many believers have
quietly absorbed the opposite idea.

If a grace is public, it is often treated as more important.
If it is dramatic, it is often treated as more spiritual.
If it is visible, it is often treated as more significant.

But the Body of Christ does not work that way.

In fact, Paul goes out of his way to show that the parts that
seem weaker, less honorable, or less visible are often treated
by God with particular care.

That means the believer who quietly carries mercy, helps, hospitality, practical service, intercession, generosity, discernment, administration, encouragement, or faithful unseen support is not carrying a "smaller" Christianity.

They may be carrying the exact grace keeping the room alive.

How many gatherings would collapse without the unseen faithful?

How many leaders would burn out without hidden supporters?

How many wounded believers would leave if mercy were absent?

How many chaotic environments would keep leaking life if nobody quietly carried order?

How many children would never be formed if hidden teachers did not keep sowing week after week?

How many moments of breakthrough were made possible because someone prayed where nobody saw?

The Body is full of graces that do not announce themselves loudly.

And thank God for that.

Because if every grace wanted the microphone, the church would become unbearable.

Sometimes the holiest thing in the room is not the person speaking.
Sometimes it is the person quietly holding the atmosphere together.

Sometimes the most Christlike grace is not the one that draws attention.
It is the one that makes other people safer, steadier, and more able to grow.

This is one of the reasons gifts must be read inside the Body.

Because the Body teaches proportion.

It reminds us that:

- not all grace is public
- not all power is loud
- not all authority is visible
- not all importance is obvious
- not all fruit announces itself in the moment

In a healthy Body, hidden grace is honored.

And when hidden grace is honored, many wounded souls begin to heal.

Because people stop believing they must become spectacular to matter.

5. CHRIST DID NOT DISTRIBUTE GIFTS TO CREATE COMPETITION

Competition is one of the clearest signs that gifts are being read through the soul instead of through the Body.

The soul asks:

- Who is greater?
- Who is more powerful?
- Who is more accurate?
- Who is more needed?
- Who gets seen?
- Who gets heard?

- Who carries the room?
- Who gets the platform?

But the Body does not ask those questions the same way.

Because a healthy body does not make the hand compete with the eye.

It does not ask whether the foot is more spiritual than the ear.

It does not ask whether the heart should be jealous of the lungs.

That would be absurd. And yet the church has often done exactly that.

Some compete over manifestations.
Some compete over revelation.
Some compete over titles.
Some compete over influence.
Some compete over who is "more anointed."
Some compete over who is more central to what God is doing.

But all of that becomes foolish the moment the Body lens is restored.

Because the question is not:

Which part is superior?

The question is:

Is the whole Body being strengthened?

A powerful meeting can still leave the Body weaker.
A dramatic gift can still leave people confused.
A strong personality can still create dependence instead of maturity.

A visible ministry can still centralize what Christ meant to distribute.

That is why Body thinking is so necessary.

It breaks the spell of comparison.

It exposes the vanity of rivalry.

It humbles the visible.

It dignifies the hidden.

It returns honor to shared life.

And it restores the reader to this truth:

Christ is not building stars. He is building a Body.

That line alone can save years of drift.

6. THE BODY IS WHERE GIFTS ARE TESTED, TRAINED, AND TRUSTED

A gift may be discovered privately.
It is usually proven relationally.

This is another reason gifts only make full sense inside the Body.

Because the Body is not only the destination of grace.

It is often the training ground of grace.

Within real Body life, a gift is not merely admired.
It is **tested**.

Not to suppress it.
Not to shame it.
Not to control it.

But to help it become trustworthy.

Inside healthy Body life:

- a word can be weighed
- a teaching can be examined
- a pattern can be observed over time
- motive can be exposed
- consistency can be seen
- fruit can be measured
- humility can be revealed
- correction can be offered
- growth can be encouraged
- extremes can be tempered
- private blind spots can be seen by others

This is how grace matures.

Not merely through excitement.
Not merely through activation.
Not merely through language of impartation.

But through **time, truth, relationship, and faithful use under Christ's headship**.

This is where many modern believers become impatient.

They want instant recognition.
Instant validation.
Instant authority.
Instant influence.

But scripture often shows something slower, safer, and more beautiful:

Grace entrusted, then observed, then strengthened, then proven.

Even in practical life, we understand this.

A man may have natural talent with tools.
But you do not hand him the cathedral roof on day one
because he swung a hammer well once.

You watch how he measures.
You watch how he listens.
You watch whether he learns.
You watch whether he rushes.
You watch how he handles correction.
You watch whether he can build straight when nobody is
clapping.

Same timber.
Very different builder.

So it is with grace.

The Body is where gifts are not only celebrated.

It is where they become safe enough to carry more weight.

7. GIFTS FIND THEIR TRUE BEAUTY WHEN THEY HELP LOVE TAKE SHAPE

At its highest level, a gift is not simply an ability.

It is a way the life of Christ becomes tangible among His
people.

That means the deepest question is not only:

What can this gift do?

It is:

What aspect of Christ's care does this gift help make visible?

A true gift may:

- strengthen the weary
- clarify the confused
- feed the hungry
- warn the drifting
- steady the fearful
- heal the bruised
- order the scattered
- encourage the tired
- protect the vulnerable
- awaken the sleeping
- equip the willing
- comfort the grieving
- build the immature
- restore the fallen
- help the Body move as one

In that sense, gifts are not merely functions.

They are **forms of loving supply**.

That is why they only make full sense inside the Body.

Because love is most clearly seen where real life is shared.

Not in abstraction.
Not in isolated self-definition.
Not in self-announcement.

But in the actual work of mutual strengthening.

A word that helps someone stand again.
A truth that keeps a family from collapse.

A mercy that gives a wounded heart room to breathe.
A practical help that lifts a crushing burden.
A hidden prayer that shifts a room.
A faithful correction that protects a soul.
A steady leader who makes peace possible.
A servant who carries weight others never noticed.

This is where gifts become beautiful.

Not when they make a person look impressive.
But when they help **God's love take form in the Body.**

And that brings us right back to the plumb line that has
been running through this whole chapter:

Every gift must still be read by the nature of God.

Is it moving in mercy?
Is it helping the suffering with compassion?
Is it patient, or is it pressuring?
Is it rooted in loving-kindness?
Is it dependable in truth?
Is it able to forgive?
Is it exercising good judgment under God?

If not, something is off in the reading.

Because even inside Body language, not everything that
appears active is necessarily healthy.

The Body is not merely a crowd.
It is a living organism under the nature of Christ.

And where that nature governs, grace becomes not only real
— but safe, nourishing, and deeply beautiful.

Guided Discovery

Before moving into the wider spiritual landscape, pause here and let this section do its work.

A gift may be in you.
A grace may be on your life.
A measure may be real.

But the mature question is not merely what you carry.

The mature question is what your grace is helping build.

Sit with that honestly.

1. When you think about grace, do you mostly think in terms of personal identity or shared responsibility?

Ask yourself:

- Do I mainly think, *What is my gift?*
- Or do I also ask, *Who is meant to be strengthened by what Christ placed in me?*
- Have I unconsciously measured spiritual value by visibility?
- Have I tied my sense of worth too closely to being recognized?

A mature heart does not deny the grace Christ has given—it simply refuses to treat that grace as private property. Grace is personal in placement, but corporate in purpose. If Christ has placed something in you, He has done so because someone, somewhere, is meant to be helped by it.

**2. Are you living connected enough for your grace
to be tested, trained, and trusted?**

Ask yourself:

- Am I meaningfully connected to real Body life?
- Do I have people who can confirm, weigh, refine, or
  correct what I believe I carry?
- Have I mistaken independence for maturity?
- Is my spiritual life becoming more relationally
  grounded—or more privately self-governed?

Healthy grace can survive being weighed. In fact, it usually
becomes stronger through it. The Body is not a threat to true
gifting—it is often the place where true gifting becomes safe
enough to carry real weight. Isolation may preserve sincerity
for a time, but relationship is usually where grace becomes
trustworthy.

**3. Do you honor hidden grace the same way you
honor visible grace?**

Ask yourself:

- Do I instinctively admire only what is public,
  powerful, or dramatic?
- Have I overlooked quieter graces like mercy, helps,
  administration, intercession, hospitality, or faithful
  support?
- Have I undervalued my own grace because it does not
  draw attention?
- Do I recognize that some of the holiest work in the
  Body happens where almost nobody sees?

In Christ, hidden does not mean lesser. Some of the most
essential graces in the Body are the ones holding the room
together without applause. The church becomes safer,

healthier, and more beautiful when visible grace is humbled and hidden grace is honored.

4. Is your grace helping love take shape—or only drawing attention to itself?

Ask yourself:

- Are people safer, clearer, steadier, or stronger because of what I carry?
- Does my contribution help the Body breathe—or does it create pressure around me?
- Is my grace moving in the nature of God's love?
- If my gift disappeared tomorrow, would what people miss most be the power—or the love it carried?

The truest beauty of a gift is not what it can display, but what it can build. When grace is under Christ, it helps God's love become tangible in real life. It strengthens, protects, nourishes, steadies, and edifies. That is where gifts stop being impressive and start becoming truly beautiful.

Section Close

A gift can be real in a person.

But it only becomes fully understandable when it is read as **living supply inside the Body of Christ**.

That is where grace finds its proportion.
That is where hidden and visible parts are rightly honored.
That is where gifts are tested, trained, and trusted.
That is where personal significance gives way to shared edification.
That is where the soul's need to be special begins to bow to Christ's desire to build.

And that matters deeply.

Because once gifts are placed inside the Body, one more truth becomes unavoidable:

not everything moving in a spiritual environment is necessarily the Holy Spirit.

There are atmospheres.
There are influences.
There are motives.
There are pressures.
There are mixtures.
There is flesh.
There is immaturity.
There is genuine grace.
And there is also the need to discern rightly.

Which means the next beam must now be laid carefully.

Because if gifts are to be understood safely, the wider spiritual environment must also be read correctly.

SECTION 5
THE SPIRITUAL LANDSCAPE MUST BE READ RIGHTLY

Gifts do not exist in a vacuum. They must be understood within the wider spiritual reality of influence, discernment, testing, and life in the Spirit.

1 Thessalonians 5:19–21 (KJV)
*"Quench not the Spirit. Despise not prophesyings. Prove all
things; hold fast that which is good."*

Section Introduction

By the time we reach the end of this first chapter, the
foundation has already been laid carefully.

We have seen that gifts do not begin with the receiver, but
with Christ Himself.
We have seen that gifts only mature safely in the
atmosphere of God's love.
We have seen that the doctrine of Christ gives spiritual
function its frame, direction, and maturity.
And we have seen that gifts only make full sense inside the
living Body, where grace is given to supply and strengthen
the whole.

Now one final beam must be set in place before we move
forward.

Because even when all of that is understood, another reality
remains:

not everything spiritual is the Spirit.

That sentence may sound obvious, but in practice it has
been one of the church's great blind spots.

Many believers have been taught to think in only two
categories:

either something is spiritual and therefore should be
welcomed,
or something is uncomfortable and therefore should be
feared.

But the New Testament gives us a far more mature way to read the landscape.

It does not tell us to reject spiritual life.
It does not tell us to mock manifestations.
It does not tell us to despise prophecy.
And it does not tell us to accept everything that carries intensity, language, confidence, or power.

Instead, it teaches something wiser.

Do not quench the Spirit.
Do not despise prophesyings.
Prove all things.
Hold fast that which is good.

That is the balance of mature spiritual life.

And that is exactly why this section must close Chapter 1.

Because before we move into the deeper study of fruit, maturity, and the nature of life in the Spirit, the reader must understand that gifts live inside a wider spiritual environment.

There is genuine grace.
There is genuine spiritual influence.
There is genuine human mixture.
There is immaturity.
There is flesh.
There is deception.
There is zeal without wisdom.
There is sincerity without formation.
And there is also the real, living, holy work of the Spirit of God.

If the spiritual landscape is not read rightly, gifts can be misunderstood in every direction.

Some will accept too much.
Some will reject too much.
Some will be impressed by power without asking about fruit.
Some will be so afraid of abuse that they shut down life itself.

Neither extreme builds the Body well.

This closing section exists to say plainly:

Gifts must never be studied as isolated functions. They must be understood inside the larger spiritual reality of discernment, testing, formation, and life in the Spirit.

That is the final framing beam of Chapter 1.

And once that beam is in place, Chapter 2 can open the next great question:

If gifts can be real, misread, immature, or mixed— what is the safest evidence that the Spirit is truly at work in a life?

That is where fruit becomes essential.

1. THE FIRST FOUR SECTIONS FORM THE FRAME—THIS SECTION TEACHES US HOW TO READ THE ROOM

The first four sections of this chapter were not separate ideas floating beside each other.

They were deliberate structural beams.

Each one established something necessary before the subject of gifts could be handled safely.

First, we learned that **gifts begin with the Giver, not the receiver.**
That guards us from ego, self-generation, and spiritual vanity.

Then we learned that **God's love is the soil true gifts grow in.**
That guards us from treating gifting as if power alone were maturity.

Then we learned that **the doctrine of Christ gives gifts their frame.**
That guards us from sincere spiritual activity without foundation, order, or direction.

Then we learned that **gifts only make full sense inside the Body.**
That guards us from private ownership, isolated identity, and self-expressive spirituality detached from shared life.

Now this fifth section gathers those four beams and asks a final, necessary question:

How do we rightly interpret what we are seeing?

Because even if a person agrees with every previous section, they can still misread the room.

They can still confuse charisma for Christlikeness.
They can still confuse intensity for the Spirit.
They can still confuse sincerity for maturity.
They can still confuse movement for health.
They can still confuse giftedness for safety.

That is why this section does not introduce a new topic unrelated to the first four.

It completes them.

It says:

- Christ is the source.
- Love is the soil.
- Doctrine is the frame.
- The Body is the context.
- **And discernment is how you read the whole environment rightly.**

Without that last piece, the house is standing—but the occupants still do not know how to judge what belongs in the room.

2. GIFTS EXIST INSIDE A WIDER SPIRITUAL REALITY

One of the most dangerous mistakes believers make is to treat gifts as if they exist in a sealed compartment.

As if spiritual function can be discussed apart from the larger realities that surround it.

But gifts do not operate in a vacuum.

They operate in people.
They operate in gatherings.
They operate in communities.
They operate in systems of influence.
They operate in seasons of maturity and immaturity.
They operate in environments where truth, error, mixture, pressure, humility, ego, love, and fear may all be present in different measures.

That means when we speak about gifts, we are never merely speaking about mechanics.

We are speaking about life.

We are speaking about people.

We are speaking about atmosphere.

We are speaking about stewardship.

We are speaking about what kind of spiritual culture is being created around the grace that is present.

This is why the New Testament repeatedly calls believers to **discern**, **judge**, **prove**, **test**, and **hold fast**.

Not because God is trying to make His people suspicious.

But because real spiritual life requires maturity.

A real gift can be present in an immature vessel.
A real moment can be mixed with human flesh.
A sincere word can still be poorly timed, poorly carried, or poorly interpreted.
A real spiritual atmosphere can still be handled in ways that create confusion rather than clarity.

That does not mean gifts are false.

It means gifts are not the only factor in the room.

And unless the wider landscape is understood, people often make simplistic conclusions:

- "It felt powerful, so it must be God."
- "It made me uncomfortable, so it must not be God."
- "They're gifted, so they must be mature."
- "They were wrong once, so nothing they carry is real."
- "The atmosphere was intense, so the Spirit was moving."
- "There was disorder, so the Spirit must have left."

These are shallow readings.

The spiritual landscape is usually more layered than that.

And that is why this section must slow the reader down.

Not to make them fearful.

But to make them wiser.

3. NOT EVERYTHING SPIRITUAL IS THE SPIRIT—AND NOT EVERYTHING STRONG IS WRONG

This is where many believers need the balance of Scripture restored.

Because once people begin to hear the phrase *not everything spiritual is the Spirit*, some swing immediately into distrust.

They begin treating discernment like suspicion.

They become tense, defensive, overly analytical, or emotionally closed.

But that is not maturity either.

There are two common overreactions in the church:

One side receives almost everything because they are afraid of quenching the Spirit.

The other side questions almost everything because they are afraid of deception.

One becomes gullible.
The other becomes brittle.

One opens every door.
The other nails the windows shut.

Neither builds a healthy house.

The New Testament path is more stable.

It gives us a holy tension that must be preserved:

- **Do not quench the Spirit**
- **Do not despise prophesyings**
- **Prove all things**
- **Hold fast that which is good**

That means the mature believer must learn to do two things at once: to remain open to the genuine work of the Spirit, and to remain sober enough to test what is being carried.

That is not unbelief.

That is stewardship.

And it is vital that we say something else clearly here:

Not everything strong is wrong.

Sometimes God corrects.
Sometimes God confronts.
Sometimes truth pierces.
Sometimes conviction exposes.
Sometimes a genuine word unsettles before it heals.

So discernment is not simply asking:

"Did that feel gentle?"

Sometimes the better question is:

"Was this aligned with truth, carried cleanly, and producing life?"

Likewise, not everything soft is safe.

Something may sound soothing and still flatter the flesh.
Something may sound affirming and still avoid truth.
Something may feel emotionally warm and still subtly
center man rather than Christ.

This is why the reader must not reduce discernment to
emotional preference.

Discernment is not:

- whatever feels exciting
- whatever feels calm
- whatever feels familiar
- whatever feels unusual
- whatever fits our tribe
- whatever flatters our expectation

Discernment must become more grounded than that.

And that deeper grounding begins to unfold in the next
chapter.

4. THIS CHAPTER PREPARES THE READER TO VALUE FRUIT ABOVE IMPRESSION

If Chapter 1 were to end without this section, some readers
would still carry the wrong instinct into the rest of the book.

They might understand the theology of gifts, but still
secretly evaluate spiritual life by impression.

By strength of personality.
By public function.
By atmosphere.
By charisma.

By confidence.
By momentum.
By language.
By visible activity.

That would be a dangerous carryover.

Because one of the central burdens of this entire book is to help the reader move from being **impressed by gifts** to being **anchored in what makes gifts trustworthy**.

That is why this final section matters so much.

It is not a detour.

It is a calibration.

It teaches the reader that before we study manifestations, ministries, operations, and functions more deeply, we must first understand this:

spiritual life must be read with discernment, not merely reaction.

And once that truth lands, the next chapter becomes unavoidable.

Because if outward spiritual activity can be real, mixed, immature, misunderstood, or misused, then the next question becomes:

What is the safest evidence that the Spirit is truly forming a life?

The answer is not first power.

The answer is not first visibility.

The answer is not first giftedness.

The answer is **fruit.**

That is why Chapter 2 does not interrupt the gifts discussion.

It protects it.

Fruit is not the side topic.

Fruit is the evidence that the root is healthy.

Fruit is what makes power trustworthy.

Fruit is what reveals whether grace is maturing in God's love or merely functioning in a gifted but unformed life.

And that is why Chapter 1 must end here:

not with fascination over gifts,
but with a reader ready to ask the right next question.

5. THE NEXT CHAPTER DOES NOT CHANGE THE SUBJECT—IT REVEALS THE SAFEST EVIDENCE

This is the final beam-line.

When the reader turns the page into Chapter 2, they must not feel like the book has changed topics.

They must feel like the book has become safer.

Chapter 2 is not leaving gifts behind.

It is answering the most necessary question raised by Chapter 1:

How do we know grace is maturing well?

If gifts begin with Christ...
If gifts grow safely only in God's love...
If doctrine gives them frame...
If the Body gives them context...
And if the spiritual landscape must be read with
discernment...

Then what should we look for first when assessing whether
spiritual life is healthy?

The answer is not the brilliance of the gift.

It is the condition of the root.

And that is why the next chapter will take us into:

GOD'S LOVE IS THE SOIL TRUE GIFTS GROW IN

Not as repetition.

But as expansion.

Not as a recycled point.

But as a necessary deepening.

Because Chapter 1 named the principle.

Chapter 2 will open the life inside it.

Chapter 1 said the soil matters.

Chapter 2 will show what grows there.

Chapter 1 warned that not everything spiritual is the Spirit.

Chapter 2 will show what the Spirit reliably produces.

Chapter 1 established the need for discernment.

Chapter 2 will give the reader one of the safest measures of all:

the fruit of the Spirit as the evidence of life in the Spirit.

And once that is understood, the rest of the book can move forward with far greater safety, clarity, and maturity.

That is how this first chapter should end.

Not merely informed about gifts.

But rightly oriented before the deeper journey begins.

Guided Discovery

Before stepping into Chapter 2, pause and ask:

1. Have I been more impressed by gifts than instructed by what makes them safe?

This is common. Gifts are often easier to notice than fruit. But maturity learns to reverse the instinct. A real gift may be present, but what makes it trustworthy is the environment it is growing in and the life it is producing.

2. Do I tend to swing toward gullibility or suspicion when spiritual things happen?

Most believers lean one direction. Some fear quenching the Spirit, so they receive almost everything. Others fear deception, so they distrust almost everything. Scripture teaches a better way: remain open, but prove all things. That is not cynicism. That is mature stewardship.

3. When I encounter spiritual intensity, what do I usually assume?

Intensity can be real, but it is not a sufficient test. Not everything spiritual is the Spirit, and not everything strong is wrong. The believer must learn to look deeper than atmosphere and ask whether truth, order, humility, and life are also present.

4. Am I ready to let the next chapter recalibrate what I look for first?

This is the turn the book is about to make. Fruit is not a lesser subject than gifts. It is one of the clearest evidences that the Spirit is truly forming a life. If you let fruit become central, your discernment becomes stronger and your view of gifts becomes safer.

Bridge to Chapter 2

Now that the frame is set, the next question becomes unavoidable:

If not everything spiritual is the Spirit, what does the Spirit reliably produce?

The fruit of the Spirit is not a side note to spiritual life.

It is the visible evidence that the root is alive.

CHAPTER 2. THE FRUIT REVEALS THE ROOT

The clearest proof of true spiritual life is not power alone, but the nature of God becoming visible over time.

Core Scripture

Galatians 5:22–23 (KJV)

"But the fruit of the Spirit is love, joy, peace, longsuffering, gentleness, goodness, faith, meekness, temperance: against such there is no law."

Secondary Anchor

Exodus 34:6 (KJV)

"And the Lord passed by before him, and proclaimed, The Lord, The Lord God, merciful and gracious, longsuffering, and abundant in goodness and truth..."

Chapter Introduction

If Chapter 1 established that the gifts begin with Christ, then Chapter 2 must establish how those gifts remain safe in the life that carries them.

Because spiritual life is not only revealed by what moves **through** a person.
It is also revealed by what has been formed **within** them.

A gift may draw attention.
A manifestation may create wonder.
A ministry may carry real weight.

But the question that must still be asked is deeper than all of that:

What kind of life is carrying it?

That is why before we move further into manifestations, ministries, and spiritual function, we must stop and look at something slower, quieter, and often more revealing:

the fruit of the Spirit.

Not the fruit of charisma.
Not the fruit of intensity.
Not the fruit of confidence.
Not the fruit of spiritual language.

The fruit of the Spirit.

And Scripture is careful here. Paul does not say *fruits* of the Spirit, as if these were disconnected spiritual traits that can be selectively developed according to personality.

He says **fruit**—singular.

One life.

One source.

One inward reality expressing itself in many visible ways.

Love.
Joy.
Peace.
Longsuffering.
Gentleness.
Goodness.
Faith.
Meekness.
Temperance.

This is not merely a list of virtues for moral improvement.

This is the evidence that the **Holy Spirit is flowing.**

The Breath Behind the Fruit

Much of the modern church has been taught to associate the Holy Spirit almost entirely with power, manifestations, impressions, atmosphere, tongues, prophecy, or miracles. And while the New Testament absolutely makes room for those realities, the Spirit of God does not merely manifest power.

He forms nature.

He does not only move **through** the believer.
He also works **within** the believer.

He convicts.
He teaches.
He leads.
He reveals Christ.
He glorifies Christ.
And over time, He forms the nature of Christ in those who yield to Him.

That is why the fruit matters so much.

The gifts may reveal what grace is doing **through** a person.
The fruit reveals what the Holy Spirit is doing **within** a person.

And this is where the connection to **Exodus 34:6** becomes deeply important.

When God declared His own nature before Moses, He did not begin with power.
He began with character.

Merciful.
Gracious.
Longsuffering.
Abundant in goodness and truth.

Before God demonstrated His works, He revealed His ways.
Before He displayed His power, He declared His nature.

That line matters.

Because if the Holy Spirit is truly the Spirit of God, then the life He produces in us will never contradict the God who revealed Himself in Scripture.

The fruit of the Spirit is not a disconnected New Testament virtue list floating in isolation from the rest of the Bible.

It is the **living evidence that the nature God revealed about Himself is beginning to take shape in us.**

The Nature Was Planted. The Breath Brings It to Life.

From the beginning, humanity was made in the image and likeness of God. That means the deepest design of human life was never meant to be separate from the nature of the Father.

In other words, the pattern was already there.

The blueprint was present before the fall distorted the house.

That is why this chapter must be read carefully.

We are not teaching that human beings naturally live in the fullness of God's nature apart from Christ. Scripture is clear that sin, self-rule, blindness, pride, fear, and corruption have deeply affected the human condition. The house may still carry traces of the original design, but left to itself, it does not remain plumb.

What we are saying is this:

God did not create humanity as something foreign to His nature.
He created us for likeness, for relationship, and for shared life.

And the Holy Spirit is the divine breath of truth that brings that intended life back into motion.

The Spirit does not create an entirely alien design inside the believer.

He awakens what was meant to live.
He restores what was meant to function.
He animates what was meant to reflect the Father.

This is why the fruit of the Spirit should not be treated as behavior management.

It is not cosmetic religion.
It is not spiritual acting.
It is not soul-level performance trying to imitate heaven.

It is the **breath of God bringing life to the nature of God within yielded ground.**

That is why, in practical life, many believers have noticed
something simple but profound: when they stop...
become aware of the presence of God...
and consciously yield to the Holy Spirit... their inner world
begins to settle.

Breathing deepens.
Pressure loosens.
Peace begins to rise.

This is not merely a nervous system trick, though the body
often participates in the mercy of God.

It is often the soul coming back under proper order.

The soul wants to rush in with its own answers.
The Spirit waits on the Word.

The soul wants to fix, control, interpret, protect, and react.
The Spirit leads in truth, peace, patience, and right
judgment.

That is why many moments of ministry, prayer, counsel, or
correction would immediately become safer if we simply
learned to stop first.

Not perform first.
Not explain first.
Not impress first.
Not react first.

Stop first.

Become aware of Him.

Allow the Holy Spirit to have the first word.

Jesus modeled this perfectly:

John 5:30 (KJV) **"I can of mine own self do nothing... as I hear, I judge..."**

That is not weakness.
That is divine alignment.

That is what mature spiritual life looks like.

The Fruit Is the Safe Place

One of the greatest mistakes believers make is assuming that the presence of a gift automatically proves the maturity of the vessel carrying it.

But the New Testament never teaches that.

A person may carry real grace and still be immature.
A person may function in a genuine gift and still be unstable.
A person may speak accurately in a moment and still lack the formed nature needed to carry that grace safely over time.

That is why the fruit matters so deeply.

The fruit of the Spirit is the safe place where we minister from.

Peace is the atmosphere.
Patience is the pace.
Gentleness is the touch.
Goodness is the moral clarity.
Faithfulness is the trustworthiness.
Self-control is the boundary line.

These are not optional extras for gentle personalities.

These are the environment of safe ministry.

They are the line in the sand we can see over, but do not cross back over.

If the fruit is absent, it is often a sign to stop and re-center.

If peace is absent... stop.
If patience is absent... stop.
If gentleness is absent... stop.
If self-control is absent... stop.

Not because the Spirit has failed, but because the soul may have started running ahead.

And sometimes the re-centering is simpler than people think.

Pause.
Breathe.
Become aware.

For some, it may be as simple as three slow breaths, allowing the soul to quiet and the inner life to return to peace.

For others, it may be the repeated inward reminder:

God's love.
God's love.
God's love.

Not as a mantra of emptiness, but as a conscious return to the headline of God's nature.

Because God's love is not merely one attribute among many.

It is the great banner under which His nature, His fruit, His truth, and His life become recognizable.

The Shape of This Chapter

This chapter will not treat the fruit of the Spirit as a detached moral checklist.

It will treat the fruit as living evidence.

Evidence that the breath of God is moving.
Evidence that the inner garden is being restored.
Evidence that the life of Christ is taking shape.
Evidence that gifts, when they come, have somewhere safe to live.

We will begin by showing that the Holy Spirit breathes life into what God already planted.

Then we will see how atonement restores the inner ground where that life can grow.

From there, we will look at how the fruit of the Spirit is the lived atmosphere of the Very Good Life—not merely admired, but cultivated.

Then we will learn why the cross teaches us to minister from peace, not pressure.

And finally, we will establish one of the most important lines in the entire book:

Every gift may be real, but only fruit makes ministry trustworthy.

Because words of wisdom, words of knowledge, prophecy, leadership, healing, discernment, teaching, and service all become safer, clearer, and more Christlike when they rise from the garden of formed nature.

The root determines the quality of the fruit.
The soil determines the health of both.

And the fruit reveals the root.

5-SECTION MASTER BEAMS

1. GRACE BREATHES LIFE INTO WHAT GOD ALREADY PLANTED

The fruit of the Spirit is not human effort behaving better—it is the divine breath awakening what God already placed within us.

This opening section establishes that the nature of God was woven into humanity at creation, and that the Holy Spirit is the divine breath of truth that awakens, animates, and cultivates that nature. Fruit is not self-manufactured morality; it is living evidence that the breath of God is flowing through yielded soil.

2. ATONEMENT RESTORES THE GARDEN OF THE HEART

The cross does not merely forgive sin—it reopens the inner ground where the life of God can grow again.

This section shows that atonement is not only the cancellation of guilt, but the restoration of inner ground. Through Christ, the damaged soil of the heart is reopened to truth, healing, conviction, and peace. The Holy Spirit works within that restored garden, bringing order where the soul once rushed ahead, and forming fruit where striving once dominated.

3. THE VERY GOOD LIFE GROWS WHERE THE FRUIT IS NURTURED

The fruit of the Spirit is not a religious checklist—it is the lived atmosphere of the Very Good Life.

This section presents the fruit as the practical experience of heaven's life taking shape within a person. The world chases externally what God has already planted internally. Fruit carries seed, but seed must be planted, nurtured, and protected over time. This is where the Very Good Life is not merely admired, but grown.

4. THE CROSS TEACHES US TO MINISTER FROM PEACE, NOT PRESSURE

True ministry does not push or pull people—it gently leads them into the peace of God's love.

This section reveals that the fruit of the Spirit is the safe place from which all ministry should flow. Peace becomes the atmosphere, patience becomes the pace, gentleness becomes the touch, and self-control becomes the boundary. The cross teaches us to release control, refuse manipulation, and lead others toward God's love without force.

5. FIVEFOLD MINISTRY MUST FLOW FROM GOD'S GARDEN OF FRUIT

Every gift may be real, but only fruit makes spiritual ministry safe, trustworthy, and truly Christlike.

This closing section brings the chapter forward into the wider argument of the book. The gifts of the Spirit and the ministries of Christ are not meant to operate outside the garden of formed nature.

Words of wisdom, words of knowledge, prophecy, healing, discernment, teaching, leadership, and helps all become trustworthy only when they rise from rooted love, peace, patience, faithfulness, and self-control.

Bridge into Section 1

So before we examine what spiritual life may look like when it speaks, moves, reveals, heals, equips, or leads... we must first ask what spiritual life looks like when it simply **lives**.

Because before the Spirit becomes visible in power,
He often becomes visible in **peace**.

Before He becomes visible in utterance,
He becomes visible in **patience**.

Before He becomes visible in ministry,
He becomes visible in **mercy, goodness, gentleness, and self-control**.

That is where we begin.

Not with striving.
Not with performance.
Not with the need to prove anything.

But with the quiet and powerful reality that **grace breathes life into what God already planted.**

SECTION 1
GRACE BREATHES LIFE INTO WHAT GOD ALREADY PLANTED

The Holy Spirit does not invent the nature of God in us—He awakens, animates, and matures what the Father planted from the beginning.

Core Scripture
Genesis 2:7 (KJV)
"And the LORD God formed man of the dust of the ground, and breathed into his nostrils the breath of life; and man became a living soul."

Section Introduction

Before we can understand spiritual gifts rightly, we must first understand something even more foundational:

Grace does not begin with ability. Grace begins with breath.

The Father made man in His likeness.
That means something of His intended nature was already planted into humanity from the beginning—not in fullness, not in maturity, not in perfect expression, but in design.

We were not made random.
We were not made empty.
We were not made without pattern.

We were made in the image of a God whose nature is revealed in **Exodus 34:6**:

And as the fuller pattern unfolds through Scripture, that same divine nature is seen in the living outflow of mercy, compassion, patience, loving-kindness, dependable truth, forgiveness, and righteous judgment.

That is not merely how God behaves...
That is who God is.

And if mankind was made in His likeness, then the seed-form of that nature belongs to the original design.

But planted nature is not the same as awakened life.

A seed may be present in the ground, but until breath, water, light, and life begin to move, what is planted remains hidden.

This is where many believers get confused.

They think grace is mostly about receiving a gift.
They think the Spirit arrives only to make someone powerful.
They think spiritual life begins when visible function appears.

But the deeper biblical picture is far more beautiful:

The Holy Spirit is not merely the distributor of gifts.
He is the divine Breath of God who brings living movement to what the Father already intended.

He breathes life into the design.
He animates the pattern.
He awakens what was planted.
He matures what was dormant.
He makes the nature of God experiential instead of
theoretical.

This is why true grace is not merely about what a person can
do.

It is about what begins to come alive in them.

Not just power.
Not just function.
Not just expression.

Life.

And this is also why the church must stop measuring grace
only by what is dramatic.

Sometimes the first evidence of grace is not a platform.
It is peace.

Sometimes the first evidence of grace is not prophecy.
It is the sudden softening of a hard heart.

Sometimes the first evidence of grace is not public gifting.
It is the deep inner stillness that comes when a person
becomes aware of God and their breathing changes before
they ever say a word.

Because the Holy Spirit is not only the One who moves
through us.

He is the One who settles us into God.

He is the Breath of Truth.
He is the Breath of Life.
He is the Breath that makes what was planted begin to live.

And if we miss that, we will build our understanding of grace around performance instead of presence.

That is backwards from the beginning.

1. GOD PLANTED HIS IMAGE BEFORE HE RELEASED HIS BREATH

The order matters: form, design, then breath.

Genesis does not present man as an accidental creature who later received a spiritual add-on.

God formed man intentionally.
God made man according to a divine pattern.
God shaped the vessel with meaning before He breathed life into it.

This matters because it shows that human life begins with **design before activation**.

The vessel was formed first.
The breath came next.
The soul became living after the breath entered.

That sequence is not random.

It reveals a spiritual principle:

God often plants structure before He releases movement.

He establishes pattern before He reveals function.
He forms identity before He manifests expression.

This is deeply important for how we understand grace.

If we start with outward function, we may assume grace begins when someone appears powerful.

But Scripture starts earlier.

Grace is not merely God giving a man something external.

Grace is God bringing divine life into what He Himself has already designed.

That means the Father's intention is older than the manifestation.

The design came first.
The breath came next.
The visible life followed.

That same principle still stands.

Before a gift is seen, something is already planted.
Before a calling is recognized, something is already formed.
Before grace becomes visible, God has already intended something in the hidden man.

This is why true ministry is not self-invention.

It is discovery under God.

It is not a man creating himself through ambition.
It is a man awakening to what God already knew.

And the same is true of God's nature.

If we were made in His likeness, then mercy was not invented later as a church concept.
Compassion was not a New Testament upgrade.
Patience was not an optional spiritual extra.
Truth was not a preference.

These things belong to the original pattern of the Father.

The Holy Spirit does not arrive to create a foreign kingdom inside man.

He comes to awaken the true one.

2. THE HOLY SPIRIT IS THE DIVINE BREATH OF TRUTH

The Spirit does not merely visit the life of God—He carries it.

From Genesis to the New Testament, the Spirit is consistently associated with breath, wind, life, movement, and divine utterance.

God breathes into Adam.
The dry bones live when breath enters them.
Jesus breathes on His disciples and says, *"Receive ye the Holy Ghost."*
At Pentecost, the Spirit comes like a rushing mighty wind.

This is not poetic coincidence.

It is theological continuity.

The Breath of God and the Spirit of God are inseparably linked throughout Scripture because the Spirit is not merely a force of activity—He is the living carrier of divine life and truth.

This is why Jesus calls Him **the Spirit of Truth**.

Truth is not merely correct information.
Truth is what can be depended on.
Truth is what does not shift under pressure.
Truth is what remains aligned with the nature of the Father.

And the Holy Spirit does not merely tell us facts about God.

He brings us into experiential contact with God's nature.

He breathes peace where anxiety ruled.
He breathes conviction where self-deception hardened the soul.
He breathes tenderness where pain built walls.
He breathes clarity where confusion had become normal.

This is why spiritual awareness often affects the body itself.

A man becomes conscious of the Holy Spirit, and his breathing naturally changes.

It slows.
It deepens.
It settles.

Not because the body is being manipulated by religious emotion, but because the soul is beginning to yield to a deeper government.

The vessel starts responding to Presence.

And this is one of the most practical signs many believers overlook:

When the Holy Spirit is given room, the whole inner world often begins to come into order.

Not always instantly.
Not always dramatically.
But truly.

The scattered mind starts gathering.
The tense body starts releasing.
The striving soul starts loosening its grip.
The inner atmosphere begins to change.

Why?

Because breath is entering the room.

The Spirit is not just bringing a message.

He is bringing life.

And this is why grace must never be reduced to visible charisma.

If the Spirit is present but a person is becoming harsher, more restless, more pressured, more proud, more brittle, or more self-exalting, something is already out of plumb.

Because the true Breath of God does not animate the flesh.

He animates what agrees with the Father.

3. EXODUS 34:6 IS THE MEASURING ROD OF WHAT THE BREATH SHOULD PRODUCE

If grace is truly breathing life into what God planted, the nature of God must become increasingly visible.

This is where discernment becomes practical.

Many believers say, "The Spirit moved."

But how do we know?

Intensity alone is not enough.
Emotion alone is not enough.
Even sincerity alone is not enough.

If the Holy Spirit is the divine Breath of God, and if that
Breath is animating what the Father originally planted in
His image-bearers, then over time there should be a
recognizable increase in the nature of God.

That is where **Exodus 34:6** becomes a line in the sand.

Not as a harsh measuring stick of condemnation.
Not as a perfection test.
But as a plumb line.

A baptism line in the sand.

A kingdom measuring rod.

When grace is truly at work, we should increasingly be able
to ask:

- Is it becoming **more merciful** or more severe?
- Is it growing in **compassion for the suffering** or merely building image?
- Is it producing **patience** or pressure?
- Is it rooted in **loving-kindness** or hidden harshness?
- Is it walking in **dependable truth** or unstable spiritual language?
- Is it releasing **forgiveness** or preserving subtle offense?
- Is it showing **righteous judgment** or reactive accusation?

This does not mean the vessel becomes perfect overnight.

It means the pendulum cannot be swinging in the opposite
direction while claiming to be led by the Spirit.

That is one of the great deceptions of immature spirituality.

People often assume that because something is energetic, bold, intense, or supernatural in tone, it must therefore be spiritual.

But the kingdom of God is not measured by intensity alone.

It is measured by **nature.**

The Breath must agree with the Father.

The Spirit does not contradict the One who sent Him.

So if what is being called "grace" is producing arrogance instead of mercy, pressure instead of patience, suspicion instead of loving-kindness, instability instead of truth, or vengeance instead of forgiveness, then whatever may be happening, it is not a trustworthy reflection of the nature of Christ.

This is why the church needs more than excitement.

It needs a plumb line.

And the safest plumb line is not merely, "Did something happen?"

It is:

"Did what happened move us further into the revealed nature of God?"

That is how grace is tested without becoming cynical.
That is how discernment stays loving instead of suspicious.
That is how the Body remains open to the Spirit without becoming naïve.

4. GRACE IS FIRST ABOUT INNER ANIMATION, NOT OUTER DISPLAY

Before grace is seen through you, it must begin to live in you.

The modern church has often trained people to recognize grace by public usefulness.

If someone teaches powerfully, they are "graced."
If someone prophesies accurately, they are "graced."
If someone leads strongly, they are "graced."
If someone gathers attention, they are "graced."

But Scripture consistently points us deeper.

Grace is not less than function.
But it is certainly more than function.

The earliest movements of grace are often hidden.

A heart that used to react begins to pause.
A man who used to dominate begins to listen.
A woman who lived in fear begins to settle in trust.
A believer who used to pray out of panic begins to pray out of presence.

That is grace too.

In fact, that is often grace in its safest and most beautiful form.

Because before grace becomes expression through the vessel, it must become government within the vessel.

The soul must learn not to rush ahead.
The body must learn not to dominate the moment.
The inner man must learn how to yield.

This is why Jesus said in **John 5:30**,
"I can of mine own self do nothing..."

That is not weakness.
That is perfect alignment.

It is the pattern of yielded life.

Jesus shows us that true spiritual life does not begin with self-generated action.
It begins with pause, hearing, agreement, and right judgment.

In other words:

He does not move first from independent will.
He moves from conscious union.

That is the atmosphere grace creates.

And that is why before we pray for someone, speak over someone, or attempt to minister in any way, there is a holy wisdom in first stopping.

Becoming aware.

Yielding.

Letting the Holy Spirit have the first word.

Not because we are trying to become passive, but because we are refusing to become presumptuous.

There is a difference.

The soul loves to rush.
The Spirit loves to govern.

And the more grace matures in a person, the more their life begins to reflect this order: not frantic first movement, but yielded first awareness.

This is why some of the most mature believers carry an unusual peace.

They are not empty.
They are not weak.
They are not disengaged.

They have simply learned that grace breathes before grace speaks.

5. TRUE SPIRITUAL LIFE BEGINS WITH AWARENESS BEFORE ACTION

The first movement of grace is often not what you do, but what you notice.

Jesus gave us a pattern in what we call the Lord's Prayer:

"Our Father which art in heaven, Hallowed be thy name..."

Many recite those words as an opening formula.

But there is something deeper happening there.

Before petition comes awareness.
Before request comes reverence.
Before speaking comes recognition.

There is a stopping.
A turning.
A conscious becoming aware of God.

That is not religious theatre.

That is spiritual alignment.

It is the soul stepping out of self-reference long enough to recognize the Presence of the Father.

And when that happens sincerely, something very practical often occurs: the inner world starts to settle.

Breathing changes.
Attention shifts.
Noise lowers.
The soul stops trying to be first.

This is not the whole of prayer.
But it is often the doorway into true prayer.

Because prayer is not merely talking toward heaven.

It is first becoming conscious of God.

And this same principle applies to ministry.

Too often believers rush to fix, rush to speak, rush to interpret, rush to perform, rush to "do something spiritual."

But mature grace often begins with a much holier instinct:

Stop first.

Become aware.

Let the Spirit have the first word.

Let the Breath settle the vessel before the vessel tries to carry the Breath.

That single adjustment can protect people from a thousand soulish mistakes.

It protects prayer from performance.
It protects ministry from self-importance.
It protects discernment from reaction.
It protects gifting from presumption.

And it also trains the whole person—body, soul, and spirit—into right order.

The body stops driving.
The soul stops narrating.
The spirit begins to wake.

This is one of the most overlooked foundations in all spiritual maturity:

awareness precedes safe expression.

That is why grace is not merely a power topic.

It is a posture topic.

It is not only about what comes through you.

It is about whether you have learned how to come under Him first.

Guided Discovery

Before moving into the rest of this chapter, pause here.

This section is not asking you whether you believe in grace. It is asking something more searching:

Have you learned to recognize grace as breath before you recognize it as function?

Sit with these questions slowly.

Write if needed.
Breathe if needed.
Don't sprint past the doorway.

1. When you think of "grace," what do you instinctively picture first?

Is it gifting, ability, ministry, and usefulness?
Or is it life, peace, presence, and the inner movement of God?

If your first thought is outward usefulness, this section is inviting a recalibration. In Scripture, grace certainly includes function—but it begins deeper than that. Grace first breathes life into the hidden man. It awakens, steadies, softens, aligns, and matures what God already planted before it ever becomes visible in ministry.

2. What tends to happen in your body and soul when you become consciously aware of God?

Do you rush? Tighten? Perform? Or do you begin to settle?

One of the quiet evidences of the Holy Spirit is that the whole inner atmosphere often begins to come into order. Breathing may deepen. Anxiety may loosen. The soul may stop pushing to be first. This does not mean every moment feels dramatic—it means grace often announces itself by settling the vessel before using it.

3. Which part of the Exodus 34:6 measuring rod most needs fresh breath in your life right now?

Mercy? Compassion? Patience? Loving-kindness?
Dependable truth? Forgiveness? Righteous judgment?

This is where grace becomes personal. The Holy Spirit is not only empowering gifts—He is maturing the nature of Christ in you. Wherever the pendulum has been swinging out of plumb, grace is able to breathe life back into alignment. The goal is not instant perfection, but increasing agreement with the Father's nature.

4. Before praying for others or stepping into ministry, do you usually pause long enough to let the Spirit have the first word?

Or do you often move from sincerity without first settling into Presence?

Many believers love God sincerely but still move too quickly from the soul. Mature grace learns to stop first. Awareness before action. Reverence before speech. Presence before performance. Letting the Spirit have the first word often protects both the minister and the person being ministered to.

5. What would change in your spiritual life if you treated grace less like a tool and more like breath?

How would your prayer life, your discernment, and your ministry feel different?

Grace would become less pressured and more relational. Prayer would become less frantic and more aware. Discernment would become less suspicious and more anchored. Ministry would become less self-generated and more yielded. You would begin to carry what is true, rather than merely trying to produce what looks spiritual.

Section Anchor

Grace is not first the power to do something for God.
Grace is first the Breath of God bringing life to what He already planted.

And when that breath is truly moving, it will not merely make a person more active.

It will make them more aligned.

More settled.
More yielded.
More truthful.
More merciful.
More safe.
More like Christ.

That is where this chapter must begin.

Because before we talk about fruit, we must understand this:

fruit is what living breath produces in planted nature.

SECTION 2
ATONEMENT RESTORES THE GARDEN OF THE HEART

The cross does not merely forgive sin —it reopens the inner ground where the life of God can grow again.

Core Scripture
Colossians 1:20 (KJV)
"And, having made peace through the blood of his cross, by him to reconcile all things unto himself..."

Section Introduction

If Chapter 2 began by showing that **grace breathes life into what God already planted**, this next section shows **why that breath can now move freely again**.

Something happened at the cross that was far deeper than many people were taught. The cross did not merely settle a legal account in heaven, erase a list of wrongs, or remove the record of guilt. It did all of that—gloriously—but it also did something deeply personal, inward, and restorative: **it reopened the garden.**

The human heart was never meant to be a battlefield of constant inner noise, overrun with shame, driven by fear, hardened by pain, and ruled by self-protection. It was made to be **ground**—holy ground, living ground, responsive ground; ground where truth could land, where the Spirit could breathe, and where God's love could grow something beautiful.

But sin did not only make us guilty. It made us fractured. It bent the inner landscape, turned the soul inward on itself, and taught the human heart to hide, brace, perform, defend, accuse, strive, and survive.

That is why atonement must be understood in more than courtroom language. Yes, the Judge is satisfied in Christ, but the **Gardener** also returns. And where the Gardener returns, the ground can live again.

If the Holy Spirit is the **Divine Breath of God**, and if the gifts are the breathings of that life, then the question is not only, **What has God given?** The deeper question is, **What kind of inner ground is that breath now landing in?**

The cross of Christ is not merely permission to be forgiven. It is the way back into peace, truth, soft ground, inner order, and a heart that can once again receive, respond, and grow.

Many believers are trying to function spiritually while still living inwardly like a locked garden—guarded, rushed, suspicious, performance-driven, and trying to produce what can only be **grown**.

But the cross says something better: **You do not have to manufacture what heaven wants to cultivate.**

The blood of Christ does not merely remove what was wrong. It restores access to what was always meant to be right. And from there, the Spirit does what breath always does: He brings life.

1. THE CROSS DOES NOT ONLY REMOVE GUILT — IT RESTORES GROUND

For many believers, atonement has been taught almost entirely in terms of **forgiveness**, and that is glorious truth. Without forgiveness, there is no peace with God. Without the blood of Christ, there is no reconciliation. Without the Lamb, there is no return.

But if we stop there, we can accidentally reduce the cross to a transaction instead of a transformation. The cross does not merely say, **"You are no longer condemned."** It also says, **"You are now able to be restored."**

This is the difference between a prisoner being legally released and a son being welcomed home.

One is acquittal. The other is reconciliation.

One removes a sentence. The other restores relationship. And relationship is where formation happens.

This is why Paul says that Christ made **peace through the blood of His cross**. Peace is not merely the absence of punishment. Peace is the restoration of right order.

Even after conversion, many people still live inwardly as if they are standing outside the garden gate. They may know the right verses, confess the right doctrines, and believe Jesus died for them, but inwardly they still brace, strive, hide, over-explain, and try to earn rest they have already been offered.

That is not because the cross failed. It is because the soul often takes time to yield to what the spirit has been given.

The cross opened the way. Now the inner man must learn to walk it.

This is why atonement is not only the cancellation of guilt.

It is the restoration of **inner ground**—ground where truth can land without being resisted, where conviction can come without collapse, where correction can happen without identity panic, where peace can settle without the soul calling it laziness, and where love can grow without constantly being uprooted by fear.

That is the garden the cross reopens. And that is why the life of the Spirit can begin to grow again.

Anchor line: The blood of Christ does not only clear your record—it softens the ground where God's life can take root again.

2. THE FALL DAMAGED MORE THAN BEHAVIOR — IT DISTORTED THE INNER LANDSCAPE

If atonement restores the garden, then we must understand what was damaged. The fall did not merely introduce bad actions. It introduced **inner disorder**.

Sin is not just what we do. It is also what it does **to us**.

It twists perception, distorts desire, disorders priority, and trains the soul to reach for control because trust feels unsafe.

This is why Adam and Eve's first instinct after sin was not worship. It was hiding, then blame, then fear. That pattern still lives in fallen human nature: hide, deflect, protect, control, justify, perform. That is the old garden.

Unless this is seen clearly, people will often try to treat spiritual life like behavior management. But the issue is deeper than conduct. The issue is **cultivation**.

A damaged garden can still produce something, but what it produces will often be mixed.

The soul can produce zeal without peace,

knowledge without gentleness,

service without joy,

correction without tenderness,

leadership without patience,

and discernment without mercy.

That is why the world—and sadly many churches—can produce intense activity without true rest.

There is motion, language, and sometimes even visible gifting, but the ground is compacted. And compacted ground cannot receive life well.

The Spirit is not trying to merely improve your old survival system. He is restoring the original order of life **In Christ**.

This is where the Exodus 34:6 measuring rod becomes so powerful. If the cross restores the garden of the heart, then what should begin to grow there? Not just spiritual activity, gifted moments, or impressive language—the nature of God.

Exodus 34:6 (KJV)
"The Lord, The Lord God, merciful and gracious, longsuffering, and abundant in goodness and truth..."

That is not merely information about God. That is the **Kingdom nature** the restored garden is meant to carry.

So the practical test becomes:

Is this inner life becoming more **merciful**?

More **gracious** toward the weak and wounded? Is there **longsuffering**, or only impatience dressed up as urgency?

Is there **goodness**, or merely usefulness?

Is there **truth**, or only forceful certainty?

Is forgiveness being released?

Is judgment becoming cleaner, calmer, and more dependable?

This is the baptism line in the sand. Not perfection, but direction. The pendulum cannot be swinging the other way while we call it maturity, because the restored garden is meant to increasingly look like the nature of the Gardener.

Atonement does not merely manage behavior—it begins restoring the inner landscape to the nature of God.

3. THE HOLY SPIRIT WORKS INSIDE THE RESTORED GARDEN, NOT OUTSIDE IT

Once the ground is reopened, the Holy Spirit does what only He can do. He breathes, hovers, settles, waters, convicts, comforts, and forms.

And importantly—He does not usually begin by making people look dramatic. He begins by making them **alive**.

This is where the "Divine Breath" theology fits like a king post in the center of the roof. The Holy Spirit is not an occasional spiritual event. He is the **Breath of Truth**.

And breath is not meant to be occasional. It is meant to be continual—daily, moment by moment, quietly sustaining what God has planted.

This is why so much of true spiritual life is not loud at first. It is subtle. You stop. You become aware. You soften. You listen. You breathe deeper. Peace begins to settle. That is not weakness. That is often the Spirit regaining first place.

Before we pray for someone, before we move, before we minister, before we answer, **we stop and allow the Holy Spirit to have the first word.** That is not passivity. That is alignment.

Jesus modeled this.

John 5:30 (KJV)
"I can of mine own self do nothing... as I hear, I judge..."

The restored garden is not the place where the soul rushes ahead trying to do something "for God."

It is the place where the inner life becomes still enough for the Spirit to lead.

This is what atonement makes possible. Without the cross, the soul stays in survival mode. With the cross, the soul can begin to yield. Without the cross, everything feels like proving. With the cross, life can begin to feel like receiving. Without the cross, ministry often starts from pressure. With the cross, ministry can begin from peace.

This is critical for the entire chapter, because gifts without restored ground can still function, but they will often carry the flavor of the old garden.

The Spirit does not merely want to use the believer. He wants to **form Christ in the believer**. That requires a garden.

The Holy Spirit does not simply visit the believer with power—He cultivates the restored heart until the life of Christ can grow there.

4. THE CROSS MAKES CONVICTION SAFE AGAIN

One of the clearest signs that the garden is being restored is this: **conviction no longer feels like annihilation.**

In damaged ground, correction feels threatening because when identity is still rooted in performance, any exposure feels like rejection. So people either harden, defend, explain, collapse, withdraw, or counterattack. This is why many believers confuse conviction with shame. But they are not the same thing.

Shame says: *You are bad, unwanted, exposed, and unsafe.* **Conviction** says: *This is not who you are in Christ. Come back into the light.*

Shame drives you from God. Conviction draws you toward Him. Shame locks the gate. Conviction opens it.

This is one of the most healing works of atonement. Through the blood of Christ, correction no longer has to mean condemnation.

Now truth can come close without destroying the heart.

Now the Spirit can put His finger on something and the soul does not have to panic.

Now repentance becomes relational, not merely emotional.

Now confession becomes cleansing, not self-humiliation.

Now growth becomes possible.

Many believers need to relearn what conviction feels like. It is not the whip of heaven. It is the hand of the Gardener—firm enough to prune, gentle enough to preserve, wise enough to know what must go, and loving enough to know what is still becoming.

Once that becomes clear, the soul stops fearing exposure quite so much, because the cross has already spoken first.

You are not being corrected to be thrown away. You are being tended because you belong.

That is a very different atmosphere. And it is exactly the atmosphere where fruit can grow.

Atonement makes truth safe enough to heal, because the cross has already removed the fear of being cast away.

5. PEACE IS NOT THE REWARD AT THE END — IT IS THE SOIL WE MINISTER FROM

This section is the hinge into what comes next. Once the garden is reopened and the Spirit begins to restore inner ground, something begins to settle that many believers have spent years trying to "arrive at."

Peace.

But peace is not merely a finish line. It is a **starting environment**. That is why Colossians says He made peace through the blood of His cross. Peace is not the luxury prize after years of striving. It is the climate of the restored garden.

This matters because many people still minister as if pressure is proof of sincerity.

They feel urgency and call it burden. They feel anxiety and call it zeal. They feel control and call it leadership. They feel intensity and call it anointing.

But the cross teaches something radically different. Christ did not redeem us so we could become more spiritually stressed.

He redeemed us so that heaven's life could begin to grow in human vessels again.

And heaven's life carries a very particular atmosphere. Not passivity. Not indifference. Not softness without strength. But peace—a peace strong enough to tell the truth, stable enough to wait, clean enough to discern, humble enough to listen, and secure enough not to manipulate outcomes.

This is why the fruit of the Spirit is not decorative. It is environmental.

Love. Joy. Peace. Longsuffering. Gentleness. Goodness. Faith. Meekness. Temperance.

That is not a religious list. That is the **atmosphere of the restored garden**.

And this is exactly where the Very Good Life begins to make practical sense, because the world keeps chasing outwardly what God has already planted inwardly.

The world chases peace by control; God grows peace by surrender. The world chases joy by stimulation; God grows joy by connection. The world chases love by demand; God grows love by nature. The world chases meaning by performance; God grows meaning by union.

That is why the Very Good Life is not first about lifestyle design.

It is about **inner cultivation**. And the cross is what reopened the ground where that cultivation can begin.

The cross does not merely promise peace one day—it restores the inner ground where peace can become the climate of life now.

Guided Discovery

Take a moment before moving forward—the key is found in the reflection.

1. When you think about the cross, do you mostly think in terms of forgiveness... or restoration?
Many believers deeply believe they are forgiven, yet still live inwardly as if they are outside the gate.

2. What does your inner ground feel like lately?
Soft? Compacted? Rushed? Defensive? Tired? Tender? Guarded? Hungry?

3. When truth comes close, what do you usually feel first?
Relief? Resistance? Shame? Defensiveness? Hope? Exhaustion?

4. If someone looked at your current spiritual atmosphere, would they say it is increasingly marked by Exodus 34:6?
Mercy, compassion, patience, loving-kindness, dependable truth, forgiveness, good judgment?

5. What would it look like this week to stop and let the Holy Spirit have the first word?
Before prayer. Before correction. Before ministry. Before advice. Before reacting. Before "trying to help."

Section Close

So the cross is not merely where sin was judged. It is where the garden was reopened.

It is where guilt was answered, yes—but also where inner ground was restored. It is where peace was made. It is where truth became safe again. It is where the soul no longer had to lead from fear. It is where the Holy Spirit could begin cultivating the life of Christ in the believer from the inside out.

And once the garden is reopened, the next question is no longer merely, **What has been forgiven?** The next question becomes, **What is now growing?**

Because the life of heaven is not measured first by noise, language, or outward activity. It is measured by **fruit**.

And that is exactly where we go next.

Because **the Very Good Life is not a religious idea to admire from a distance. It is what grows when the fruit of the Spirit is nurtured in restored ground.**

SECTION 3
THE VERY GOOD LIFE GROWS WHERE THE FRUIT IS NURTURED

The fruit of the Spirit is not a religious checklist—it is the lived atmosphere of the Very Good Life.

Core Scripture

Galatians 5:22–23 KJV
"But the fruit of the Spirit is love, joy, peace, longsuffering, gentleness, goodness, faith, meekness, temperance..."

The Very Good Life does not begin outside a person. It begins where the Holy Spirit breathes life into what God already planted. The world spends its strength chasing love, joy, peace, patience, kindness, goodness, faithfulness, gentleness, and self-control as though they are distant treasures. But in Christ, these are not foreign things we must manufacture. They are the fruit of restored life.

Fruit is not decoration. Fruit is evidence. A tree does not prove its health by announcing itself loudly. It proves its life by what grows from it over time.

The same is true within the heart.

When grace breathes life into God's nature, and atonement reopens the garden of the heart, the fruit of the Spirit becomes the visible atmosphere of the inner life. This is where the Very Good Life begins to become livable. Not merely believed. Not merely admired. Grown.

1. Fruit Reveals What Has Been Nurtured

Fruit does not appear because someone demands it. Fruit grows where life is tended.

This is why the fruit of the Spirit cannot be reduced to a religious checklist. A checklist can measure behavior for a moment, but fruit reveals what has been forming over time. A person may act patient once because they are being watched.

A person may speak gently once because the situation is easy. But formed fruit carries a different weight. It appears when pressure comes, when disappointment speaks, when the soul wants to rush ahead, and when the body wants immediate relief.

Fruit reveals the garden.

If love is being nurtured, love begins to appear. If peace is being guarded, peace begins to govern. If patience is being practiced, patience begins to lengthen the soul's fuse. If gentleness is being formed, truth can be carried without bruising what God is healing.

This is why the Very Good Life cannot be faked for long. The atmosphere eventually tells the truth.

2. The World Chases Outside What God Grows Inside

Much of the world's striving is a search for the fruit of the Spirit without the Spirit.

People chase joy through entertainment. They chase peace through control. They chase love through approval. They chase patience by removing every irritation. They chase goodness by comparing themselves to someone worse. They chase faithfulness through personal discipline alone. They chase self-control through willpower until the will grows tired.

But the Very Good Life works from a different source.

God does not merely hand us an improved behavior plan. He restores the inner ground where His own life can grow.

The Holy Spirit does not simply stand outside us giving instructions. He breathes within us, convicts us, comforts us, steadies us, and teaches the soul how to come back under the peace of God.

The world keeps trying to staple fruit to branches.

The Spirit grows it from the root.

3. Fruit Carries Seed

Fruit is not only evidence of life. Fruit carries seed.

This matters because the fruit formed within one person becomes nourishment and possibility for others.

A peaceful person can help settle a troubled room. A patient person can create space for repentance. A gentle person can make truth easier to receive. A faithful person can become a living signpost that God can be trusted. A self-controlled person can protect others from the damage of ungoverned impulse.

Fruit multiplies by being lived.

This is why God's love must be more than an idea. Love that has been formed begins to carry the seed of the Kingdom into every relationship it touches.

It does not need to force itself into the soil of another person's heart. It simply offers the taste of a different atmosphere.

And sometimes one taste of real peace awakens hunger for God.

4. Seed Must Be Planted, Nurtured, and Protected

Seed does not become fruit just because it exists.

A seed may carry life, but life must be planted. It must be watered. It must be protected from weeds, heat, neglect, and trampling feet.

In the same way, the nature of God planted within humanity must be nurtured by the Holy Spirit, guarded by truth, and protected from the old patterns that once dominated the soul.

This is where many believers grow weary. They expect fruit to appear instantly because they have believed the right truth. But truth is not only meant to be agreed with. Truth must be received, practiced, tested, and allowed to reshape the inner life.

A garden grows by rhythm.

The heart does too.

Prayer waters the ground.

Scripture brings light.

Repentance pulls weeds.

Forgiveness clears old roots.

Worship lifts the atmosphere.

Obedience trains the soul to trust the Spirit's lead.

Community gives the fruit room to be tested, strengthened, and shared.

The Very Good Life is not rushed into existence. It is grown by walking with the Spirit daily.

5. The Fruit Becomes the Atmosphere of the Very Good Life

The fruit of the Spirit is the atmosphere people were created to breathe.

Love gives the heart safety. Joy gives the soul strength. Peace gives the inner life room to settle. Patience gives relationships time to heal. Gentleness makes truth approachable. Goodness makes trust possible. Faithfulness creates stability. Meekness keeps strength humble. Temperance gives desire a proper boundary.

This is not small fruit.

This is the life of heaven taking shape inside a human being.

When this fruit is nurtured, the Very Good Life stops being a distant concept and becomes a present atmosphere. It begins in the unseen place, but it does not stay hidden. It affects the face, the tone, the pace, the choices, the words, the home, the ministry, and the way a person carries strength.

This is why fruit must come before public function.

A gift may open a door, but fruit determines whether people are safe inside the room.

Guided Discovery

Question 1: Why is the fruit of the Spirit more than a religious checklist?

Because fruit is not merely behavior we perform for a moment. It is the evidence of life being formed within us over time. A checklist can measure what we did. Fruit reveals what has been growing.

Question 2: Why does the world often chase externally what God wants to grow internally?

Because people long for love, joy, peace, and stability, but often seek them through control, approval, entertainment, or achievement. God restores the inner ground so these things can grow from His life within us.

Question 3: Why does fruit need to be nurtured and protected?

Because seed carries life, but it must be planted, watered, guarded, and given time. The heart must be tended through prayer, truth, repentance, forgiveness, obedience, and daily awareness of the Holy Spirit.

Question 4: How does fruit affect ministry and relationships?

Fruit creates atmosphere. Peace settles. Patience gives room. Gentleness protects. Faithfulness builds trust. Self-control sets boundaries. Without fruit, even real gifting can become unsafe.

Question 5: What makes the Very Good Life grow?

The Very Good Life grows when the Holy Spirit breathes life into God's nature within us, and we continue to nurture that life until the fruit of the Spirit becomes the atmosphere we live from.

Bridge Into Section 4

Once the fruit of the Spirit becomes the atmosphere of the inner life, ministry begins to change.

We no longer minister from pressure, panic, control, or the need to produce results. We begin to minister from peace. The cross teaches us that love does not manipulate people into life. It lays itself down, trusts the Father, and gently leads others toward the garden God is restoring.

That is where we turn next.

SECTION 4.
THE CROSS TEACHES US TO MINISTER FROM PEACE, NOT PRESSURE

True ministry does not push or pull people—it gently leads them into the peace of God's love.

Core Scripture — John 20:21–22 KJV
"Then said Jesus to them again, Peace be unto you: as my Father hath sent me, even so send I you. And when he had said this, he breathed on them, and saith unto them, Receive ye the Holy Ghost."

The first thing Jesus released after the cross was not urgency. It was peace.

He did not return to frightened disciples demanding immediate courage, visible results, or spiritual performance.

He stood among them and said, **Peace be unto you.** That moment gives us more than comfort—it gives us the nature of true ministry. Ministry in Christ does not begin with pressure. It begins with the settled presence of the risen Christ.

1. PEACE IS THE FIRST ATMOSPHERE OF TRUE MINISTRY

The cross did not create a ministry of panic. It revealed a ministry of peace.

Jesus did not save through manipulation, emotional force, or spiritual pressure. He laid His life down, revealed the Father, and made a way for love to enter where striving had ruled. That means the first atmosphere of true ministry is not intensity—it is **peace.**

If ministry begins in pressure, it will often reproduce pressure. If it begins in fear, it will spread fear. If it begins in insecurity, it will quietly search for outcomes to prove itself. But if it begins in the peace of Christ, it carries another spirit.

It becomes steady without becoming passive, gentle without becoming weak, and clear without becoming harsh.

This is why the cross matters so deeply here. The cross is not only where sin was dealt with. It is also where the spirit of coercion was exposed.

Jesus did not force hearts open. He did not control people into transformation. He made a way for truth and love to reach the heart without violating it.

That is the first lesson: peace is not the absence of ministry. Peace is the proper atmosphere of ministry.

2. THE CROSS EXPOSES THE SPIRIT OF CONTROL

The cross teaches us that God does not build His kingdom through control.

Jesus ministered from surrender, not striving. He spoke what He heard from the Father. He did what He saw the Father doing. He did not need to manufacture movement to prove heaven was near. He carried heaven because He remained yielded.

That is the pattern for us.

To live **In Christ** is to flow in the anointed presence of God's love like Jesus.

That means ministry must never be driven by soul-pressure, insecurity, or the need to secure outcomes. It must not push people into agreement, pull people into dependence, or create emotional force so something appears spiritual.

This is where many sincere believers drift without realizing it.

Concern can become control. Burden can become pressure. Passion can become force. Care can become overreach. The outward actions may still look spiritual, but the inward atmosphere has changed.

The cross calls us back to surrendered strength.

True ministry gently leads people toward God's love and trusts the Holy Spirit to do what only the Holy Spirit can do.

3. THE FRUIT OF THE SPIRIT MAKES MINISTRY SAFE

This is where the fruit of the Spirit becomes more than private character. It becomes the safe place from which all ministry should flow.

Peace becomes the atmosphere.

Patience becomes the pace.

Gentleness becomes the touch.

Self-control becomes the boundary.

These are not decorative virtues. They are the inner conditions that make spiritual ministry trustworthy.

Without peace, ministry becomes anxious.
Without patience, it becomes forceful.
Without gentleness, it bruises.
Without self-control, it crosses lines while calling itself care.

That is why the fruit must come before the force.

A person can be passionate and still peaceful. A person can be direct and still gentle. A person can correct and still carry compassion. A person can lead and still refuse control.

That is what formed fruit looks like in motion.

The gift may be real, but if the atmosphere is wrong, the experience can still wound. The cross teaches us that spiritual function without formed nature may still move powerfully, but it will not consistently feel like Jesus.

4. EXODUS 34:6 IS THE MEASURING ROD OF MINISTRY

This is where the nature of God becomes the measuring line again.

Everything that claims to be ministry must be tested in the light of God's revealed nature. Exodus 34:6 is not just a beautiful description of the Father—it is the baptism line in the sand for discernment.

If something claims to represent God, it must be measured by the kind of God He says He is.

Is it mercy-full?
Is it compassion helping the suffering?
Is it patience—or is it pressure?
Is it rooted in loving-kindness?
Is it dependable truth?
Is it releasing forgiveness?
Is it carrying good judgment?

This is not a call to unrealistic perfection. None of us carry this flawlessly at all times. But the plumb line cannot be swinging in the opposite direction while we still call it spiritual maturity.

If ministry consistently produces fear, confusion, pressure, control, humiliation, or dependency, something is off in the atmosphere—even if the language sounds spiritual.

This is what makes discernment practical.

We are not merely asking, *Was something powerful?* We are asking, *Did it carry the nature of God's love in Christ?*

That question protects the Body.

5. WE ARE SERVANTS, NOT SAVIORS

The cross also teaches us to release the burden of outcomes.

We can pray, serve, teach, warn, comfort, confront, encourage, and lay hands on people—but we cannot become the inward force of transformation for another person.

When we try to force change, we step beyond our grace. When we try to carry what belongs to God, ministry becomes heavy.

The peace of Christ protects both the one ministering and the one being ministered to.

It reminds us that we are servants, not saviors.
Witnesses, not owners.
Gardeners, not manufacturers of fruit.

We plant. We water. God gives the increase.

That one truth removes a great deal of false pressure from ministry.

We are called to be faithful, not controlling. We are called to be available, not all-powerful. We are called to reveal God's love, not replace God's role in someone else's transformation.

When this settles into the heart, ministry becomes lighter without becoming shallow. It becomes stronger without becoming forceful. It becomes freer without losing responsibility.

6. THE BODY OF CHRIST IS BUILT BY PEACEFUL GRACE

The Body of Christ is not built by pressure. It is built by grace flowing through people whose inner garden is being formed by God's love.

True ministry does not drag people toward God. It reveals enough of His nature that hearts begin to trust Him again.

When ministry flows from peace, people can breathe. They can listen. They can heal. They can grow. They can begin to recognize that God's love is not another burden laid upon their shoulders, but the atmosphere where life becomes whole again.

That is why the fruit must come before the force. That is why peace must govern the gift. That is why the cross teaches us to minister from rest, not recoil.

The gift may be real. The calling may be genuine. The burden may be sincere. But if the atmosphere is wrong, the experience will still wound.

The cross teaches us a better way: surrendered strength, peaceful authority, gentle truth, and love that refuses to manipulate.

This is the kind of ministry that feels like Jesus.

Guided Discovery

1. Where have I mistaken pressure for spiritual passion?

Pressure often appears when I believe the outcome depends on me instead of trusting God to work through peace, truth, and love.

2. What atmosphere do people experience when I try to help them?
They should experience safety, patience, clarity, and peace—not control, anxiety, guilt, or emotional force.

3. Where do I need to release control and trust the Holy Spirit more?
 I need to notice where I am trying to force change, fix people too quickly, or carry burdens God never asked me to carry.

4. How does the cross reshape my understanding of ministry?
The cross shows me that true ministry lays down control and reveals God's love through surrender, mercy, truth, and peace.

5. What fruit must be strengthened in me before my gift becomes safer for others?
Peace, patience, gentleness, and self-control must deepen in me so my ministry reflects Christ, not pressure.

Take a moment before moving forward—the key is found in the reflection.

When ministry flows from peace, the gift no longer needs to prove itself. It becomes a servant of God's love.

And that brings us to the closing beam of this chapter: **fivefold ministry itself must never operate outside the garden of formed fruit.**

When ministry flows from peace, the gift no longer needs to prove itself. It becomes a servant of God's love.

Fivefold ministry itself must never operate outside the garden of formed fruit.

SECTION 5
FIVEFOLD MINISTRY MUST FLOW FROM GOD'S GARDEN OF FRUIT

Every gift may be real, but only fruit makes spiritual ministry safe, trustworthy, and truly Christlike.

Core Scripture
Galatians 5:22–23 (KJV)
"But the fruit of the Spirit is love, joy, peace, longsuffering, gentleness, goodness, faith, meekness, temperance: against such there is no law."

This closing section brings the chapter forward into the wider argument of the book.

The gifts of the Spirit and the ministries of Christ were never meant to operate outside the garden of formed nature. Grace may be present. Function may be real. Influence may be visible. But if the inner life is not being shaped by the Spirit, the very thing meant to help can begin to harm.

That is one of the great lessons of the Very Good Life:

Power without fruit can still move—but it cannot be fully trusted.

Words of wisdom, words of knowledge, prophecy, healing, discernment, teaching, leadership, and helps all become truly safe when they rise from rooted love, peace, patience, faithfulness, and self-control.

The Spirit does not merely want to *manifest through us*—He wants to *form Christ within us*.

Fruit is not the decoration around ministry.
Fruit is the climate ministry was always meant to breathe in.

1 GIFTS MAY FUNCTION BEFORE CHARACTER FULLY FORMS

A thing can be spiritually active before it is spiritually mature.

This is where many people get confused.

They assume that because something moved powerfully, it must also be safe. Because a word was accurate, they assume the vessel is healthy. Because someone carries authority, they assume the inner life has already been deeply formed.

But scripture and experience both tell us otherwise.

A person may speak something true and still carry impatience.
A person may lead strongly and still carry insecurity.
A person may discern sharply and still wound unnecessarily.
A person may help faithfully and still drift into resentment.
A person may teach accurately and still lack gentleness.

This is why the fruit of the Spirit must remain the measuring rod.

The issue is not merely, **"Did something spiritual happen?"**
The deeper question is, **"What kind of nature carried it?"**

If the ministry feels hurried, pressured, proud, controlling, cold, self-exalting, or unstable, the gift may still be functioning—but the garden needs attention.

The Father is not only interested in what flows *through* us. He is deeply interested in what is growing *in* us.

2 FIVEFOLD MINISTRY WAS NEVER MEANT TO GROW IN STRIVING

Christ gives ministries to build the Body, not to create dependency, pressure, or spiritual theatre.

Ephesians 4 shows us that apostles, prophets, evangelists, pastors, and teachers are gifts from Christ to His Body. But those ministries were never meant to become titles searching for a platform. They were meant to become mature expressions of Christ's care.

That means fivefold ministry must grow in the same garden as every other grace.

An apostolic gift without patience can become forceful.
A prophetic gift without gentleness can become cutting.
A teaching gift without love can become heavy.
A pastoral gift without truth can become soft in the wrong places.
An evangelistic gift without peace can become driven by urgency more than discernment.

The ministry itself may be real.
But if it is not rooted in the fruit of the Spirit, it can begin to pull people by pressure rather than lead them by peace.

Jesus never ministered from inner panic.

He moved with urgency when needed, but not with anxiety.
He spoke strongly when needed, but not from ego.

He corrected sharply when needed, but not from instability.
He carried authority without needing to prove He had it.

That is the pattern.

True ministry does not merely express a role. It reveals a nature.

3 FRUIT IS THE SAFETY SYSTEM OF SPIRITUAL POWER

Fruit makes ministry breathable.

This is one of the simplest ways to say it, and one of the most important.

When fruit is present, people can breathe around a gift.

Love makes people feel valued, not used.
Joy keeps ministry from becoming grim and performative.
Peace removes the subtle hum of pressure.
Longsuffering gives room for growth.
Gentleness keeps truth from bruising unnecessarily.
Goodness keeps motives clean.
Faithfulness makes ministry dependable over time.
Meekness carries strength without domination.
Temperance keeps power inside healthy boundaries.

This is why fruit is not a "nice extra."

It is the Spirit's built-in safety system.

A real gift can gather attention.
Only fruit can build trust.

A real gift can create moments.
Only fruit can sustain environments.

A real gift can impress the room.
Only fruit can help the room heal.

And in the wider argument of this book, that matters deeply.

Because the goal is not to raise impressive ministers.
The goal is to see the **Body of Christ become livable,
breathable, and beautiful again.**

4 GOD'S GARDEN IS THE MEASURING ROD FOR ALL MINISTRY

The ministry may look spiritual, but does it smell like God's
nature?

This is where Exodus 34:6 quietly becomes one of the
strongest discernment tools in the whole book.

If ministry is to flow **In Christ**—in the anointed presence of
God's love like Jesus—then it must increasingly reflect the
nature of the One it claims to represent.

So the line in the sand becomes simple:

Is it **merciful**—or merely forceful?
Is it **compassionate**—or only impressive?
Is it **patient**—or subtly pressuring?
Is it **loving-kindness**—or merely polished presentation?
Is it **truthful and dependable**—or exaggerated and
unstable?
Is it **forgiving**—or does it quietly keep score?
Is it **just and rightly weighted**—or is it reactive and self-
serving?

No ministry is carried perfectly.
No vessel is fully finished.

But the pendulum cannot be swinging in the other direction and still claim maturity.

This is not a standard of condemnation.
It is a standard of alignment.

It gives the believer a way to discern not only whether something is powerful, but whether it is being carried in the spirit of Christ.

And that matters, because the Kingdom that endures forever is not built merely on power displays.

It is built on the nature of God.

5 THE GARDEN MUST GROW BEFORE THE TREE CAN CARRY WEIGHT

The stronger the ministry, the deeper the roots must go.

This is where Chapter 2 naturally hands the whole structure into the next movement of the book.

If the fruit of the Spirit is the visible atmosphere of healthy inner life, then the next question becomes:

How does that inner life actually become strong enough to carry increasing grace?

That is where many believers stall.

They may understand gifts.
They may admire fruit.
They may desire maturity.
But they do not yet understand the deeper internal building blocks that stabilize the soul, strengthen the spirit, and

prepare the whole life to carry more without collapsing under it.

Fruit is the garden in bloom.
But before bloom, there must be strengthening in the root system.

Before wide branches, there must be inner formation.
Before shelter for others, there must be strengthening within.

So Chapter 2 closes here, not with ministry as the final goal, but with formation as the necessary bridge.

Because before the house can carry more weight, the inner frame must be strengthened.

And that leads us exactly where we need to go next.

GUIDED DISCOVERY

1. Have I ever mistaken visible gifting for full maturity?

Yes—many of us naturally assume visible grace means inward maturity, but scripture teaches us to discern more carefully. A gift may be real while the inner life is still being formed.

2. Which fruit of the Spirit most affects whether I feel safe around a ministry expression?

Peace, gentleness, patience, and faithfulness often determine whether ministry feels safe and trustworthy. These fruits create the atmosphere where grace can be received without pressure.

3. Do I tend to admire power more quickly than I discern nature?

It is easy to notice what is powerful before asking whether it is Christlike.

This question helps slow the soul down and measure what is happening by God's love rather than by impact alone.

4. Where might God be inviting me to value formation as much as function?

God may be shifting my focus from chasing impact to becoming a vessel that can carry impact safely. He often deepens the roots before He increases the visible weight.

5. If my current grace increased tomorrow, would my inner roots be ready to carry it well?

If the roots are still shallow, the loving answer is not shame —it is deeper formation. God is not trying to expose weakness to condemn us, but to strengthen us for what is ahead.

BRIDGE TO CHAPTER 3

The fruit of the Spirit shows us what healthy life looks like when the garden is alive.

But fruit is not magic.
It grows from deeper inner strengthening.

So before we move further into gifts, ministries, and function, we must step beneath the visible bloom and examine the hidden graces that stabilize the believer from within.

Because the next stage of maturity is not merely learning how to *express* grace.

It is learning how to be *built strong enough* to carry it.

The inner building blocks of spiritual maturity that prepare a believer to carry all other gifts well.

Using **2 Peter 1:5–7**, chapter 3 explores **faith, virtue, knowledge, temperance, patience, godliness, brotherly kindness, and charity** as inner graces that help stabilize the believer.

This is the formation chapter—
the sapling growing into a tree strong enough to shelter others.

CHAPTER 3. THE FOUNDATIONAL GRACES OF THE SPIRIT

Before a tree can carry fruit for others, it must become strong enough not to split under the weight.

Core Scripture
2 Peter 1:5–7 (KJV)
"And beside this, giving all diligence, add to your faith virtue; and to virtue knowledge;
And to knowledge temperance; and to temperance patience; and to patience godliness;
And to godliness brotherly kindness; and to brotherly kindness charity."

The gifts of God are real, but not everything real is yet ready to carry weight well.

A believer may begin to sense grace, function, insight, burden, discernment, or even unusual spiritual sensitivity long before their inner life has become stable enough to carry those things safely. This is why Scripture does not only show us gifts—it also shows us formation.

It does not only show us power—it shows us process. It does not only show us what can flow through a person—it shows us what must be built within them.

That is where this chapter lives.

If Chapter 1 established the ground the gifts grow in, and Chapter 2 showed us that fruit reveals the root, then Chapter 3 brings us to the strengthening structure of the tree itself.

Here the life of Christ is no longer merely planted. It is beginning to take shape. The sapling is becoming a trunk. The inner fibres are thickening. The first strong limbs are beginning to form.

This is the formation chapter.

This is where the believer begins to become the kind of person who can carry more without becoming unstable.

Peter gives us one of the clearest inner building sequences in the New Testament. He does not describe random spiritual qualities floating in isolation. He gives us a progression.

Faith is not meant to remain alone. It is to be built upon. Virtue is added. Then knowledge. Then temperance. Then patience. Then godliness. Then brotherly kindness. Then charity. Each grace strengthens the next, and together they form a life that can stand, endure, discern, and love well.

This is not merely a list to admire.

It is an inner architecture.

It is the hidden timbering of spiritual maturity.

These graces are not the visible fruit itself, though they will eventually support fruit. They are not yet the broader branching functions of the Body, though they will prepare a believer to carry them.

They are the strengthening trunk and the first weight-bearing limbs—the formed inner nature that keeps a person from bending every time pressure, praise, misunderstanding, temptation, or spiritual responsibility increases.

Without this kind of formation, a real grace may still be present, but the vessel remains vulnerable.

A person may have insight, but not restraint.
A person may have zeal, but not patience.
A person may have conviction, but not kindness.
A person may have burden, but not stability.
A person may have movement, but not maturity.

And when that happens, what should have become shelter can become strain.

But when these foundational graces are allowed to form deeply, something beautiful begins to happen. The believer becomes less reactive, less easily moved by impulse, less dependent on emotional weather, and more able to remain steady under the pressures of life and ministry.

The soul begins to lose some of its old tyranny. The inner man becomes less scattered. The life of Christ begins to hold shape.

This is how a sapling becomes a tree strong enough to shelter others.

This chapter matters because many believers want to understand gifts before they understand weight-bearing maturity. They want to know what they are called to do before they have learned how to remain stable while doing it.

But Scripture is wiser than our excitement. God is not only interested in expression. He is interested in endurance. He is not only forming moments... He is forming people.

And that is good news.

Because the goal is not to become impressive.

The goal is to become trustworthy.

The goal is not merely to move in something spiritual.

The goal is to become the kind of person through whom the life of Christ can move consistently, safely, and fruitfully.

In this chapter, we will walk through these foundational graces as living realities, not abstract virtues.

We will see how faith begins the journey, how virtue gives it moral direction, how knowledge brings light, how temperance gives restraint, how patience teaches endurance, how godliness aligns the inner life with heaven, how brotherly kindness makes spiritual life relationally safe, and how charity crowns the whole structure with the mature nature of God's love.

This is the chapter where the inner tree thickens.

This is where what was planted begins to hold.

This is where spiritual maturity stops being a vague idea and starts becoming a formed life.

IN THIS CHAPTER

1. FAITH IS THE ROOT OF ALL SPIRITUAL BUILDING

Faith is the first yes of the inner life—the beginning point where trust in God makes all true growth possible.

2. VIRTUE, KNOWLEDGE, AND TEMPERANCE FORM INNER STRENGTH

These graces begin to shape the moral and practical structure of the believer, turning desire into disciplined direction.

3. PATIENCE AND GODLINESS TEACH A LIFE TO STAND

Spiritual maturity is not proven in moments of inspiration, but in what remains steady under pressure, delay, and testing.

4. BROTHERLY KINDNESS MAKES MATURITY SAFE FOR OTHERS

A formed life must become relationally trustworthy, not merely personally strong.

5. CHARITY CROWNS THE WHOLE STRUCTURE

The highest grace is not power, knowledge, or endurance—but the mature love of God made visible in a human life.

What Peter gives us here is not a ladder of self-improvement, but a living sequence of grace. These are not merely traits to collect. They are the strengthening work of the Spirit within a yielded life.

As each one is added, the inner man becomes more stable, more usable, and more able to carry what God may later entrust.

Before we move into the visible functions of the Body, we must first let the inner structure rise.

Before the great limbs spread, the trunk must thicken.

Before others can safely rest in the shade, the tree must learn how to stand in the wind.

So we begin where all true building begins:

with **Faith**.

SECTION 1
FAITH IS THE ROOT THAT REACHES FOR WHAT GOD HAS SAID

Before strength is seen in the branches, trust must first go down deep into the unseen.

Core Scripture

2 Peter 1:5 (KJV)
"And beside this, giving all diligence, add to your faith virtue..."

Faith is the first inner movement in this progression because it is the first true reaching of the heart toward God. Before virtue can stand, before knowledge can guide, before patience can endure, there must first be trust.

Faith is the root beneath the surface. It is the hidden reach of the inner man toward the Word, the character, and the nature of God.

And scripture is clear that this is not a minor matter.

Hebrews 11:6 (KJV)
"But without faith it is impossible to please him: for he that cometh to God must believe that he is, and that he is a rewarder of them that diligently seek him."

It is impossible to please God—and impossible to truly find the Very Good Life—without first believing **that He is** who He says He is, and that He rewards those who diligently seek Him.

That one verse gives us the whole direction of this section.

Faith is not optional.
Faith is relational.
Faith is directional.
Faith moves.
Faith comes to God.
Faith believes He is.
Faith expects that His nature is good enough to be worth seeking.

This chapter is about the **foundational graces of the Spirit**—the inner building blocks that prepare a believer to carry the life of Christ well.

If Chapter 2 was the garden where fruit grows, Chapter 3 is the strengthening of the inner structure. Here the sapling begins to become something more than tender. Here the trunk begins to form. Here the limbs begin to strengthen. What starts as inward life begins to become inward stability.

And the first thing that must be strengthened is faith.

Faith is not merely agreement with doctrine. It is not religious optimism. It is not pretending something is true because we want it to be. In scripture, faith is a living response to what God has said. It is trust placed in the One who cannot lie. It is the inner leaning of the soul and spirit toward God's nature, even when the visible world has not yet caught up.

Put simply:

Faith is a confident expectation in God's love.

Not in vague possibility.
Not in human optimism.
Not in emotional momentum.
Not in the soul's demand for instant relief.

Faith is a confident expectation in the goodness, dependability, and revealed nature of the Father.

That is why faith comes first in Peter's progression.

Without faith, everything that follows becomes strained. Virtue becomes willpower. Knowledge becomes information. Temperance becomes self-punishment. Patience becomes grim endurance. Godliness becomes performance. Brotherly kindness becomes selective niceness. Charity becomes sentiment.

But when faith is alive, every other grace grows from living connection rather than human effort.

Faith is the root that reaches before the tree can rise.

1. FAITH DID NOT BEGIN AT YOUR NEXT PROBLEM — IT BEGAN AT CREATION

Faith is often taught as though it begins when life goes wrong. Scripture presents something much deeper. Faith did not begin as a crisis tool. Faith began as part of the original design of life with God.

Before fear entered the garden, trust was already meant to be the atmosphere of human life.

Man was not created first for anxiety, reaction, or self-preservation. Man was created for relationship. He was made to live from God, walk with God, receive from God, and trust the One who gave him life.

In that sense, faith is not merely the answer to a fallen world. Faith is part of the architecture of the original one.

This matters deeply.

Because if faith is only seen as a response to trouble, then it will always feel like emergency equipment. But if faith is seen as part of the original design, then it becomes something much richer: the restoration of the soul and spirit to their proper posture before God.

That fits the tree language of this chapter beautifully.

A natural tree does not grow by panicking at the wind. It grows by remaining anchored in the soil while reaching toward the light.

So too the believer.

The believer grows toward God from a life anchored in the soil of God's love.

That is why Chapter 2 and Chapter 3 belong together so naturally.

The fruit of the Spirit reveals the life in the tree.
But faith is the first root that reaches downward and upward at once—anchored in love, yet growing toward the light.

Faith did not begin at your next problem.
Faith began in the heart of creation, where man was first made to live in trusting dependence upon the God who is.

2. FAITH BEGINS WHERE GOD'S CHARACTER BECOMES MORE REAL THAN YOUR FEAR

Faith does not begin when circumstances improve. It begins when the heart starts trusting the nature of God more than the noise around it.

Many people think faith begins when they feel strong. Scripture shows the opposite. Faith often begins while a person still feels weak, uncertain, or surrounded by contradiction. The beginning of faith is not emotional confidence. It is a decision of inner direction.

It is the moment when the heart says:

God is still true, even here.

That is why faith is deeply connected to the revealed nature of God. If God were unstable, faith would be foolish. If His character changed with mood, faith would be dangerous. But because His nature is dependable, faith becomes the safest foundation a person can build on.

This is why your larger framework matters so much in this book. The believer is not asked to trust a vague force. The believer is invited to trust **the Father revealed in Christ,** whose nature is mercy, compassion, patience, loving-kindness, truth, forgiveness, and justice. Faith is not floating in empty space. It is rooted in the known goodness of God.

Faith begins when fear is no longer allowed to be the loudest voice in the room.

3. IN THE DOCTRINE OF CHRIST, FAITH IS NOT STATIC — IT IS FAITH TOWARD GOD

This is one of the most important clarifications in the whole subject.

The Doctrine of Christ does not merely say **faith**.

It says:

Hebrews 6:1 (KJV)
"Therefore leaving the principles of the doctrine of Christ, let us go on unto perfection... of repentance from dead works, and of faith toward God..."

That small word matters.

Not merely faith....but
Faith toward God.

The language itself implies movement.

Faith is not meant to sit still as an internal religious idea. Faith is directional. Faith turns. Faith leans. Faith comes. Faith moves toward the One it has begun to trust.

This fits perfectly with the first doctrine listed beside it.

Repentance is a turning **from**.
Faith is a moving **toward**.

Both are directional.
Both are relational.
Both are living.

This is why biblical faith is never mere mental agreement. It is not simply believing something *about* God. It is the heart beginning to move toward Him.

Toward His truth.
Toward His nature.
Toward His ways.
Toward His love.
Toward His life.

This is where many spiritual journeys either strengthen or stall.

A person may admire truth without moving toward it.
A person may agree with doctrine without leaning into it.
A person may say they believe in God while still letting fear, self-rule, or soul-habit remain the true direction of the inner life.

But real faith changes direction.

It begins to orient the whole inner man toward God.

4. FAITH IS NOT PASSIVITY — IT IS AN INNER LEANING THAT CHANGES DIRECTION

Biblical faith is not sitting still and hoping something nice happens. It is an active inward leaning that changes how a person walks, chooses, and endures.

Peter does not say, "Have faith and stop there." He says, **"add to your faith..."** That means faith is the starting grace that opens the door for movement. It is not the end of the journey. It is the first inner alignment that makes growth possible.

In practical life, faith often looks very ordinary before it looks impressive.

It looks like staying steady when panic wants to rule.
It looks like obeying a small instruction before seeing the larger outcome.
It looks like praying before reacting.
It looks like pausing before speaking.
It looks like taking the next right step when the full map has not yet appeared.

That is why your own definition of wisdom fits beautifully here:

Wisdom is the next right step.

Faith often does not receive the whole blueprint first. It receives enough light for the next timber. Enough grace for the next cut. Enough clarity for the next move. The soul often wants certainty before obedience. Faith is willing to obey because it has already settled who God is.

Faith is not passive.
Faith is directional.
Faith changes where the inner man leans.

And over time, that inward leaning changes the whole structure of a life.

5. FAITH MUST BE DILIGENTLY STRENGTHENED OR IT REMAINS A SAPLING

Peter says, **"giving all diligence..."** That means spiritual growth is not accidental. The seed may be given by God, but strengthening requires cooperation.

This is an important balance.

We do not manufacture grace.
But we do participate in its formation.

Faith may begin as a genuine response to God, but if it is never fed, exercised, tested, and reinforced, it can remain shallow. A shallow faith may still be sincere, but it will struggle when strong winds come.

It may love the idea of God, but collapse under pressure. It may speak spiritual language, but have little root when contradiction appears.

This is where Hebrews 11:6 becomes even more practical.

He is not only a God who exists.
He is a God who rewards those who diligently seek Him.

That means diligence is not legalism here.
Diligence is relational pursuit.

It is the repeated movement of the heart toward the One who is already good.

That is why this chapter uses the **sapling into shelter** language.

A sapling is alive.
A sapling is real.

A sapling matters.
But a sapling cannot yet carry weight.

The goal is not to shame the sapling. The goal is to strengthen it.

Faith is strengthened when it is exercised in real conditions. It is strengthened when the believer remembers what God has done.

It is strengthened when truth is chosen over emotional momentum.

It is strengthened when obedience happens before visible reward.

It is strengthened when delay does not become abandonment.

Every time the believer chooses to remain aligned with God's nature in the middle of tension, the trunk thickens a little more.

And this is vital for the chapters ahead.

Because the gifts of the Spirit may manifest suddenly. But inner strength is usually formed gradually.

If the tree is to carry shelter for others, the roots must go deep first.

6. FAITH CREATES THE INNER PLATFORM THAT MAKES VIRTUE POSSIBLE

Peter's sequence matters. He does not start with virtue. He starts with faith, then says to add virtue.

Why?

Because virtue without faith can become moral strain.

A person may try to live uprightly without real trust in God, but the result is often pressure, image management, or religious exhaustion. Outward effort may still be visible, but inward rest is missing. The life begins to feel like performance instead of transformation.

Faith changes that.

Faith says:

I trust the nature of the One I am following.
I trust His way is life.
I trust obedience is not loss.
I trust surrender is not destruction.

From that place, virtue becomes something more than behavior modification. It becomes the strengthening of moral courage from a place of trust.

It becomes the soul learning to align with what the spirit now believes. It becomes the first visible firmness rising from an invisible root.

This is why faith must come first in the formation chapter.

Before the tree can stand upright, it must first be anchored. Before the limbs can stretch, the trunk must know where the root is drawing from.
Before virtue becomes visible, faith must become settled.

Faith is not flashy.
But it is load-bearing.

7. TRUE FAITH ALWAYS PULLS THE BELIEVER TOWARD CHRISTLIKENESS

Real faith does not merely seek outcomes. It seeks alignment.

This is one of the great corrections needed in spiritual teaching. Many people have been taught to think of faith mainly as a mechanism for receiving things—breakthrough, healing, provision, doors opening, outcomes changing. While God certainly does move in these areas, biblical faith is deeper than outcome management.

Faith is first relational before it is circumstantial.

Faith trusts God enough to move toward His nature.

That means real faith will not only ask,
"What can I receive?"
It will increasingly ask,
"What am I becoming?"

This matters deeply in a book about gifts.

Because spiritual gifting can attract attention quickly.
But faith asks a better question than visibility.

Faith asks:

Am I becoming stable enough to carry what God gives?
Am I becoming safe enough for others to rest under my branches?
Am I becoming more aligned with the nature of Christ, or only more interested in spiritual function?

That is why this chapter is not merely about spiritual capacity. It is about spiritual formation.

Faith is the first grace in this progression because it is the grace that turns the whole tree toward the light.

Without it, the growth may still be active, but crooked. With it, the entire inner structure begins to rise in the right direction.

And when faith is rightly rooted, the next grace can be added without strain.

Virtue.

Guided Discovery

1. Have I mostly treated faith as something for problems, or have I seen it as part of the original design of life with God?
If I only think of faith when I need help, I may still be living as though self-rule is normal and trust is occasional. But scripture shows that trust was meant to be part of the original atmosphere of life with God from the beginning.

2. What am I currently trusting more than the revealed nature of God?
Fear, delay, pressure, disappointment, and visible circumstances often try to become the loudest voices. Faith begins when I become honest about what has been shaping my reactions more than God's character.

3. Am I living in faith toward God, or only agreement about God?
It is possible to believe certain truths and still remain inwardly stationary. Faith toward God means my heart is moving, leaning, and orienting itself toward His nature, His truth, and His ways.

4. Where in my life is God asking me for the next right step rather than the full blueprint?
Faith usually grows through movement, not total

explanation. The next right step may be small, but obedience in the small often strengthens the whole inner structure.

5. Has my faith been growing deeper roots, or have I mostly been living on spiritual agreement alone?
Agreement can sound right without being load-bearing. Rooted faith becomes visible in steadiness, obedience, endurance, and peace under pressure.

6. What pressure in my life is currently revealing the strength—or weakness—of my inner root system?
Pressure does not create the root, but it reveals it. The places where I wobble most often show where God wants to strengthen trust more deeply.

If someone rested under the shade of my current spiritual life, would they feel steadiness or strain?

This chapter is not about private spirituality alone. The goal is to become the kind of person who can carry weight, offer shelter, and reflect the nature of Christ safely.

Faith is where the inner life first reaches for God in the unseen.

But faith is not meant to remain alone.

Once trust is rooted, the next grace must begin to rise through the trunk—
not merely believing what is right,
but gaining the inner courage to stand in it.

And that brings us naturally into Section 2:

SECTION 2
VIRTUE IS THE FIRST STRENGTH THAT GROWS FROM FAITH

Faith reaches toward God, but virtue is the first visible strength that begins to form when that trust takes root.

Core Scripture

2 Peter 1:5 (KJV)
"And beside this, giving all diligence, add to your faith virtue..."

Before we go further, we need to make this word simple.

Virtue is the strength behind purpose.

It is a fascinating word because its expression shifts with the object being described, but the common thread is the **inner strength that enables something to fulfill what it was made for.**

A knife has virtue when it cuts well.
A bridge has virtue when it carries weight safely.
A tree has virtue when it stands, grows, and bears fruit.
A believer has virtue when the life of Christ within begins to form enough inner strength to live, stand, and respond in alignment with what God intended.

That is why Peter places it here.

He does not say, *start with gifting*.
He does not say, *start with visibility*.
He does not say, *start with influence*.

He says:

...add to your faith virtue.

Because once faith has turned the life toward God, something must begin to form that gives that faith **shape, strength, and carrying power**.

Faith is not meant to remain a fragile idea.

It is meant to become a life that can stand.

That is what virtue begins to do.

Before the tree grows tall enough to be admired, it must grow strong enough not to bend to every wind.

That is why this second grace matters so deeply.

A believer may sincerely trust God, yet still be unstable in response, inconsistent in conduct, or easily pulled by old appetites, old wounds, or old habits of the soul. Faith may be present, but if virtue is not being formed, the life remains spiritually tender in all the wrong places.

Faith connects.
Virtue stabilizes.

And in the architecture of spiritual maturity, this is one of the first great transitions:

not merely *believing in God's love*,
but beginning to **stand like someone who has.**

1. VIRTUE IS NOT JUST "BEING GOOD" — IT IS INNER STRENGTH TAKING SHAPE

Virtue is often reduced to the idea of "being good."

That is not wrong, but it is too thin if left there.

In the deeper sense Peter is using it, virtue is more than outward niceness or religious restraint.

It is **moral strength, inner excellence, formed responsiveness**, and **stability of nature** beginning to emerge in the believer.

But even underneath those spiritual expressions, the simpler idea still holds:

Virtue is the inner strength that enables a thing to fulfill its purpose.

That is why it belongs immediately after faith.

Faith turns the life toward God.
Virtue begins strengthening the life so it can actually move in that direction without collapsing under pressure.

This is not about trying harder to appear holy.

This is about the life of Christ beginning to produce **spiritual backbone**.

Faith says,
"I trust God."

Virtue begins to say,
"Therefore I will stand differently."

This is where trust begins to take shape in conduct.

This is where belief starts affecting reflex.

This is where the soul starts learning that it cannot keep reacting the old way if the spirit is now turning toward the Father.

A seed hidden in the ground is alive before anyone sees it.

But once it takes root, pressure begins to produce form.

The shell breaks.
The root pushes downward.
The shoot pushes upward.

And in that first struggle, strength begins.

That is virtue.

Not polished religion.
Not image management.
Not public spirituality.

Virtue is the first strong response of a life that has truly begun turning toward God.

It is the early trunk beginning to stiffen.

It is the sapling learning not to collapse under weather.

It is the first visible sign that faith is becoming inhabitable.

And this matters because many believers want fruit before formation.

But fruit grows best on wood that can carry weight.

Faith is the root.
Virtue is the first strengthening fiber in the stem.

2. VIRTUE FORMS WHEN FAITH IS TESTED IN REAL CONDITIONS

A tree does not become strong in a greenhouse forever.

At some point, it must face wind.

In the same way, virtue is not formed in theory.
It is formed in **contact with reality**.

Faith toward God is the inward turn.
Virtue is what begins to form when that inward turn meets real life:

when the old habit calls,
when the pressure rises,
when the offense lands,
when the fear returns,
when the temptation whispers,
when the soul wants to panic,
when the body wants relief,
when the world offers a shortcut.

This is where virtue begins to grow.

Not because you never feel the pull—

but because **you no longer agree with it the same way.**

That is an important distinction.

Virtue does not mean the absence of temptation.
It means the emergence of a stronger inner agreement with what is true.

The old reflex may still knock.

But another voice is beginning to answer.

The soul may still rush.

But the spirit is beginning to steady the wheel.

This is why virtue cannot be separated from diligence.

Peter says,
"giving all diligence..."

That means spiritual growth is not passive drift.

Grace is given.
But formation is cooperated with.

God supplies the life.
You supply the willingness to stay turned toward the light.

The seed carries the design.
But the soil, water, pressure, and time all matter.

A man becomes patient by choosing patience under
irritation.
A woman becomes steadfast by continuing under pressure.
A believer becomes trustworthy by repeatedly choosing
what is aligned with God's love when other options are
easier.

That is virtue being formed in real weather.

And this is where the chapter's tree language becomes
deeply useful:

Roots grow in darkness.
Strength grows in resistance.
Branches grow toward light.

If there is no resistance, there is often very little real
strengthening.

If everything is always easy, much remains shallow.

But if faith remains turned toward God in the middle of pressure, virtue begins to harden the inner grain.

3. VIRTUE IS THE DIFFERENCE BETWEEN SPIRITUAL DESIRE AND SPIRITUAL WEIGHT-BEARING

Many believers sincerely desire good things.

They want truth.
They want peace.
They want holiness.
They want usefulness.
They want to be led by the Spirit.
They want to be safe carriers of grace.

But desire alone is not yet weight-bearing.

A sapling may be alive, but that does not mean it can yet carry fruit, support branches, or shelter birds.

In the same way, a believer may be genuinely alive in faith, but still too unformed to carry certain responsibilities safely.

This is why virtue is essential.

Virtue is what begins to make a life **load-bearing**.

It is what gives structure to sincerity.

It is what keeps spiritual aspiration from collapsing under pressure.

Without virtue, a person may mean well but remain easily swayed.
Without virtue, gifts may arrive before character can carry them.
Without virtue, insight may exceed maturity.

Without virtue, emotion may outrun wisdom.
Without virtue, zeal may outrun love.

That is how spiritual strain fractures branches.

But virtue thickens the trunk.

It teaches the inner life to hold shape.

This is why in the broader argument of this book, the graces of 2 Peter 1:5–7 are so important before we move further into the gifts set in the church.

Because God may plant potential early—

but safe carrying capacity must still be formed.

A person may have moments of power before they have patterns of maturity.

A person may touch something real in the Spirit before their nature is yet stable enough to hold that reality well.

Virtue is part of how God protects both the person and the people around them.

It is the grace that starts teaching the tree how to bear weight without splitting.

Not all growth is upward.
Some growth is strengthening.

And often, that is the growth that matters most next.

4. TRUE VIRTUE GROWS FROM GOD'S LOVE, NOT SELF-HARDENING

There is a counterfeit version of virtue.

It looks strong on the outside, but it is brittle inside.

It is built from willpower alone.
It is built from pride.
It is built from fear of failure.
It is built from image maintenance.
It is built from religious pressure.
It is built from self-protection dressed up as discipline.

That kind of "strength" can look impressive for a while.

But it often becomes harsh, defensive, rigid, or secretly exhausted.

That is not the virtue Peter is describing.

True virtue grows from the same source as true faith:

God's love.

If Chapter 1 established that gifts must grow in the soil of God's love, and Chapter 2 established that fruit reveals the root, then Chapter 3 must make clear that even the foundational graces themselves are not built by self-salvation.

They are formed by grace in cooperation with truth.

Virtue is not you becoming hard.

Virtue is you becoming **whole enough to remain aligned.**

It is not emotional shutdown.
It is not pretending not to feel.
It is not suppressing the soul until it becomes a prisoner.

It is the spirit learning to lead.
It is the soul learning to follow truth.
It is the body learning it is not in charge.

That is a very different thing.

The strength of virtue is not the strength of concrete.

It is the strength of living wood.

It has grain.
It has flexibility.
It can bend without snapping.
It can endure seasons.
It can carry life.

That is why the tree metaphor works so well here.

A tree is not strong because it is rigid.
A tree is strong because it is rooted, living, and responsive to
what is real.

So too with virtue.

**Virtue is living strength under the government of
God's love.**

It is the kind of strength that can still be gentle.
The kind of firmness that can still be patient.
The kind of resolve that can still be kind.
The kind of structure that does not lose tenderness.

That is Christlike strength.

And that is the kind that can be trusted.

5. BEFORE THE TREE CAN SHELTER OTHERS, THE INNER WOOD MUST BE FORMED

One of the great temptations in spiritual life is wanting visible usefulness before invisible formation.

We want fruit before root depth.
We want branches before trunk strength.
We want influence before inward stability.
We want usefulness before hidden shaping.

But God is not in a hurry to grow a tree that will split in its first storm.

The Father is after something more durable than fast spiritual appearance.

He is forming lives that can eventually **carry, cover, and shelter**.

That is why virtue matters.

Before a tree gives shade, its inner fibers must strengthen.

Before it holds nests, it must survive seasons.

Before it bears fruit in abundance, its trunk must learn how to carry weight.

In the same way, before a believer becomes a safe source of encouragement, correction, teaching, leadership, discernment, or spiritual support for others, something must be formed within.

Not perfection.

But integrity.

Not flawlessness.

But dependable grain.

Not image.

But inward substance.

This is where many frustrations in spiritual growth begin to make sense.

Sometimes what feels like delay is actually strengthening.

Sometimes what feels like hiddenness is actually formation.

Sometimes what feels like "Why am I not doing more yet?" is actually the mercy of God building the trunk before the branch spread.

Because once a tree begins to widen, the demands increase.

Once people lean on you, weight increases.

Once fruit appears, responsibility increases.

Once grace becomes visible, scrutiny increases.

So the Father often strengthens what no one sees first.

That is not rejection.

That is craftsmanship.

The Carpenter knows wood.

And He knows exactly how much grain must be formed before the structure can safely hold what is coming.

Faith turns the life toward God.
Virtue begins forming the inner wood.

And once the inner wood is strong, the next grace can grow with far greater safety.

That is why Peter's order is not accidental.

It is organic.

It is living.

It is architectural.

And it is kind.

Guided Discovery

1. In simple terms, what does virtue mean in this chapter?
Virtue means the inner strength that enables something to fulfill what it was made for. In the believer, it is the strengthening of the inner life so faith can become stable, dependable, and load-bearing.

2. Why does Peter place virtue immediately after faith?
Because faith turns the life toward God, but virtue begins to give that faith shape and strength. Without virtue, faith may be sincere but still unstable under pressure.

3. How does virtue form in everyday life?
Virtue forms when faith meets real conditions—pressure, temptation, fear, offense, fatigue, and old habits—and the believer keeps turning toward truth instead of agreeing with the old reflexes.

4. What is the difference between true virtue and self-made religious strength?
True virtue grows from God's love and grace, making a person strong yet tender, stable yet alive.

Counterfeit virtue is driven by pride, fear, image, or pressure, and usually becomes brittle or harsh.

5. Why might hidden seasons of strengthening actually be the mercy of God?
Because God often forms the inner wood before allowing greater visibility or responsibility. What feels like delay may actually be preparation for safe fruitfulness and lasting spiritual weight-bearing.

Bridge Into Section 3

If **faith** is the root reaching toward God,
and **virtue** is the first strengthening of the inner wood,
then the next grace must teach the growing tree **how to rightly recognize what is true.**

Because strength without understanding can still grow crooked.

And that is why Peter says next:

"and to virtue knowledge."

SECTION 3
KNOWLEDGE TEACHES
THE GROWING TREE
WHAT TO REACH FOR

Knowledge does not replace faith or virtue—it gives them direction, helping strength grow toward what is true.

Core Scripture
2 Peter 1:5 (KJV)
"And beside this, giving all diligence, add to your faith virtue; and to virtue knowledge;"

The order matters.

Faith is the root that takes hold beneath the surface.
Virtue is the inner strength that pushes upward through resistance.
But once life begins to rise, something else becomes necessary:

direction.

A tree may have life in it.
A tree may have strength in it.
But unless that life and strength are guided toward what is real, the growth can still become twisted, stunted, or misdirected.

That is where knowledge enters the sequence.

Knowledge, in this progression, is not merely the collecting of facts.
It is not spiritual trivia.
It is not the pride of being able to quote what others have said while never becoming what Christ is forming.

In this chapter, knowledge is the light-sensitive intelligence of spiritual growth.

It is the God-given capacity to recognize what is true, what is useful, what is healthy, what is aligned, and what is worth reaching toward.

Every seed begins as a root... but not every root finds the right light unless truth teaches the direction.

That is why Peter does not say to add knowledge before faith.
And he does not place it before virtue.

A person can know many things and still not move.
A person can understand doctrine and still remain unchanged.
A person can explain truth and still lack the inner strength to follow it.

But once faith has taken hold, and virtue has begun to supply the strength behind purpose, knowledge becomes the next grace that keeps the growing life from reaching in the wrong direction.

Knowledge teaches the growing tree what to reach for.

And in spiritual life, what you reach for eventually shapes what you become.

1. KNOWLEDGE IS NOT INFORMATION ALONE — IT IS TRUTH RECOGNIZED IN THE RIGHT DIRECTION

A tree does not grow because it has data. It grows because it responds to light.

This is one of the great confusions in spiritual life.

Many people hear the word *knowledge* and immediately think of stored information.
Definitions.
Verses.
Teachings.
Books read.
Sermons heard.
Concepts understood.

Those things matter.
But Peter is not merely describing an educated believer.

He is describing a formed believer.

Knowledge in this progression is not simply *what you know*.
It is the growing ability to recognize what is true in a way that actually guides your movement.

That distinction matters more than most people realize.

A person may know scripture and still move in fear.
A person may know doctrine and still react from pride.
A person may know principles and still reach for approval, control, comfort, or self-protection.

That is because information can sit in the mind while the soul still steers the life.

But true spiritual knowledge begins to change the steering.

It begins to retrain the inner reach.

It teaches the believer not only what is true in theory, but what is true enough to trust, true enough to obey, and true enough to build a life around.

Proverbs 1:7 (KJV)
"The fear of the Lord is the beginning of knowledge..."

This verse is often misunderstood, as though knowledge begins when a person becomes afraid of God.

But in this context, *fear* is not terror.
It is reverence.

It is the recognition that God is worthy of being trusted, listened to, honored, and followed.

To revere something is to recognize its worth.
And that kind of recognition deepens through lived knowing.

That is why the fear of the Lord is the *beginning* of knowledge.

Knowledge begins when the heart stops treating God casually.

It begins when faith turns toward Him, not merely believing that He is real, but believing that **He is who He says He is**.

Hebrews 11:6 (KJV)
"But without faith it is impossible to please him: for he that cometh to God must believe that he is, and that he is a rewarder of them that diligently seek him."

Faith is the movement toward God.
Reverence is the posture that receives Him rightly.
Knowledge begins when both are present.

This is why spiritual knowledge cannot be reduced to
intelligence.

A clever man may be full of ideas and empty of wisdom.
A well-read believer may still be unstable in crisis.
A person may be sharp with words and yet blind in
direction.

Because knowledge, in the kingdom, is not proven by how
much truth you can repeat.

It is proven by what your life reaches toward when the light
is not obvious.

When pressure comes... what do you move toward?
When disappointment comes... what do you interpret it
through?
When desire rises... what do you call good?
When opportunity appears... what do you measure it
against?

That is where knowledge reveals itself.

Not in the classroom only.
In the turning.

Not merely in what you can explain.
In what you can recognize.

Not merely in what sits in your memory.
In what governs your direction.

The growing tree must learn what light is.

Because not everything bright is life. And not every open
door leads upward.

Knowledge is not merely stored truth—it is truth recognized clearly enough to guide the next reach.

2. KNOWLEDGE TEACHES THE SOUL TO STOP CALLING DARKNESS LIGHT

The soul will reach for what feels familiar unless truth retrains what it calls good.

This is where this grace becomes deeply practical.

The soul is a pattern-maker.
It learns through repetition, memory, pain, relief, reward, fear, habit, and emotional association.

That means if the soul has been trained in the wrong environment, it can become highly skilled at reaching for the wrong light.

A person can call relief peace.
A person can call numbness rest.
A person can call control wisdom.
A person can call flattery love.
A person can call excitement purpose.
A person can call avoidance patience.
A person can call passivity faith.

This is why knowledge is necessary.

Because the soul often mislabels what it is reaching for.

And if the labels are wrong, the direction will be wrong.

The branch may look alive for a while... but it will keep bending toward distortion.

Isaiah 5:20 (KJV)
"Woe unto them that call evil good, and good evil; that put darkness for light, and light for darkness..."

That is not only a cultural warning.
It is an inner warning.

One of the deepest works of God in a believer's life is to retrain the soul's definitions.

To teach us again what peace really is.
What love really is.
What strength really is.
What patience really is.
What success really is.
What spiritual maturity actually looks like.

Without this retraining, the believer may be sincere but unstable.

The tree may be growing... but toward a false sun.

This is where the Word of God becomes more than a religious text.

It becomes a measuring rod.

It becomes the straight line beside the trunk.

It becomes the sunlight test.

Not everything that feels urgent is important.
Not everything that feels spiritual is the Spirit.
Not everything that feels strong is virtue.
Not everything that feels right is truth.

Sometimes the soul wants quick fruit.
God is growing enduring wood.

Sometimes the soul wants immediate relief.
God is forming rooted life.

Sometimes the soul wants confirmation of what it already prefers.
God is teaching the branch to turn toward what is real.

That is why knowledge often feels like correction before it feels like comfort.

Because it first exposes false light.

And false light is dangerous precisely because it often feels convincing.

John 8:31–32 (KJV)
**"If ye continue in my word, then are ye my disciples indeed;
And ye shall know the truth, and the truth shall make you free."**

Notice the sequence.

Continue.
Then know.
Then become free.

Knowledge is not instant because freedom is not instant.

Truth must be continued in long enough to retrain what the soul has learned to trust.

This is why discipleship matters.

This is why doctrine matters.

This is why repeated exposure to truth matters.

Because knowledge is not only about revelation.
It is about reorientation.

Knowledge retrains the soul by teaching it to stop chasing what glitters and start recognizing what gives life.

3. KNOWLEDGE GIVES VIRTUE A TARGET WORTH ITS STRENGTH

Strength without direction can become waste, pride, or collision.

Virtue is the strength behind purpose.
It is the inner force that helps something become what it was made to be.

But strength alone is not enough.

A strong branch can still grow into the wrong space.
A strong man can still build the wrong house.
A passionate believer can still pour themselves into a direction God never asked for.

That is why Peter says:

"and to virtue knowledge."

Knowledge gives virtue a worthy target.

It tells strength what to support.

Without knowledge, virtue can become intensity without alignment.
Effort without clarity.
Passion without proportion.
Movement without maturity.

A person may feel stirred.
They may feel called.
They may feel urgent.
They may feel spiritually alive.

But if they have not yet learned what truth actually looks like in motion, they may end up spending real strength on the wrong branch.

That is exhausting. And often confusing. Because people then assume the problem was the strength. But many times the problem was not lack of effort.
It was lack of direction.

They were sincere.
But sincerity alone does not make the line plumb.

Hosea 4:6 (KJV)
"My people are destroyed for lack of knowledge…"

That is a strong verse.

Not merely inconvenienced.
Not merely slowed down.

Destroyed.

Why?

Because life can be spent building what truth would never have supported. This is why knowledge is mercy.

It saves years.
It saves energy.
It saves heartbreak.
It saves people from mistaking spiritual momentum for spiritual maturity.

A growing tree does not need more random force.
It needs light it can trust. The same is true in the believer's life.

Before you reach higher… know what is above you.
Before you stretch farther… know what is feeding you.
Before you carry more… know what is true.

Virtue is the strength behind purpose.

But knowledge now asks:

Which purpose?
Whose purpose?
What kind of fruit will this direction eventually produce?

Those are knowledge questions. And if they are ignored, strength may become a servant to impulse, ego, tradition, pain, or pressure. But when knowledge is present, virtue becomes beautiful. Because strength is no longer just force.

It becomes faithful growth.

Knowledge does not weaken virtue—it keeps strength from spending itself on the wrong branch.

4. KNOWLEDGE IN CHRIST IS RELATIONAL, NOT MERELY CONCEPTUAL

The deepest knowledge in scripture is not merely knowing about God, but learning how to walk with Him.

There is a kind of knowledge that fills the head. And there is a kind of knowledge that forms the life. Scripture consistently pushes us toward the second.

This is crucial in a book like this, because we are not merely building a theological filing cabinet. We are building a life that can carry heaven safely.

The Hebrew and biblical sense of *knowing* is often deeper than modern usage.
It frequently carries relational weight.

It implies intimacy, familiarity, tested trust, and lived awareness.

That means spiritual knowledge is not complete when you can explain the concept. It begins to mature when you have walked with the Person.

Jeremiah 9:23–24 (KJV)
"Let not the wise man glory in his wisdom...
But let him that glorieth glory in this, that he
understandeth and knoweth me..."

That is not anti-wisdom.
It is anti-boasting in detached wisdom.

The goal is not merely to know things about God.
The goal is to know God well enough that His nature begins to shape your own.

This fits the whole sequence beautifully.

Faith trusts Him.
Virtue rises in response.
Knowledge begins to recognize Him.

Not just in scripture.
In life.

In correction.
In peace.
In timing.
In conviction.
In restraint.
In open doors.
In closed doors.
In the fruit produced by a path.

This is where knowledge becomes lived discernment.

You begin to notice:

That felt exciting, but it did not carry peace.
That looked powerful, but it did not smell like love.
That opportunity was open, but it pulled me away from truth.
That correction stung, but it brought clarity.
That delay was frustrating, but it protected me.

That is not merely concept retention. That is relational knowledge maturing. And that kind of knowing becomes deeply stabilizing. Because the believer is no longer just reacting to circumstances.
They are learning the ways of God.

Psalm 103:7 (KJV)
"He made known his ways unto Moses, his acts unto the children of Israel."

Many want the acts.
Few learn the ways.

But the growing tree needs the ways. Because acts can be admired from a distance. Ways must be walked. This is where the phrase *In Christ* becomes more than a doctrinal label. It becomes the environment of learning.

To live *In Christ* is not merely to agree with Christ.
It is to remain connected to Him long enough that His truth becomes your instinctive direction.

That is when the branch begins to bend toward the right light almost naturally.

Spiritual knowledge matures when truth is no longer merely studied, but recognized through ongoing life with God.

5. THE RIGHT LIGHT PRODUCES THE RIGHT FRUIT

What the tree reaches for in secret will eventually be seen in what it bears in public.

Knowledge is not an end in itself. It is a directional grace.

Its purpose is not to make the believer impressive.
Its purpose is to help the believer grow straight enough to bear trustworthy fruit. That is the payoff.

Because eventually, hidden direction becomes visible outcome.

Roots are hidden.
Strength is internal.
Direction is subtle.

But fruit is public.

What you repeatedly reach toward becomes what you eventually reproduce.

If you keep reaching toward applause, you will bear performance.
If you keep reaching toward control, you will bear pressure.
If you keep reaching toward comfort, you will bear shallowness.
If you keep reaching toward truth, you will bear stability.
If you keep reaching toward God's love, you will bear safety.
If you keep reaching toward Christ, you will bear something that feels like home.

This is why knowledge is not merely a middle step. It is a protecting step. It protects the future fruit. It protects the later branches. It protects the wider canopy. Because a mature tree will eventually hold weight beyond itself.

Birds will rest there.
Shade will be found there.
Fruit will be taken from there.
Storms will test there.

So the direction of early growth matters more than it first
appears.

Matthew 7:16 (KJV)
"Ye shall know them by their fruits..."

Fruit reveals root.
But fruit also reveals direction.

What has this life been reaching toward? That is why this
grace is so important in the sequence.

Faith begins the connection.
Virtue supplies the strength.
Knowledge teaches the direction.

And once direction is rightly established, the next grace
becomes inevitable. Because once a tree has begun reaching
toward the right light consistently, it must now learn
something else: how to govern its own growth.

How to stop overreaching.
How to hold its form.
How to keep appetite from becoming excess.

Which is exactly where Peter takes us next.

Temperance.

Because once you know what to reach for...
you must also learn how to restrain what would still try to
reach everywhere else.

**Knowledge teaches the branch where life is found—
so the fruit that follows can be trusted.**

GUIDED DISCOVERY

**1. What is the difference between information and
spiritual knowledge?**
Information can fill the mind without changing direction.
Spiritual knowledge is truth recognized clearly enough to
guide what I reach for, trust, obey, and build around.

**2. Why does knowledge come after faith and virtue
in 2 Peter 1:5?**
Because faith roots me in God, virtue gives me strength to
rise, and knowledge then teaches that growing strength
where to go. Without the first two, knowledge can remain
intellectual instead of transformational.

**3. How can the soul mistake false light for true
light?**
The soul often calls familiar things "good" because of habit,
pain, fear, relief, or desire. It can mistake relief for peace,
control for wisdom, or flattery for love unless truth retrains
its definitions.

4. Why is knowledge necessary for virtue?
Because strength without direction can become wasted
effort, pride, or misaligned passion. Knowledge gives virtue
a target worth its strength.

**5. What does it mean that knowledge in Christ is
relational?**
It means I am not just learning ideas about God—I am
learning His ways through walking with Him. Over time,
His truth becomes familiar enough to shape my instincts
and decisions.

6. How does knowledge affect future fruit?
What I repeatedly reach toward in secret becomes what I eventually bear in public. Knowledge protects future fruit by teaching early growth to bend toward what is true.

BRIDGE INTO SECTION 4

Once the growing tree begins to recognize the right light, another challenge appears.

Not every branch should keep extending without restraint.

Even healthy growth must learn boundaries.
Even true appetite must be governed.
Even living things can overreach if they are not disciplined.

So Peter's next word is not accidental.

After knowledge comes **temperance**.

Because once truth teaches the direction...
self-government must teach the pace.

SECTION 4

TEMPERANCE KEEPS THE TREE FROM GROWING WILD

Strength without restraint can still become dangerous. Temperance is the inward governance that keeps growth aligned with life.

Core Scripture

2 Peter 1:6 (KJV)
"And to knowledge temperance; and to temperance patience; and to patience godliness;"

Temperance is one of those words that can sound smaller than it is.

To many readers, it may first sound like mere moderation, or perhaps an old religious word tied to self-denial. But in the progression of spiritual formation, temperance is far more vital than that. It is not merely the ability to say no. It is the ability to remain governed.

A tree may have strong roots. It may begin to rise with purpose. It may stretch toward the light with real vigor. But if it grows without order, without containment, without wise regulation, it becomes unstable. Branches overextend. Weight distributes poorly. Growth becomes impressive, but unsafe.

That is what temperance prevents.

Faith reaches toward God.
Virtue gives strength behind purpose.
Knowledge gives light and understanding.

But temperance teaches all that strength and understanding how to stay governed.

Without temperance, growth can still become wild.

1. TEMPERANCE IS STRENGTH UNDER GOVERNMENT

Temperance is not weakness.

It is not passivity.
It is not lifeless restraint.
It is not fear of desire.

Temperance is strength that has learned who is in charge.

In the natural life, a person may have strong emotions, sharp thoughts, real gifts, powerful appetites, and deep ambition. None of those things are automatically evil. The problem is not always the presence of power. The problem is what governs it.

A river within its banks gives life.
A river without banks becomes destructive.

Temperance is the bank.

This is why spiritual maturity is not measured merely by intensity. A person may be passionate, gifted, persuasive, intelligent, or deeply zealous—and still be ungoverned. If desire is stronger than direction, if reaction is stronger than wisdom, if appetite is stronger than purpose, the life may still be moving, but it is not yet safe.

Temperance is what teaches inner strength to stay under right rule.

Not suppressed.
Not denied.
Governed.

And in the doctrine of Christ, that government is not fear-based control. It is alignment under the Spirit of Truth, in the atmosphere of God's love.

2. TEMPERANCE TEACHES DESIRE TO SERVE PURPOSE

The body has desires.
The soul has desires.
The flesh has impulses.
The mind has cravings.
The emotions have reactions.

Temperance does not pretend these do not exist.

It teaches them their place.

This matters deeply, because many believers assume maturity means the absence of desire. But scripture does not teach that. Maturity is not the disappearance of impulse. It is the ordering of impulse.

A horse may be powerful, but if it cannot be bridled, it cannot carry a rider safely.
A fire may be useful, but if it cannot be contained, it burns the house down.

Temperance is what keeps power useful.

This is why temperance must follow knowledge. Once light begins to come, once understanding increases, the next danger is misuse. Knowledge can inflate. Insight can accelerate confidence.

Revelation can make a person feel further along than they really are. But temperance slows the life enough to remain teachable, sober, and rightly paced.

It teaches the believer to ask...

Not merely, *Can I do this?*
But, *Should I?*
Not merely, *Is this available?*
But, *Is this aligned?*
Not merely, *Do I feel this strongly?*
But, *Who is leading right now?*

That is not repression.

That is maturity learning to steer.

3. TEMPERANCE PROTECTS THE TREE WHILE IT IS STILL FORMING

Young growth is often fast growth.

When a tree is young, it can shoot upward quickly, especially when conditions are favorable. But fast growth is not the same as stable growth. If the trunk is not strengthening, if the roots are not deepening, if the weight is not balancing, the very thing that looks like progress may later become a weakness.

Temperance protects the forming life from premature collapse.

This is one of the hidden mercies of God.

There are times when the Spirit will slow a person down, not because He is withholding life, but because He is protecting structure. What feels like frustration may actually be mercy.

What feels like delay may actually be reinforcement. What feels like limitation may actually be the Father strengthening the trunk before adding more branches.

Many people want expansion before government.
God often gives government before expansion.

Because what grows fast without temperance often breaks under its own weight.

This applies to gifting.
It applies to influence.
It applies to relationships.
It applies to money.
It applies to opportunity.
It applies to ministry.

The issue is not whether growth is happening. The issue is whether the inner structure can carry what is coming.

Temperance says:

Not yet.
Not like that.
Not at that pace.
Not without deeper roots.

That voice may feel restrictive to the flesh. But to the Spirit, it is protection.

4. TEMPERANCE IS THE INNER BOUNDARY THAT KEEPS LOVE TRUSTWORTHY

A person can sincerely love God and still wound others if they are not governed.

This is one of the most important reasons temperance matters.

Because without temperance, even good intentions can become intrusive. Passion can become pressure. Conviction can become harshness. Desire to help can become control. Boldness can become impulsiveness. Even truth, when ungoverned, can be delivered without mercy, timing, or wisdom.

Temperance places a holy boundary around expression.

It asks:

How should this be said?
When should this be said?
How much should be said?
Is this for now?
Is this for them?
Is this coming from love, or from my own need to act?

That kind of inward boundary is not the enemy of love.

It is what makes love safe.

A mature tree does not crush everything around it with unchecked spread. It grows in such a way that others can come near, rest beneath it, and benefit from what it has become.

That is what temperance begins to form in a believer. Not merely private restraint, but relational safety.

It keeps strength from becoming domination.
It keeps confidence from becoming pride.
It keeps desire from becoming demand.
It keeps movement from becoming chaos.

Temperance makes growth livable.

5. TEMPERANCE PREPARES THE LIFE TO ENDURE

There is a reason the sequence continues:

"...and to temperance patience..."

Temperance is what prepares a believer for endurance.

Because patience is not possible if a person cannot govern themselves.

If every impulse must be obeyed, patience will fail.
If every discomfort must be escaped, patience will fail.
If every craving must be satisfied, patience will fail.
If every emotional wave becomes a steering wheel, patience will fail.

Temperance teaches the inner life how to remain under direction long enough for patience to become possible.

It teaches the body that hunger is not always an emergency.
It teaches the soul that discomfort is not always danger.
It teaches the emotions that intensity is not always truth.
It teaches the mind that speed is not always wisdom.

That is why temperance is such a crucial hinge in the progression.

Without it, the life may have sincere faith, emerging strength, and increasing knowledge—but still lack stability. With it, the believer becomes increasingly able to carry weight without immediately reacting, forcing, fleeing, or grasping.

Temperance is the beginning of inward steadiness.

And inward steadiness is what makes patience possible.

GUIDED DISCOVERY

1. What is temperance in this progression?
Temperance is inward government. It is the grace that
teaches strength, desire, and knowledge to remain under
right rule rather than growing wild.

2. Why must temperance come after knowledge?
Because once understanding increases, the next danger is
misuse, overconfidence, or ungoverned acceleration.
Temperance teaches light how to stay safe.

3. Is temperance the absence of desire?
No. Temperance does not erase desire. It teaches desire to
serve purpose and remain aligned under the Spirit of Truth.

**4. Why is temperance important for relationships
and ministry?**
Because without temperance, even sincere love or
conviction can become pressure, control, or harm.
Temperance makes maturity safe for others.

**5. How does temperance prepare the way for
patience?**
It teaches the believer to remain governed under discomfort,
delay, and pressure, making endurance possible without
reacting impulsively.

Temperance does not make the tree smaller.

It makes the tree safer.

And once a life has learned not only how to grow, but how to
remain governed while growing, it is finally ready for the
next grace—the one that proves whether strength can stand
when the wind does not stop.

SECTION 5
PATIENCE AND GODLINESS TEACH A LIFE TO STAND

Spiritual maturity is not proven in moments of inspiration, but in what remains steady under pressure, delay, and testing.

Core Scripture

2 Peter 1:6 (KJV)
"...and to temperance patience; and to patience godliness;"

By this point in Peter's progression, the tree is no longer a fragile shoot.

Faith has already taken root in the soil of God's love.
Virtue has supplied inner strength toward purpose.
Knowledge has given direction and recognition of what is true.
Temperance has restrained that growth so the life does not become wild, impulsive, or self-governed.

Now Peter adds the next two strengthening beams:

patience and **godliness**.

And he places them together for good reason.

Because self-control alone can restrain a person for a while.
But only patience teaches a life how to endure over time.
And only godliness teaches that enduring life how to remain
aligned with the Father while it waits.

Temperance may stop the hand.
Patience steadies the heart.
Godliness turns the face in the right direction while
standing still.

This is where spiritual maturity stops being about moments
and starts becoming about **condition**.

Anyone can look strong in a moment of excitement.
Anyone can sound spiritual in a moment of revelation.
Anyone can feel sincere when inspiration is fresh.

But the real question is:

What remains when the moment stretches?

What remains when the answer delays?
When the prayer is not yet visible?
When the pressure continues?
When the misunderstanding lingers?
When the soul wants relief but heaven is still forming
something deeper?

That is where patience and godliness do their work.

They teach a life to stand.

Not rigidly.
Not proudly.
Not stubbornly.

But steadily.

Like a tree that no longer bends with every wind because the
trunk has thickened and the roots have gone deeper.

1. PATIENCE IS NOT PASSIVITY—IT IS STRENGTH THAT CAN REMAIN

Biblical patience is often misunderstood.

It is not resignation.
It is not emotional shutdown.
It is not pretending pressure does not exist.
And it is certainly not the lazy version of "whatever will be, will be."

Patience is active endurance.

It is the inward strength to remain rightly aligned while time, difficulty, or resistance press against the soul.

James 1:3–4 (KJV)
***"...the trying of your faith worketh patience.
But let patience have her perfect work, that ye may be perfect and entire, wanting nothing."***

That is a weighty line.

The trying of faith does not prove faith failed.
It is often how faith becomes formed.

Patience is what happens when faith is forced to remain standing long enough to become substance in the inner man.

This is why patience cannot be skipped.

A believer who only knows inspiration may still collapse in delay.
A believer who only knows insight may still wobble under contradiction.
A believer who only knows desire may still become unstable when outcomes do not arrive quickly.

Patience is where faith becomes durable. It is where the soul learns that urgency is not always wisdom.
It is where desire learns that timing matters.
It is where expectation is refined until it no longer demands control.

Temperance may say, *Do not react.*
Patience says, *Remain here without losing your alignment.*

That is a much deeper work.

2. GODLINESS IS NOT RELIGIOUS IMAGE—IT IS GOD-ALIGNED PRESENCE

Peter does not stop at patience.

He adds **godliness**.

That matters because endurance alone can still harden a person if the heart is not facing the right direction.

A man can endure and become bitter.
He can endure and become proud of how much he has survived.
He can endure and make his pain part of his identity.
He can endure and still become dry, sharp, suspicious, or self-protective.

So patience by itself is not the goal.

Patience must be joined to **godliness**.

Godliness is not religious performance.
It is not looking spiritual.
It is not vocabulary, tone, posture, or public appearance.

Godliness is the inward orientation of a life that has learned to remain turned toward God.

It is reverence expressed in direction.
It is the life beginning to carry the Father's nature more consistently.
It is not merely avoiding sin.
It is becoming increasingly aligned with what is true, clean, stable, and like Christ.

1 Timothy 4:8 (KJV)
"...godliness is profitable unto all things, having promise of the life that now is, and of that which is to come."

That line is beautiful in the context of this chapter.

Godliness is not just future-focused.
It has promise **for the life that now is**.

In other words, godliness is not only about heaven later. It is about heavenly alignment now. This is where your larger framework keeps quietly humming under the boards: to be **In Christ** is not merely to believe something doctrinally.
It is **to begin flowing in the anointed presence of God's love like Jesus.**

That is what godliness is moving toward.

Not religion.
Alignment.

Not image.
Likeness.

Not performance.
Presence.

3. PETER KNEW THE DIFFERENCE BETWEEN IMPULSE AND STEADINESS

This is where Peter becomes very important again.

Because Peter did not write about patience and godliness as a naturally measured man. He wrote as someone who knew what it was to react first and understand later.

Peter knew what it was to speak too quickly.
To resist what Jesus was saying because it did not fit his expectation.
To act from emotion.
To pull a sword in the garden.
To promise what he could not yet sustain.
To collapse under pressure in the courtyard.

Peter knew what unsteady zeal looked like. And because of that, he also came to know what formed steadiness looked like.

After the resurrection, after the breaking, after the restoration, something changed.

The man who once rushed ahead learned to wait in Jerusalem.
The man who once reacted in fear learned to stand in boldness.
The man who once denied under pressure later endured opposition, imprisonment, correction, and responsibility without losing his direction.

That is not personality polish. That is formation. Peter became a man who could stand. Not because he was naturally calmer than before.
But because grace had worked deeper than impulse.

That is why his progression here carries so much weight. He is not saying, Here is a nice spiritual sequence to memorize.

He is saying, in effect:

This is what happened to me when Christ kept forming me past my reactions.

Faith became tested.
Strength became restrained.
Restraint became endurance.
Endurance became alignment.
And alignment became a life that could remain under weight without falling apart.

That is lived doctrine.

That is spiritual architecture.

4. PATIENCE AND GODLINESS TURN MOMENTS INTO CHARACTER

There is a great difference between having a spiritual moment and becoming a spiritually formed person.

Moments can be powerful.
Moments can be real.
Moments can change direction.

But moments alone do not build character.

Character is built when truth remains under repetition.

When faith remains under delay.
When restraint remains under provocation.
When peace remains under misunderstanding.
When obedience remains under inconvenience.
When reverence remains when no one is watching.

That is where patience and godliness do their finest work.

They turn revelation into habit.
They turn desire into continuity.
They turn private sincerity into lived consistency.

This is why a believer can have a genuine encounter with God and still need years of formation afterward. Because the encounter may awaken the seed.
But patience and godliness help grow the trunk.

And the trunk is what carries the weight later.

Without patience, the life remains emotionally weather-driven.
Without godliness, the life may still endure but drift in its inner posture.

Together, they create something stronger: a believer who is not merely passionate, but dependable. A believer who is not merely moved, but anchored. A believer who does not only begin well, but can continue well.

That is the kind of life that can later carry greater responsibility without cracking.

5. A LIFE THAT CAN STAND BECOMES SAFE TO BUILD ON

This section matters far beyond personal devotion. Because the whole argument of this book is moving toward function.

Gifts.
Ministries.
Expressions.
Responsibilities in the Body.

And none of those are safe in unstable hands.

A person may have insight.
A person may have intensity.
A person may have charisma.
A person may even have genuine spiritual sensitivity.

But if they cannot remain under pressure...
If they cannot endure delay without becoming offended...
If they cannot hold alignment when misunderstood...
If they cannot stand when their emotions are not being rewarded...

Then the structure is not yet ready to carry weight.

And if Peter could do it... then anybody can.

Patience and godliness are what make a life load-bearing.

This is where the tree stops merely growing upward and starts becoming structurally reliable.

It can take wind.
It can take season.
It can take waiting.
It can take pruning.
It can take drought without assuming God has vanished.

That kind of life becomes trustworthy.

Not because it never feels.
But because it no longer obeys every feeling.

Not because it never struggles.
But because it knows where to face while it struggles.

That is one of the clearest signs of maturity.

Not dramatic power.
Not spiritual vocabulary.
Not visible intensity.

But the quiet ability to remain rightly aligned over time. That is a life that can stand.

Guided Discovery

1. What does patience mean in this chapter?
Patience is not passive waiting, but active endurance—the inward strength to remain rightly aligned under pressure, delay, and testing.

2. Why does Peter place patience after temperance?
Because self-control may restrain reaction for a moment, but patience teaches the life how to remain steady over time when pressure continues.

3. What is godliness in this context?
Godliness is not religious appearance, but inward alignment with the Father—a life increasingly turned toward God in thought, posture, and response.

4. Why is Peter such a strong example here?
Because Peter knew what it was to react impulsively, fail under pressure, and then be formed by Christ into a man who could endure, remain, and stand.

5. Why do patience and godliness matter for what comes next?
Because they make the life structurally reliable. Before maturity becomes relationally safe for others, it must first become steady enough to carry weight.

Bridge Forward

A life that can stand is no longer merely growing. It is becoming stable.

But Peter is still not finished.

Because maturity is not complete when a man becomes strong enough to endure.

A formed life must also become **safe in relationship**.

It is one thing to be personally disciplined.
It is another thing to become a person others can actually trust, rest around, and grow near.

That is why the next branch matters so much. Because once the trunk is strong, the question becomes:

What kind of shelter does it create for others?

SECTION 6

BROTHERLY KINDNESS MAKES MATURITY SAFE FOR OTHERS

A formed life must become relationally trustworthy, not merely personally strong.

Core Scripture
2 Peter 1:7 (KJV)
"And to godliness brotherly kindness..."

Brotherly kindness is where maturity begins to feel safe.

Up to this point in the chapter, the inner life has been under construction. **Faith** laid the root. **Virtue** gave the stem strength. **Knowledge** taught the tree where light is found. **Temperance** kept the growth from becoming wild. **Patience** taught it to endure the seasons. **Godliness** turned that endurance upward, so the whole life began to lean toward the Father.

But spiritual maturity is not complete when a man can stand alone.

It is not enough to be disciplined.
It is not enough to be stable.
It is not enough to be reverent.
It is not enough to be inwardly strong.

If the life being formed in Christ does not become safe, warm, and dependable for other people, then the tree is still growing for itself.

That is why Peter does not stop at godliness.

He moves next into **brotherly kindness**.

This is not sentimental softness.
This is not surface niceness.
This is not social polish dressed up as spirituality.

Brotherly kindness is the grace that makes maturity relationally usable.

It is the evidence that what God has built in you is no longer only strengthening *you*—it is now beginning to shelter others. A tree is not called mature merely because it is tall. A tree becomes truly valuable when something can rest beneath it.

That is where Peter is taking us now.

Brotherly kindness is the widening of spiritual maturity into human touch, tone, patience, warmth, and practical care. It is the moment the inner life becomes a place where other people can breathe.

And that matters deeply in the Body of Christ.

Because a strong man who is not safe can still wound people.

A gifted man who is not gentle can still scatter people.
A disciplined man who is not kind can still make truth feel
like threat.
A spiritually serious man who lacks tenderness can still
leave bruises while calling it righteousness.

But brotherly kindness changes the atmosphere.

It takes strength and clothes it with warmth.
It takes truth and delivers it with mercy.
It takes conviction and makes it approachable.
It takes maturity and turns it into shelter.

This is why brotherly kindness belongs near the top of the
ladder.

It is not one of the first visible signs of growth because it is
not merely personality. It is the fruit of many deeper graces
already formed. It is what happens when patience has had
time to soften the edges. It is what happens when godliness
has bowed the heart low enough before God that it no longer
needs to stand over men.

Real brotherly kindness is not weakness.

It is restrained strength made safe by love.

It is the kind of presence that does not make people feel
managed, measured, or threatened. It makes them feel seen,
carried, and given room to breathe while truth still remains
intact.

And in a book about gifts, ministries, and maturity, this
section matters more than it first appears.

Because if the tree is going to shelter others, this is where
the branches stop becoming personal achievement and start
becoming communal blessing.

1. BROTHERLY KINDNESS IS THE FIRST RELATIONAL PROOF THAT MATURITY IS REAL

A person can appear spiritual in private and still be unsafe in relationship.

That is one of the great blind spots in spiritual formation.

Some people can pray deeply, study much, fast long, endure hardship, and speak with conviction—but still be difficult to live with, hard to receive from, or emotionally sharp in ways they do not even recognize.

Why?

Because inward strength alone is not the final proof of Christlike maturity.

Relationship is.

Peter's progression makes that plain.

He does not end with godliness, as if reverence toward God alone completes the structure. He moves from vertical alignment into horizontal expression. That means a mature life must eventually become visible in the way it handles people.

This is deeply consistent with the whole testimony of Scripture.

1 John 4:20 (KJV)
"If a man say, I love God, and hateth his brother, he is a liar..."

John does not allow spiritual language to remain abstract. He brings it back to people.

If love for God does not show up in the way we treat those near us, then something in our claimed spirituality is still incomplete, distorted, or self-deceived.

That is not condemnation. That is calibration.

Brotherly kindness is part of that calibration.

It asks simple but searching questions:

Can people approach you without bracing?
Do people leave you more settled, or more tense?
Does your strength create peace, or pressure?
Does your maturity make room, or make demands?
Do people feel corrected by your tone before they ever hear your truth?

These are not small questions.

These are measurements of whether maturity has become relationally trustworthy.

A man can have correct doctrine and still lack brotherly kindness.
A woman can carry real discernment and still be difficult to receive from.
A leader can be accurate, disciplined, and sincere, and still create an atmosphere that exhausts people.

But when brotherly kindness is present, maturity stops feeling like a wall and starts feeling like a doorway.

Truth is still truth.
Boundaries are still boundaries.
Correction is still possible.
Conviction is still real.

But now the atmosphere changes. People do not merely encounter your convictions. They encounter your care.

That is why brotherly kindness is such an important proof.
It reveals whether the tree is becoming inhabitable.

And in the Body of Christ, inhabitable matters.

Because Jesus did not merely carry truth.

He was approachable.

Children came near Him.
Sinners ate with Him.
The weak reached for Him.
The broken wept around Him.
The fearful found courage in His presence.

He was holy without becoming inaccessible.
Strong without becoming harsh.
Clear without becoming cold.

That is the shape of mature brotherly kindness.

Not soft on truth.
Not loose in conviction.
Not passive in the face of disorder.

But safe.

And a safe life is a powerful life.

Because when people feel safe, they can hear.
When they can hear, they can receive.
When they can receive, they can grow.

Brotherly kindness is one of the first relational proofs that the life of Christ is becoming visible in a human being.

2. BROTHERLY KINDNESS IS NOT NICENESS—IT IS STRENGTH WITH A GENTLE TOUCH

The modern world often confuses kindness with weakness.

Scripture does not.

Biblical kindness is not the absence of backbone.
It is not avoidance.
It is not appeasement.
It is not fear of conflict.
It is not smiling while truth is abandoned.

Brotherly kindness is strength that has learned how to touch
without crushing. That is very different. A man without
strength cannot truly be gentle—he is simply limited.
But a man with strength under control can be gentle,
because he could push harder and chooses not to.

That is maturity.

That is why kindness belongs so high in Peter's progression.
It is not entry-level emotion. It is refined power.

It is what happens when **virtue** has become stable,
knowledge has become wise, **temperance** has become
governing, **patience** has become settled, and **godliness**
has become humble.

Now the life no longer needs to prove itself.

So it can become tender without becoming weak.

This is why Paul speaks the way he does:

Ephesians 4:2 (KJV)
*"With all lowliness and meekness, with
longsuffering, forbearing one another in love..."*

Notice how relational maturity is described.

Not dominance.
Not pressure.
Not emotional force.
Not sharpness mistaken for boldness.

But lowliness.
Meekness.
Longsuffering.
Forbearance.
Love.

These are not the marks of a powerless life. They are the marks of a powerful life that has been surrendered.

A surrendered life does not need to win every exchange.
It does not need to dominate every room.
It does not need to make every correction publicly.
It does not need to prove how right it is.
It does not need to turn every disagreement into a courtroom.

It knows what it carries. And because it knows what it carries, it can move with calm.

Brotherly kindness carries that calm.

It listens before reacting.
It considers before speaking.
It corrects without humiliating.
It protects without controlling.
It confronts without wounding for sport.
It stays warm even when truth must be strong.

That last line matters. Because many people can be kind while things are easy. But brotherly kindness in the Spirit remains present when tension rises.

It is one thing to be pleasant in peace.
It is another to stay gentle in misunderstanding.
It is another to remain honorable when someone is immature.
It is another to preserve dignity when truth requires friction.

That is where brotherly kindness proves itself. Not in convenience.

In contact.

The strongest branches are not the ones that wave in the wind when no one is near. They are the ones that can bear weight without breaking what rests on them. This is also why brotherly kindness is essential for leadership, ministry, and gifting.

A person may carry revelation.
A person may carry authority.
A person may carry discernment.
A person may carry prophetic sharpness.

But if brotherly kindness is absent, the same grace that could have built people can end up bruising them.

That does not make the grace false. It makes the vessel unfinished. Brotherly kindness is what makes the vessel safe to pour from. And the more real the gift, the more necessary that safety becomes.

The greater the strength, the greater the need for a gentle hand.

3. BROTHERLY KINDNESS MAKES THE BODY OF CHRIST FEEL LIKE FAMILY

Peter does not simply say kindness. He says brotherly kindness.

That matters.

This is not generic human courtesy.
This is not social etiquette.
This is not public politeness.

This is familial grace.

It is the kind of kindness that treats others not as interruptions, rivals, audiences, or projects—but as brothers and sisters in the same household of God. That shifts the whole atmosphere. When family is rightly understood, people are not merely assessed for usefulness.
They are valued for belonging.

That is a major correction for spiritual communities.

Because the moment the Body of Christ becomes merely a platform for gifting, a machine for productivity, or a hierarchy of visibility, it stops feeling like home.

And the Father did not design His house to feel like a factory.

He designed it to feel like family.

Ephesians 2:19 (KJV)
"Now therefore ye are no more strangers and foreigners, but fellowcitizens with the saints, and of the household of God;"

That phrase matters: **the household of God**.

A household is relational.

A household has proximity.
A household has patience.
A household has shared burdens.
A household has ordinary touchpoints.
A household has repeated opportunities for mercy.
A household reveals character because you cannot perform
forever in a home.

**Brotherly kindness is what keeps the household
from becoming a battlefield of personalities.**

It teaches us how to carry one another.

Not by pretending weakness is strength.
Not by denying truth.
Not by enabling disorder.

But by remembering that formation takes time, and
everyone in the house is still under construction. That is a
deeply useful lens. Because once you realize the people
around you are still being built, you stop expecting finished
rooms in unfinished houses.

You become less shocked by rough edges.
You become less reactive to immaturity.
You become less quick to label.
You become more patient with process.
You become more careful with tone.

Brotherly kindness gives grace to process.

And if there is any place that should understand process, it
is the Body of Christ.

We are not the museum of completed saints.

We are the living worksite of the Father.

Some are still being framed.
Some are being rewired.
Some are under repair.
Some are being stripped back to the studs.
Some are finally getting windows where walls once stood.

And if we forget that, we start treating people as
disappointments when they are actually construction zones.

**Brotherly kindness keeps the foreman voice from
becoming the only voice.**

It remembers that even when something needs correcting,
the goal is still a home. That is why this grace is so crucial in
communities, churches, ministries, and leadership
structures.

Without brotherly kindness, people may gather but not
bond.
They may attend but not trust.
They may serve but not feel seen.
They may stay busy while still feeling alone.

But when brotherly kindness is present, something deeper
forms.

The room softens.
The pace steadies.
The walls stop feeling cold.
People begin to breathe again.

And suddenly the Body of Christ feels less like an event and
more like a family.

That is not small.

**Brotherly kindness is one of the clearest signs that
maturity is becoming communal.**

4. BROTHERLY KINDNESS PROTECTS TRUTH FROM BECOMING A WEAPON

Truth is holy.

Truth matters.
Truth must be spoken.
Truth must not be compromised.
Truth is one of the great anchors of maturity.

But truth handled by an unsoftened soul can become a blade in the wrong hands. This is one of the reasons brotherly kindness is so necessary. Because spiritual people often love truth—but not all spiritual people have yet learned how to deliver truth in a way that heals.

Some use truth to expose without restoring.
Some use truth to win arguments rather than win people.
Some use truth to relieve their own frustration.
Some use truth as permission to be sharp.
Some call harshness "boldness" and coldness "discernment."

But heaven does not confuse these things.

Ephesians 4:15 (KJV)
"But speaking the truth in love, may grow up into him in all things, which is the head, even Christ:"

Notice that Paul ties this directly to growth. Truth in love is not optional etiquette. It is part of growing up into Christ. That means if truth is present but love is absent, maturity is still incomplete.

Brotherly kindness is one of the graces that keeps truth from mutating into a weapon.

It slows the hand.
It checks the motive.
It tests the tone.
It asks whether this word is being given to heal, restore, clarify, protect, or simply discharge irritation.

That is a critical question.

Because many accurate words have done unnecessary damage simply because the spirit in which they were delivered was wrong. The content may have been right. But the climate was wrong. And climate matters.

A seed may be true, but if the soil is frozen, it will not root well.

Brotherly kindness helps create relational soil where truth can land without immediately triggering defense.

That does not mean everyone will receive it.

Some will still resist.
Some will still harden.
Some will still react.

But your responsibility is not control of outcome. Your responsibility is faithfulness of spirit. And that spirit matters especially in correction.

Galatians 6:1 (KJV)
"Brethren, if a man be overtaken in a fault, ye which are spiritual, restore such an one in the spirit of meekness..."

That is stunning. Paul says the truly spiritual are not proven by how fiercely they expose.

They are proven by how gently they restore.

That does not erase boundaries.
That does not remove consequences.
That does not eliminate seriousness.

But it sets the spirit.

The goal is restoration. Brotherly kindness remembers that.
It knows that every hard word should still carry the scent of
hope.

It knows that correction without dignity can humiliate
rather than heal.
It knows that exposure without covering can wound more
deeply than necessary.
It knows that people often hear tone before they hear
content.
It knows that the right word at the wrong temperature can
still miss its purpose.

This is why brotherly kindness is not ornamental.

It is protective.

It protects people from unnecessary harm.
It protects leaders from becoming hard.
It protects truth from being misrepresented.
It protects communities from growing brittle.
It protects maturity from becoming proud.

It keeps the branch from becoming a spear.

And that is one of the most practical graces in the entire
structure.

5. BROTHERLY KINDNESS PREPARES THE TREE FOR ITS FINAL CROWN

Peter is building in sequence.

Every grace matters.
Every grace supports the next.
Nothing here is random.

Brotherly kindness is not the final grace in the list.

It is the last major relational threshold before the crown.

That is deeply revealing.

Because before Peter speaks of **charity**—the mature love of God made visible—he first gives us **brotherly kindness**.

Why?

Because universal love must first become dependable in actual relationships.

It is easy to speak grandly about love in theory.
It is harder to be patient with actual people.
It is easy to preach charity in abstraction.
It is harder to live with warmth, steadiness, and practical care in repeated contact.
It is easy to love humanity in general.
It is much harder to love the brother in front of you.

Brotherly kindness trains the heart in that practical field.

It teaches maturity how to touch people.
It teaches truth how to travel through tone.
It teaches strength how to make room.
It teaches reverence toward God how to become dependable toward others.

In that sense, brotherly kindness is the branch system preparing for fruit. The tree is no longer merely standing. It is learning to host life. And that is exactly where Peter wants us before he brings us to charity.

Because charity is not vague benevolence.
It is not emotional intensity.
It is not poetic sentiment.

It is the mature, governing love of God expressed through a formed life.

But if brotherly kindness is absent, a person may try to jump to "love" while still being relationally rough, impatient, inaccessible, or subtly self-centered. Peter prevents that jump.

He makes sure the structure is safe before he crowns it.

That is wise.

Because heaven's highest love is not meant to rest on an unstable frame. Brotherly kindness is one of the final stabilizers. It tells us that before the full crown of love can rest visibly on a life, that life must first become livable for others.

Not merely admirable.

Livable.

That is a strong word.

Can people walk with you?
Can they grow near you?
Can they fail near you and still find dignity?
Can they receive correction without being crushed?
Can they bring weakness without being despised?
Can they rest under your strength without being controlled by it?

If the answer is increasingly yes, then brotherly kindness is doing its work.

And if brotherly kindness is doing its work, the crown is near.

Because the tree that can shelter others is almost ready to bear its highest fruit.

GUIDED DISCOVERY

1. Does my maturity feel safe to other people, or merely strong?
A mature life should not only stand firm—it should create room for others to breathe, heal, and grow.

2. Do I deliver truth in a way that restores, or in a way that relieves my frustration?
Brotherly kindness tests not only what is said, but the spirit, tone, and temperature it is carried in.

3. Do people around me feel managed, measured, or genuinely cared for?
Relational safety is one of the clearest proofs that inward maturity is becoming outwardly usable.

4. Am I trying to jump to "love" in theory while still lacking warmth in practice?
Brotherly kindness is the proving ground where lofty language becomes dependable human presence.

5. Is my life becoming a place where others can rest without fear?
The tree is nearing its crown when the branches no longer just reach upward—but begin to shelter what is beneath them.

SECTION BRIDGE

Brotherly kindness makes maturity safe for others.

It turns inward formation into outward shelter.
It makes truth approachable.
It makes strength gentle.
It makes the Body feel like family.
It prepares the structure for its highest expression.

But Peter does not end with relational warmth alone. There is still one grace above all the rest.

One crown above every branch.
One final completion above strength, knowledge, discipline, endurance, reverence, and even brotherly kindness.

Because the highest maturity is not merely a life that can stand.
It is a life through which the very love of God becomes visible.

And that is where the whole tree was always meant to land.

The highest grace is not power, knowledge, or endurance—but the mature love of God made visible in a human life.

SECTION 7
CHARITY CROWNS THE WHOLE STRUCTURE

The highest grace is not power, knowledge, or endurance—but the mature love of God made visible in a human life.

Core Scripture
2 Peter 1:7 (KJV)
"...and to brotherly kindness charity."

The final word in Peter's ladder is not accidental.

He does not end with strength.
He does not end with knowledge.
He does not end with endurance.
He does not even end with brotherly kindness.

He ends with **charity**.

1. CHARITY IS MORE THAN A WORD —IT IS LOVE MADE VISIBLE

To many modern readers, that word can feel smaller than it once did. It may call to mind a collection tin, a donation box, or a handout given in passing. But in scripture, the word carries far more weight than that.

In the older sense, **charity is not the loose change in your pocket—it is the visible manifestation of love becoming real heart-delivered support for the suffering.** It is not merely the act of giving. It is the formed expression of a heart rightly aligned.

There is **a charity**… and then there is **actual charity**.

One may wear the name.
The other carries the nature.

That is why the KJV's use of **charity** is so powerful here. Peter is not simply repeating himself after brotherly kindness by adding a vague word for love. He is bringing the entire structure to its highest expression.

Brotherly kindness is relational affection. It is warmth among the branches. It is maturity becoming safe for others. But **charity** is something greater still. It is the whole tree reaching its intended form. It is the life of God becoming visible in the fruit, the shade, and the nourishment the tree now offers.

2. AGAPĒ MUST BE UNDERSTOOD THROUGH GOD'S NATURE, NOT MODERN SENTIMENT

The Greek word beneath this is **agapē**—often described in Christian circles as unconditional love. That phrase can be helpful, but it can also become misleading if it is left undefined. God's love is not careless. God's love is not permissive confusion. God's love is not sentiment without wisdom. God's love is not the removal of all boundaries.

God's love is good, and good requires truth, order, and sound judgment.

This is where many people lose the line.

If love is detached from truth, it becomes subjective.
If love is detached from wisdom, it becomes unstable.
If love is detached from righteousness, it becomes dangerous.

What feels good to one person may not be good for another.
What appears compassionate in the moment may actually enable destruction.
What presents itself as kindness may quietly become compromise.

That is why love must have rails.

And the rails are not man-made rules meant to choke life. They are the revealed nature of God.

3. EXODUS 34:6 REVEALS THE GUARDRAILS OF TRUE CHARITY

This is why **Exodus 34:6** matters so deeply to the whole framework of this book.

Exodus 34:6 (KJV)
"And the Lord passed by before him, and proclaimed, The Lord, The Lord God, merciful and gracious, longsuffering, and abundant in goodness and truth..."

Here the Father names Himself in qualities, not abstractions. He reveals the atmosphere of His own nature:

- **Mercy**
- **Grace / Compassion**
- **Longsuffering / Patience**
- **Goodness / Loving-kindness**
- **Truth**

And as the wider scriptural witness continues, **forgiveness and justice** are not absent from that revelation—they are implied in its outworking. God's love is not shapeless. It is not undefined energy. It has recognizable attributes. It has dependable expression. It has moral beauty. It has judgment that protects what is truly good.

This is why, in the language of this book, **agapē is best understood as God's Good.**

Not merely a feeling.
Not merely affection.
Not merely goodwill in theory.

But the active, wise, self-giving, truth-governed goodness of God made visible in life.

That is charity.

4. WITHIN GOD'S GUARDRAILS, AGAPĒ IS FREE BECAUSE IT IS ALREADY ALIGNED

And within God's guardrails, agapē may rightly be called unconditional—not because it has no boundaries, but because once it is truly formed in the nature of God, it no longer needs external restraint in the same way.

As Paul says of the fruit of the Spirit, *"against such there is no law"* (Galatians 5:23).

True divine love does not become dangerous when left free, because it is already governed from within by the character of God.

A true charity should reflect those qualities.
A true charity should carry mercy.
A true charity should carry compassion.
A true charity should carry patience.
A true charity should carry goodness.
A true charity should carry truth.
A true charity should carry forgiveness rightly.
A true charity should carry justice where needed.

Otherwise it may wear the language of care while lacking the nature of God.

5. CHARITY IS THE CROSSING POINT WHERE GROWTH BECOMES OUTWARD GOOD

This is why Peter places charity last.

Faith turns the life toward God.
Virtue gives it strength.
Knowledge gives it recognition.
Temperance gives it restraint.
Patience teaches it to remain.
Godliness aligns it with the Father's nature.
Brotherly kindness makes that maturity safe in relationship.

But **charity** is where all of it becomes rightly ordered for the good of others.

Charity is not merely what a mature believer feels.
Charity is what a mature believer becomes.

This is also where the deeper line in the sand appears.

At every lower stage, a person can still quietly use spiritual growth for self-reference.

Faith can still be about getting my answer.
Knowledge can still be about being right.
Strength can still be about being impressive.
Patience can still be about proving endurance.
Even brotherly kindness can still be selective and familiar.

But charity forces the crossing.

This is the place where **mammon must meet the line in the sand**.

This is where personal gain, personal image, personal ambition, and personal advantage must look across into another kingdom and decide whether they will cross over.

This is where a person must choose whether life will remain a system of exchange built around self-preservation, or become a vessel of God's good flowing outward. This is where what we have called success must look back and see the difference.

Mammon asks,
"What returns to me?"

Charity asks,
"What reflects the Father?"

Mammon calculates.
Charity gives wisely.

Mammon gathers.
Charity nourishes.

Mammon uses people.
Charity becomes shelter.

Mammon can imitate generosity for image.
Charity serves because love has become nature.

6. WITHOUT CHARITY, THE TREE STOPS AT ITSELF

This is why this final grace is the game changer.

Without charity, the tree may still be alive—but it has not yet reached its intended maturity.
Without charity, the structure may still stand—but it has not yet become a dwelling of blessing.
Without charity, spiritual development may still be real—but it does not yet fully look like Christ.

Without charity, the fruit stays with the tree, and the seed never gets to spread.

Brotherly kindness makes a life safe.
Charity makes that life look like Christ.

And this is the completed picture Peter is building toward.

A life **In Christ** is not merely a person with beliefs.
It is not merely a person with gifting.
It is not merely a person with discipline.
It is not merely a person with moral effort.

It is **a life formed by grace—**

the divine influence on the heart and the reflection in the life—

until the goodness of God begins to move through it in recognizable ways.

7. THE TREE OF LIFE STANDS IN THE FLOW OF GOD'S CHARITY

That is the tree of life.

Not a frantic tree.
Not a performative tree.
Not a decorative tree.

A living tree.

Its roots run deep into the unseen flow.
Its trunk has been strengthened through process.
Its branches have learned to hold weight.
Its shade has become safe for others.
Its fruit now carries the nature of the seed from which it
came.

And if we were to speak of it in the language of this book, we
could say it this way:

**A life in God's love, In Christ, becomes a tree of life
whose roots are planted in the flow of the river of
God's charity.**

Not charity as a label.
Not charity as performance.
Not charity as occasional sentiment.

But charity as the living current of the Father's own nature—
flowing in **mercy, compassion, patience, goodness,
truth, forgiveness, and justice**—until what was once
planted as faith has now become a mature and fruitful life.

This is the crown of the structure.
This is the top of the tree.
This is the difference between growth and fullness.

And this is why Peter ends here.

Because the final evidence of spiritual maturity is not what a person can do.

It is what kind of life now flows through them.

GUIDED DISCOVERY

1. Why does Peter end with charity rather than stopping at brotherly kindness?
Because brotherly kindness makes maturity relationally safe, but charity is the highest formed expression of God's own nature flowing through a life.

2. Why can the word love become confusing in modern language?
Because it is often used for emotion, preference, attraction, or sentiment, while biblical charity points to mature, truth-governed, self-giving goodness.

3. How does Exodus 34:6 help define true charity?
It gives the revealed qualities of God's nature—mercy, compassion, patience, goodness, and truth—which act as the safety rails for what divine love actually looks like.

4. What is the line in the sand between mammon and charity?
Mammon asks what returns to self, while charity asks what reflects the Father and becomes real support, shelter, and good for others.

5. What is the final evidence of a life formed in Christ?
Not merely gifts, strength, or knowledge, but the visible flow of God's good through a mature life that has become safe, fruitful, and Christlike.

CHAPTER 3 CLOSE

The tree is now standing.

What began as faith has become structure.
What began as turning has become formation.
What began as inward grace has become outward fruit.

Peter's ladder has shown us that spiritual maturity is not built in one dramatic moment, but in the steady layering of graces that shape a life strong enough to carry weight, safe enough to shelter others, and mature enough to reflect the Father's nature.

This is the inner formation of the believer.

But once the inner structure is formed, another question must be asked:

How does that formed life function within the wider Body?

Because grace is not only grown within a believer.
Grace is also **set within the Church**.

And that is where we now turn next.

In the next chapter, we move from the formation of the inner life to the placement of spiritual function—into the ministries, roles, and callings that God has set in the Body for the building up of all.

The tree has grown. Now we must learn how it stands in the forest.

CHAPTER 4. THE GIFTS SET IN THE CHURCH

Chapter Introduction

**God once placed a flaming sword at the gate of the garden.
Now, through Christ, the gate is open again—and all that is needed to walk in is a heart set ablaze by His love.**

Core Scriptures:
"And God hath set some in the church, first apostles, secondarily prophets, thirdly teachers, after that miracles, then gifts of healings, helps, governments, diversities of tongues."
— 1 Corinthians 12:28 (KJV)

"Therefore if any man be in Christ, he is a new creature: old things are passed away; behold, all things are become new."
— 2 Corinthians 5:17 (KJV)

If Chapter 3 gave us the trunk and strengthening limbs of inner formation, Chapter 4 shows us the great structural branches God has set in the living organism of His church.

Paul is not merely listing spiritual experiences or handing out religious titles. He is showing us that the new creation is not an idea, but a functioning body.

The church is not a crowd gathered in a room. It is a living organism under one Head, supplied by what God Himself has placed within it.

This is why Paul's words must be read carefully. We often hear terms like apostles, prophets, or governments as if they belong to a distant religious vocabulary, or worse, to a culture of self-promotion and spiritual branding.

But Paul does not begin with human ambition. He begins with divine placement: **"God hath set…"**

These are not self-appointed identities. They are functions of supply, given for the health, order, strengthening, and maturing of the Body of Christ.

When rightly understood, they stop sounding mysterious and start becoming recognizable all around us.

And this is where the lens of **2 Corinthians 5:17** becomes so powerful. **"Behold"** means look again.

See it. Recognize it. In Christ, all things are not merely improved—they are made new. A new order has begun. A new organism now exists in the earth. A new kind of life is flowing.

The old guarded garden has been reopened in Christ, and what once stood behind the flaming sword is now entering the world through a people made alive by God's love.

The gifts set in the church are not strange additions to Christian life; they are visible signs that the new creation has already begun.

In this chapter, we will step into that living structure and begin to recognize the great limbs God has set in His tree.

We will start at the doorway, where Paul reminds us that these gifts are not built by ego or platform culture, but placed by God for the sake of the Body.

From there, we will look at the first three structural functions—apostles, prophets, and teachers—as the strongest formative limbs of the church, not merely as titles but as real and recognizable channels of supply.

We will then move into miracles and healings, not as spiritual spectacle, but as the compassionate power of God's kingdom breaking into human weakness.

After that, we will uncover the quiet strength of helps and governments, where some of the most overlooked and powerful gifts hold the whole Body together in daily life.

By the end of the chapter, the reader should not merely know the list—they should begin to **see the living organism of the Body of Christ with new eyes.**

1. GOD HAS SET THESE GIFTS IN THE CHURCH, NOT IN HUMAN AMBITION

These functions are not self-appointed identities—they are placed by God for the health, order, and supply of the Body.

2. THE FIRST THREE FORM THE STRONGEST STRUCTURAL LIMBS

Apostles, prophets, and teachers provide foundational direction, alignment, and formation in the living church.

3. MIRACLES AND HEALINGS REVEAL THE COMPASSIONATE POWER OF GOD'S KINGDOM

These are not spiritual entertainment—they are signs of God's love breaking into human weakness.

4. HELPS AND GOVERNMENTS HOLD THE BODY TOGETHER IN DAILY LIFE

Some of the most powerful gifts in the church are not the loudest—they are the ones that make the whole organism work.

5. TONGUES AND THE WHOLE BODY TEACH US TO SEE A NEW CREATION ORDER

The gifts are not random spiritual phenomena—they are signs that the old order has passed and a living Body now exists under one Head.

Chapter 3 showed us the inner formation of the believer. Peter walked us through the graces that strengthen the life from within—**faith, virtue, knowledge, temperance, patience, godliness, brotherly kindness, and charity.**

Those were not random spiritual words, but the growth rings of maturity. They showed us that before a tree can carry outward weight, it must first be strengthened in its inner fibers. Before a life can safely carry gifts, it must first be formed by grace.

Now the tree begins to spread.

SECTION 1
GOD HAS SET THESE GIFTS IN THE CHURCH

These functions are not self-appointed identities—they are placed by God for the health, order, and supply of the Body.

Core Scripture
1 Corinthians 12:28 (KJV)
"And God hath set some in the church, first apostles, secondarily prophets, thirdly teachers, after that miracles, then gifts of healings, helps, governments, diversities of tongues."

1. GOD SETS—MAN RECEIVES

The starting point is not desire, gifting, personality, or opportunity. The starting point is God.

"And God hath set..."

That one phrase quietly removes a thousand counterfeit pressures. These roles are not built by ambition, secured by networking, or proven by platform—they are placed. Positioned. Assigned within a living Body that already belongs to Christ.

A man may feel called, stirred, or burdened—but the setting is still God's work. The Body is not self-organizing; it is divinely arranged. When this is seen clearly, striving begins to fall away, and alignment becomes the pursuit instead.

You do not become something to be seen—you become available to be placed.

2. THE BODY DEFINES THE NEED, NOT THE INDIVIDUAL

These gifts exist because the Body requires supply.

Apostles are not titles to carry—they are functions that build where something must begin. Prophets are not personalities —they are voices that bring alignment where something has drifted. Teachers are not performers—they are stabilizers where understanding must take root.

Every function listed is a response to a need already present within the Body of Christ.

This means the gift is never about self-expression—it is about supply.

Remove the Body, and the gift loses its purpose. Remove the need, and the function has nothing to serve. The moment a gift turns inward, it begins to distort. But when it stays connected to the life of the Body, it remains clean, useful, and life-giving.

The question is not, "What am I?"
The question is, "What is needed—and where has God placed me to supply it?"

3. IDENTITY FLOWS FROM PLACEMENT, NOT PERFORMANCE

When gifts are misunderstood, identity becomes unstable.

People begin to build identities around what should only be functions. Titles replace substance. Visibility replaces formation. And slowly, the focus shifts from being part of a Body to being seen as something within it.

But in God's order, identity is not built from function—function flows from identity already secured in Christ.

You are not an apostle, prophet, or teacher as a personal possession. You are a member of the Body, and within that Body, God may place you in a function that supplies others.

This keeps the heart safe.

Because when the function is not active, the identity does not collapse. And when the function is active, the glory does not attach to the person.

Everything stays anchored "In Christ," where it belongs.

4. AMBITION BUILDS PLATFORMS— GOD BUILDS BODIES

Human ambition always leans toward visibility.

It asks: *How do I grow this? How do I expand this? How do I be seen?*

But God's pattern is different.

He builds bodies, not platforms. He forms connection, not comparison. He establishes supply lines, not stages.

This is why the phrase **"God hath set"** is so protective. It guards the church from becoming a performance culture and restores it as a living organism.

In a body, no part competes. The eye does not strive to be the hand. The hand does not envy the voice. Each part simply functions in alignment with the Head, and the whole Body grows through what every part supplies.

Ambition asks to be something.
Love asks to serve something.

And only one of those can sustain the Body.

5. GIFTS EXIST TO SUPPLY LIFE, NOT TO DEFINE WORTH

The final safeguard is this: gifts do not determine value—they express supply.

Every believer is already complete "In Christ." The gift does not make a person more important; it simply reveals how that person contributes to the life of others.

This removes both pride and insecurity at the same time.

There is no need to elevate one function above another, because the Body cannot function without all of them. The unseen supports often carry the greatest weight, even if they receive the least attention.

Heaven measures differently.

The question is never, "How visible is this?"
The question is, "How much life does this supply?"

And in that measurement, the whole Body is honored.

GUIDED DISCOVERY

1. What does "God hath set" reveal about where gifts come from?

It reveals that every true function in the Body originates from God's intentional placement, not human ambition, preference, or effort. This removes pressure to "become" something and instead invites a posture of alignment—recognizing that God positions each part where it can best supply life within the Body.

2. Why can't a gift be understood apart from the Body?

Because every gift exists to meet a real need within a living system. Detached from the Body, the gift loses both its purpose and its clarity. It is only in connection—with people, with need, and under Christ as Head—that the function becomes meaningful, healthy, and effective.

3. What happens when identity is built on function instead of Christ?

Identity becomes fragile and performance-driven, rising when the function is visible and falling when it is not. But when identity is anchored "In Christ," the function becomes a steady expression of life rather than a source of personal worth, keeping the heart grounded and secure.

4. How does ambition distort spiritual function?

Ambition shifts the focus from serving others to elevating self. It builds platforms instead of strengthening the Body, turning what was meant to be a supply line into a stage. Over time, this disconnect weakens both the individual and the community it was meant to support.

5. What is the true measure of a gift in operation?

Not how visible, impressive, or recognized it is—but how much life it supplies. A true gift strengthens, supports, and builds others up in God's love.

In this way, the quiet, unseen functions often carry the greatest weight in the health of the whole Body.

Bridge to Section 2

If God is the One who sets these gifts, then the order in which they are named is not random.

There is structure within the placement.

And at the front of that structure stand three foundational limbs—apostles, prophets, and teachers—through which direction, alignment, and formation begin to take shape in the living Body.

SECTION 2
THE FIRST THREE FORM THE STRONGEST STRUCTURAL LIMBS

Apostles, prophets, and teachers provide foundational direction, alignment, and formation in the living church.

The structure of the Body does not begin with activity—it begins with alignment.

Before the church moves, it must be shaped. Before it expands, it must be framed. And before it carries others, it must be built on something that can hold weight without bending under pressure.

This is why Paul names these first.

"First apostles, secondarily prophets, thirdly teachers..." (1 Corinthians 12:28, KJV)

Not as a hierarchy of value, but as a sequence of **support**—like the order of construction or the growth of a tree. The trunk must form before the branches can safely spread.

And underneath it all is the pattern Jesus revealed:

The greatest love is not found in position, but in laying down one's life so that others can stand.

These are the structural limbs...

1. APOSTLES ESTABLISH DIRECTION AND PATTERN

Apostles are sent ones—builders who carry the blueprint of what God is forming.

Jesus did not begin with a system—He began with people. ***"And when it was day, he called unto him his disciples: and of them he chose twelve, whom also he named apostles."*** (Luke 6:13, KJV)

They were not self-appointed. They were formed in relationship, then sent with clarity.

This is the apostolic pattern.

Apostles do not merely start things; they establish what kind of thing is being built. They carry

pattern, alignment, and forward movement. Where there is no apostolic foundation, activity may increase, but direction becomes unclear.

An apostolic function asks:
What is God actually building here?
And are we building it His way?

Without this, the Body risks becoming busy but misaligned—like a structure assembled without reference to the original design.

Apostles keep the build true.

2. PROPHETS MAINTAIN ALIGNMENT WITH GOD'S HEART

If apostles carry the pattern, prophets keep the connection alive.

"But he that prophesieth speaketh unto men to edification, and exhortation, and comfort." (1 Corinthians 14:3, KJV)

That is the steady pulse of the prophetic.

Not performance.
Not platform.
But strengthening, lifting, and steadying the Body.

The prophetic function keeps the church from drifting into form without life. It brings present alignment—reminding the Body not just what is true, but what is alive now in the Spirit.

They ask:
Is this still flowing from God's heart?
Or have we slipped into routine without relationship?

Where this function is absent, the structure may remain, but the life begins to thin.

Prophets keep the build alive.

3. TEACHERS FORM UNDERSTANDING AND STABILITY

Teachers take what has been established and make it understandable, livable, and transferable.

"And they continued stedfastly in the apostles' doctrine..." (Acts 2:42, KJV)

"And they, continuing daily with one accord... and breaking bread from house to house..." (Acts 2:46, KJV)

This is the rhythm of the early church—truth taught, shared, lived, and repeated until it became part of daily life.

Teachers bring clarity where there could be confusion. They slow things down enough for truth to take root.

And as Hebrews reminds us:
"Therefore leaving the principles of the doctrine of Christ, let us go on unto perfection..." (Hebrews 6:1–2, KJV)

You cannot move on from what has never been **previously laid**.

A teacher asks:
Do the people understand what is being built?
Can they live it, not just hear it?

Where teaching is weak, people may be inspired but not formed. And what is not formed cannot stand under pressure.

Teachers make the build strong.

Together, these three functions form the primary framework of the living Body.

Apostles give direction.
Prophets maintain alignment.
Teachers establish understanding.

Each one supports the other.
Each one lays itself down so the others can stand.

Remove one, and the structure begins to lean. Remove two, and it becomes unstable. Remove all three, and what remains may still look like a church—but it will struggle to carry the weight of real life.

This is not about titles. It is about supply.

Everyone wants a title.
Fewer are willing to become support.

But this is the way of Christ—life gained by being given.

God did not design His Body to depend on personality, charisma, or platform. He designed it to be built, aligned, and formed—so that His love could move through it in a way that is both powerful and safe.

The disciples became apostles.
The prophets strengthened the people.
The teachers anchored truth into daily life.

That's not theory—that's a living pattern.

The tree does not argue about its trunk.
It grows because the structure is there.

And when these limbs are in place, the rest of the gifts can extend outward—without breaking the very thing they were meant to support.

GUIDED DISCOVERY

1. What does "sequence of support" reveal about how the Body is built?
It shows that each role exists to uphold the others. The structure grows through mutual support, not personal elevation.

2. What do the apostles in Luke 6:13 show us about how this role begins?
They were first disciples—formed in relationship with Jesus—then sent. Apostolic function flows from formation, not ambition.

3. According to 1 Corinthians 14:3, what is the true purpose of the prophetic?
To edify, exhort, and comfort—strengthening and aligning the Body rather than drawing attention to the individual.

4. What pattern do we see in Acts 2:42–46 about teaching?
Truth was taught daily, shared relationally, and lived out in community until it became part of everyday life.

5. Why is it important that foundations are "previously laid"?
Because true growth depends on what has already been established. Without a clear foundation, maturity cannot be sustained.

———

With the structural limbs in place, the Body is no longer just forming—it is ready to express.

Now the question becomes not just *how it is built*,
but *how the life of God begins to move through it in visible ways*.

And this is where the branches begin to spread...

SECTION 3. MIRACLES AND HEALINGS REVEAL THE COMPASSIONATE POWER OF GOD'S KINGDOM

Where God's love is allowed to flow, power does not need to be forced—it arrives.

Core Scripture
"Heal the sick, cleanse the lepers, raise the dead, cast out devils: freely ye have received, freely give." — Matthew 10:8 (KJV)

Secondary Anchor

"And Jesus went about... healing all manner of sickness and all manner of disease among the people." — Matthew 4:23 (KJV)

There is something in every person that leans forward when they hear about miracles. Not curiosity alone—but hope. A quiet thought that says, *"What if that could happen here... what if that could happen for me?"*

That instinct is not misplaced. It is the echo of God's love reaching into a world that knows it needs restoring.

But this is also where things can become unclear. Some have seen too much hype and quietly stepped back. Others have stepped out in faith, prayed, believed—and when nothing seemed to shift, something inside them pulled back as well.

So this section is not here to impress—it's here to steady the ground. Because miracles were never meant to be chased as moments or measured as results. They belong to a living Kingdom—one that flows through relationship, formation, and the steady work of God's love *in Christ*.

And once that foundation is understood, the whole subject begins to open up without confusion or pressure.

1. THESE WORKS BEGIN IN THE HEART OF GOD, NOT IN HUMAN DISPLAY

A good build always starts from the source of supply, not from what's visible on the surface.

Miracles don't begin in a prayer line—they begin in the heart of God.

Jesus didn't move because a moment needed filling. He moved because compassion stirred. Over and over, Scripture shows it—*He was moved*, and then He healed. That order matters.

It quietly removes pressure. We're not here to manufacture outcomes—we're learning to step into what is already flowing.
And when that settles in, everything softens. Less striving. More alignment. Less performance. More presence.

2. HEALING REVEALS WHAT GOD DESIRES—WHOLENESS, NOT JUST MOMENTS

In **Gospel of Luke 17:11–19**, ten lepers were cleansed—but only one returned, and Jesus said to him, ***"your faith has made you whole."***

Ten received something real. One entered something deeper.

It's the difference between patching a wall and restoring the whole house. One fixes what's seen. The other restores what holds everything together.

God's love always leans toward wholeness.

So when a moment feels incomplete, it doesn't always mean nothing happened. Sometimes it means something deeper has begun.
Wholeness is not rushed—it is formed.

3. MIRACLES CONFIRM THE KINGDOM—THEY DO NOT REPLACE FORMATION

No builder skips the foundation and expects the structure to stand.
Moments matter—but what sits underneath matters more.

There is a real place for stepping out, praying, and believing in the moment. That should never be undervalued.
But when nothing seems to shift, it is not always a failure—it is often a doorway.

A deeper prayer life. A stronger rooting in faith. A clearer alignment with God's love.

When foundation is laid, **what once felt hit-and-miss begins to carry weight and consistency.**

4. DEEP HEALING FLOWS FROM TRANSFORMED HEARTS

There is a healing that relieves—and a healing that restores.

Deep healing happens when God's love *in Christ* reaches the heart—where identity sits, where wounds have settled, where beliefs have been quietly shaping life.

When that place is touched, things don't just improve—they realign.

Like resetting a frame that's been slightly off for years, everything begins to sit properly again.
And from that place, life starts to flow differently—not forced, but formed.

5. JESUS IS THE BENCHMARK— AND THE INVITATION

Jesus healed **all** who came to Him. That is not pressure—it is direction.
It shows what a life fully aligned with God's love looks like.

And then He says in **Gospel of John 14:12** that **greater works would follow.**
Not because we become greater—but because we learn to live *in Him.*

This is where it lands.
We are not learning techniques—we are learning to live *in Christ,* **flowing in the anointed presence of God's love like Jesus.**

And as that becomes natural... what flowed through Him no longer feels distant—it begins to find expression through us.

GUIDED DISCOVERY

1. Where do miracles and healings truly begin?
They begin in the heart of God, not in human effort, emotion, or expectation. This means the starting point is not "trying harder," but becoming more aware of His compassion and learning to respond to it. When you see healing this way, it shifts you from pressure into partnership—joining what God is already doing rather than attempting to create something yourself.

2. What is the difference between healing and wholeness?
Healing often addresses a specific condition or moment, while wholeness reaches deeper into the person's life, identity, and relationship with God. A person can experience healing yet still carry fear, confusion, or disconnection—but wholeness restores alignment across the whole life. It brings peace, clarity, and stability, not just relief.

3. How should we understand moments where nothing seems to happen?
Rather than seeing them as failures, they can be understood as invitations. They often reveal areas where deeper foundation is needed—whether in prayer, faith, understanding, or alignment with God's love. These moments can actually strengthen the structure of a person's life, preparing them to carry something more consistent and lasting.

4. Where does lasting, deep healing take place?
Lasting healing takes place in the heart—where beliefs are formed, where wounds are stored, and where identity is shaped. When God's love in Christ reaches this place, it doesn't just change symptoms—it reshapes how a person sees God, themselves, and their life. From there, outward change begins to follow naturally.

5. What is the true goal in this area of life?
The goal is not to become someone who performs miracles,
but to become someone who lives *in Christ.*

As a life becomes aligned with God's love, what flows
through that life becomes increasingly natural, steady, and
trustworthy.

Power is no longer something to strive for—it becomes a
byproduct of alignment.

**When the foundation is God's love, miracles are no
longer something we try to make happen—they
become something that finds us already aligned.**

BRIDGE INTO SECTION 4

If miracles and healings reveal the visible movement of
God's compassion, there is another side of the Body that is
just as vital—but far less noticed.

Because not everything that builds the Kingdom happens in
moments of power.
Much of it happens quietly, steadily, and consistently—
holding everything together behind the scenes.

**And without this hidden strength, even the most
powerful moments would have nowhere to land.**

SECTION 4. HELPS AND GOVERNMENTS HOLD THE BODY TOGETHER IN DAILY LIFE

Some of the most powerful gifts in the church are not the loudest—they are the ones that make the whole organism work.

Core Scripture
"But now hath God set the members every one of them in the body, as it hath pleased him." — 1 Corinthians 12:18 (KJV)

"Thy Father which seeth in secret himself shall reward thee openly." — Matthew 6:4 (KJV)

There is a tendency to chase what is seen while overlooking what sustains. Flashy finishes draw attention, but without daily maintenance, even the strongest build begins to wear. The kingdom of God does not operate on visibility—it operates on supply.

Helps and governments are the hidden framework of the Body. They are the beams behind the wall, the systems under the floor, the steady hands that keep everything moving when no one is watching. Without them, vision stalls, gatherings strain, and even the most anointed moments struggle to land.

Many look for what they have not been given, while overlooking what God has already placed in their hands.

But grace always fits its assignment. The one called to administration will feel out of place carrying a message on a stage not built for them, just as the one called to teach may feel stretched under the weight of systems and structure. This is not weakness—it is design.

God never intended the Body to function through duplication, but through supply.

1. DESIGN, NOT COMPARISON

No part of the Body is greater than another—only different in function. Apostles, prophets, teachers, miracle workers, helpers, healers, administrators, and intercessors are not competing roles, but converging streams.

When comparison enters, clarity leaves. But when design is honoured, strength begins to flow.

You cannot move into what was never given—and you do not need to. What has been placed in you carries everything required for your part in the build.

2. THE POWER OF WHAT IS DONE IN SECRET

The kingdom places a high value on what is unseen. Not to hide it—but to form it.

What is done in private is not ignored by the Father—it is established by Him. And in the right time, He brings recognition—not to expose you, but to rightly position you. Not because you need affirmation, but because **the Body is strengthened when each part is seen and valued.**

There is a quiet confidence in being known by God before being known by man.

3. HELPS: LOVE IN MOTION

Helps is often underestimated because it looks practical—but in truth, it is love made visible.

It is not just setting up chairs or making coffee. It is seeing what is needed and stepping in without being asked. It is carrying responsibility not because you have to, but because you love to.

This is where the heart begins to align closely with the Father.

Because the Father is always looking for ways to supply.

Helps says, *"I see the gap—and I will become the bridge."*

4. GOVERNMENTS: ORDER THAT PROTECTS LIFE

Where helps supplies movement, governments supply structure.

Administration is not restriction—it is protection. It creates pathways where life can flow without confusion, waste, or unnecessary strain. **It holds things together so that what God is doing can continue without collapse.**

Without order, even good things can break under their own weight.

But when structure is in place, growth becomes sustainable.

5. ONE BODY, MANY EXPRESSIONS

Paul does not present these gifts as a hierarchy, but as a living organism. Each part contributes, each part depends, and each part strengthens the whole.

The visible and the invisible work together.
The platform and the preparation.
The voice and the support.

And when they move in unity, the Body begins to function as it was always designed—alive, connected, and flowing in God's love.

GUIDED DISCOVERY

1. Where might you be overlooking what God has already placed in your hands?
There are often areas in your life where grace is already present, but familiarity has hidden its value. What feels "normal" to you may actually be your assignment. Taking a moment to recognize this can bring clarity, confidence, and direction without striving for something new.

2. Do you feel pressure to operate outside your natural design? Why?
Pressure often comes from comparison, expectation, or environment. Identifying where that pressure is coming from allows you to release it and return to the place where your strength flows more naturally, consistently, and with far less strain.

3. What does "serving because you love to" look like in your daily life?
There is a clear difference between obligation and love-led action. One drains, the other energizes.

Reflecting on this helps you recognize where your service is flowing from, and where a simple shift in alignment could bring more life into what you're already doing.

4. How do you respond when your contribution is unseen or unrecognized?
Your response in these moments reveals where your validation is rooted. When it is anchored in the Father, consistency replaces frustration, and quiet faithfulness becomes a place of strength rather than discouragement.

BRIDGE INTO SECTION 5

When this kind of life begins to take shape, something quietly shifts.

People are no longer waiting to be asked while others are waiting for them to step forward. The tension between "being given a role" and "finding something to do" begins to dissolve.

Because a life lived In Christ does not move with spiritual blinders on. It sees what is needed.
It responds when love leads.
It flows—not from a need to be needed, but from knowing enough to *want to*.

This is where charity and grace begin to take over—not as ideas, but as the divine influence on the heart and the reflection in the life. And when that happens, the Body is no longer driven by instruction alone...

It begins to reveal a completely different order of life. Not just a functioning church— but a living, breathing new creation. Which leads us directly into what that life actually is.

SECTION 5. TONGUES AND THE WHOLE BODY TEACH US TO SEE A NEW CREATION ORDER

The gifts are not random spiritual phenomena—they are signs that the old order has passed and a living Body now exists under one Head.

Core Scripture

"Therefore if any man be in Christ, he is a new creature: old things are passed away; behold, all things are become new." — 2 Corinthians 5:17 (KJV)

"For as the body is one, and hath many members... so also is Christ." — 1 Corinthians 12:12 (KJV)

There is a point where the gifts stop appearing as isolated expressions and begin to reveal a shared life.

A new order.

Not built on outward form...
but flowing from inward connection.

Tongues, perhaps more than any other gift, have been misunderstood, overemphasized, or avoided altogether. Yet when seen in the context of the whole Body, they become far less confusing—and far more meaningful.

Not as a badge of spirituality...
but as part of a living system of communication between heaven and earth.

1. TONGUES AT PENTECOST — LANGUAGE THAT BUILDS BRIDGES

At Pentecost, the disciples spoke in tongues—but what stood out was not just how they spoke, but what was heard.

Each listener understood in their own language. What was not native to the speaker became clear to the hearer. This raises a simple but important question:

Can tongues be expressed in a known language?

It appears they can.

Because the miracle was not locked into sound—it was found in understanding.

**Tongues, at their root, are not about sounding spiritual...
they are about making something of God known.**

Sometimes beyond the speaker.
Sometimes beyond the listener.
But always within the reach of God.

2. WHAT WAS SPOKEN — WORDS THAT POINTED TO GOD

The focus at Pentecost was not the phenomenon—but the message.

Those listening heard truth that pointed them toward God.

It stirred recognition.
It awakened awareness.
It drew hearts upward.

Tongues, in this sense, are not empty sounds—they carry direction.

They encourage.
They reveal.
They turn attention toward God's love.

If what is being expressed does not build, lift, or point toward truth...
then something has drifted.

Because the purpose has always been clear:

To edify, not to impress.

3. INTERCESSION — A LANGUAGE BEYOND LIMITATION

Not all prayer is public.

Not all communication with God is formed in structured words.

Jesus Himself often stepped away to pray alone.

There is a place where language reaches its limit... and yet the need to express remains.

This is where intercession lives.

A place where the Spirit helps carry what the mind cannot fully articulate.

Tongues, in this context, are not something to perform—but something to participate in.

Not always initiated...
often responded to.

A quiet awareness.
A yielding.
A flow that moves deeper than thought.

Not replacing understanding—
but supporting it.

4. IS TONGUES THE ONLY EVIDENCE OF THE SPIRIT?

This is where confusion has often taken root.

Some have taught that tongues are the required evidence of receiving the Holy Spirit.

But the wider witness of Scripture shows something broader.

The Spirit reveals Himself in many ways:

- love
- boldness
- wisdom
- transformation
- conviction
- unity

Tongues may be a sign...
but they are not The sign.

Because the clearest evidence of the Spirit has always been a life being shaped into the nature of Christ.

Not one expression...
but a whole life.

5. A SUPERNATURAL BODY, HELD TOGETHER IN UNITY

There are many expressions within the Body that reach beyond natural explanation. Much of what is received in prayer—insight, understanding, direction—often arrives from beyond personal experience.

This should not feel strange.

It should feel expected.

Because the Body is not sustained by human ability alone... but by a living connection with God.

There is much we do not yet understand about the depth of the spiritual realm. But this we do know:

When hearts come together in unity, God moves.

Provision flows.
Clarity comes.
Strength increases.

There is no lack in the kingdom of God.

And even when language differs—whether understood or not—God understands both the expression and the heart behind it.

One may speak in a language another does not know... while another prays in a way the first does not recognize...

Yet both are heard.

Both are received.

Because the source is one.

GUIDED DISCOVERY

1. What is your current understanding of tongues—and where might it need refining?
Take a moment to identify where your understanding has been shaped—whether by teaching, experience, or assumption. Growth often begins by revisiting familiar ground with fresh perspective and allowing truth to settle more clearly.

2. Do you focus more on how something spiritual appears, or what it produces?
It is easy to be drawn to outward expression, but lasting value is always found in what is built within and released toward others. Shifting your focus to fruit and outcome helps anchor your discernment.

3. How comfortable are you with prayer that goes beyond structured words?
There may be areas where control has limited expression. Learning to yield, listen, and respond can open a deeper, more honest connection with God that is not dependent on perfect wording.

4. Do you measure spiritual life by one expression, or by the whole transformation of a life?
A single sign can never carry the weight of a whole life. Consider how love, patience, truth, and consistency reveal the Spirit's work in a far more complete way.

5. How aware are you of your connection to the wider Body of Christ?
Your life is not designed to function in isolation. Growing awareness of shared life brings both confidence and responsibility, allowing you to participate more fully in what God is building.

BRIDGE TO CHAPTER 4 CLOSING SUMMARY

At this point, the picture becomes clear.

The gifts are not isolated abilities given to individuals for personal expression.

They are **functions of a living Body**.

A Body not built on ambition...
but placed together by God.

A Body not sustained by pressure...
but supplied through connection.

A Body not waiting to be activated...
but already alive in Christ.

From apostles to helps...
from wisdom to healing...
from structure to service...
and even to the quiet, often unseen flow of intercession—

Every part reveals the same truth: This is a new creation order.

Not many lives trying to work together...
but one life expressed through many.

And when that life is aligned...

The Church is no longer something people attend.

It becomes something they **are**.

CHAPTER 4 — CLOSING SUMMARY

THE GIFTS FORM A LIVING HOUSE, NOT A DISPLAY ROOM

What God has set in the Church was never meant to be observed from a distance—it was meant to be lived from within.

This chapter has not been about identifying roles so people can label themselves. It has been about recognizing how a living Body actually functions when it is aligned **In Christ**.

From the moment we saw that ***"God hath set...",*** the tone was established: this is not human ambition dressed in spiritual language—this is divine placement for real supply.

The structure has been laid carefully.

The first three—**apostles, prophets, and teachers**—form the strongest structural limbs. Not as a hierarchy of value, but as a sequence of **support**.

What is sent must first be laid. What is revealed must be aligned. What is taught must be built upon something real. You cannot move forward from what has never been previously laid. These are not titles to carry—they are burdens to bear for the sake of others.

From there, **miracles and healings** opened a window into the compassionate power of God. Not as spectacle, not as hit-and-miss moments, but **as expressions of God's love meeting human need.** They remind us that the Kingdom is not theory—it touches pain, restores what is broken, and reveals that heaven is not distant, but willing to move.

Then **helps and governments** quietly held the entire structure together. The unseen joints. The steady hands. The daily faithfulness that keeps everything from falling apart. These are the gifts that rarely draw attention, yet **without them, nothing stands.** Here we saw that a life lived **In Christ** does not wait to be asked—it sees, responds, and supports. Not from a need to be needed, but from a heart aligned with God's love.

And finally, **tongues** and the whole Body brought us to see something deeper—a **new creation order**.

The gifts are not random spiritual expressions scattered across individuals. They are evidence that the old isolated life has passed, and a connected, Spirit-led Body now exists under one Head. Whether through language understood, prayer offered in secret, or the many unseen workings of the Spirit, the direction is always the same—toward God's love, toward unity, toward life.

What begins to emerge, when all of this is seen together, is not a list—but a **house**.

A living house.

A house where:

- Christ is the Head
- Love is the atmosphere
- Truth is the framework
- Grace is the flow through every room
- And every member supplies something real

This is why the gifts must never be separated from formation.

Because without the inner graces from the previous chapter, the gifts can become unstable.

Without love, they can become loud but empty.
Without truth, they can drift.
Without patience and maturity, they can damage what they were meant to build.

But when formed in God's love...

The apostle builds safely.
The prophet speaks clearly.
The teacher grounds deeply.
The healer restores gently.
The helper strengthens quietly.
The whole Body moves as one.

There is also a quiet correction that runs through this entire chapter.

The Body does not gather around a man waiting to be given a job.

And the man does not stand waiting for the Body to volunteer.

Both are looking at each other when they should be looking **to Christ**.

Because in a life lived **In Christ**, the question is no longer:
"What role do I have?"

It becomes:
"What has been placed in my hands today—and how can I let God's love flow through it?"

We all receive the same thing each day:
A portion of time.
A measure of grace.
An opportunity to love.

And in that simple rhythm, the Body builds itself.

So the chapter closes not with instruction, but with invitation.

Step out of observation.
Step out of comparison.
Step out of waiting.

Step into the flow.

Because the gifts are already set.
The Head is already established.
The supply is already present.

The only question that remains is:

Will you align your life with God's love and take your place
In Christ—
not as a title...
but as a living part of the Body?

Bridge to Next Chapter

If Chapter 4 has shown us how the Body functions together, then what remains is even deeper:

How does a life become stable enough to carry this without collapsing under it?

Because before the gifts can flow safely, the inner life must be formed properly.

And that takes us into the next layer of the build...
not the outer structure—but the **inner strength that holds it all together**...

CHAPTER 5. THE ASCENSION GIFTS OF CHRIST

These are not branches trying to stand out—they are branches trained to help the whole tree rise.

CORE SCRIPTURE

"Wherefore he saith, When he ascended up on high, he led captivity captive, and gave gifts unto men...
And he gave some, apostles; and some, prophets; and some, evangelists; and some, pastors and teachers;
For the perfecting of the saints, for the work of the ministry, for the edifying of the body of Christ:
Till we all come in the unity of the faith, and of the knowledge of the Son of God, unto a perfect man, unto the measure of the stature of the fulness of Christ."
— Ephesians 4:8, 11–13 (KJV)

God once placed a flaming sword at the gate of the garden. Now, through Christ, the way stands open—and what was once guarded is now entered by a heart set ablaze with His love.

This is where **The Gifts Of Christ** begins to come into full view.

The earlier chapters have laid the ground well. We have seen
the foundation of grace, the formation of the inner life, and
the shaping of a believer through the foundational graces of
the Spirit. From there, we stepped into what God has set **in**
the Body—living functions, daily supply, the movement of
life through many members working together.

But now we come to something deeper.

Not just what flows *through* the Body...
but what Christ has given *to* the Body.

In **Ephesians 4**, we are not looking at scattered
expressions of gifting.

We are seeing the intentional provision of Christ Himself—
the way He ensures that His Body does not merely exist, but
grows, strengthens, and reaches maturity In Christ.

When Christ ascended, He did not leave behind instructions
alone. He gave people—living expressions of His ongoing
care, order, and building pattern.

These are not titles to pursue or positions to climb into.
They are gifts given for the sake of others, shaping the whole
Body toward unity, stability, and fullness.

This is why they are rightly understood as **The Gifts Of
Christ**.

Not because they belong to men...
but because they are given *by Christ*,
to reveal His heart,
and to build His Body into His likeness.

1. CHRIST GAVE PEOPLE TO THE BODY TO ESTABLISH GROWTH

These are not replacements for Christ, nor intermediaries that stand between Him and His people. They are expressions of His ongoing work—men and women shaped in such a way that their lives help others grow in alignment with Him. Their purpose is not to gather followers, but to form people.

This section will anchor the reader in the reality that Christ is still actively building His Body. He does this not only through inward transformation, but through outward provision—placing people within the Body who carry pattern, direction, and clarity.

The focus shifts from identity to function: not who they are called, but how they help the Body grow.

2. THE PURPOSE IS MATURITY, NOT ACTIVITY

Movement can look like growth, but they are not the same. A life can be full of activity and still remain unchanged in its nature. This section will gently separate busyness from true spiritual formation.

Here we unfold "the perfecting of the saints" as a process of alignment, strengthening, and completion. The goal is not constant motion, but steady transformation into the likeness of Christ.

This brings the reader back to the heart of the book: not doing more for God, but becoming more aligned with His love In Christ.

3. WITHOUT FORMATION, THE BODY DRIFTS

Where structure is absent, instability quietly takes hold. Without clear formation, the Body can become vulnerable to confusion, imbalance, and shifting ideas—even while appearing alive and active on the surface.

Drawing from the warning of being "tossed to and fro," this section will help the reader recognize that drift is not always dramatic—it is often subtle. Without the equipping Christ has provided, growth becomes uneven, and truth becomes difficult to hold onto.

Formation is not control—it is stability.

4. TRUTH AND LOVE FORM THE GROWTH ENVIRONMENT

Growth does not happen in harshness, nor in softness without substance. It happens where truth and love remain together. This section will establish that both are essential, and neither can produce maturity on its own.

Truth gives direction. Love provides the environment where that direction can be received. Truth without love hardens, and love without truth drifts—but together they create the conditions where a life can grow safely and strongly In Christ.

This is the atmosphere of a healthy, living Body.

5. EVERY PART SUPPLYING CREATES A LIVING BODY

The end goal is not a few strong individuals, but a fully joined and living Body. This section brings everything back into unity—where every part has value, every connection matters, and every supply contributes to life.

Here we see that maturity is not measured by isolation, but by connection. Each part both gives and receives, strengthening the whole.

This is where the structure becomes alive—not just a framework, but a functioning organism, growing together in God's love In Christ.

BRIDGE TO SECTION 1

The garden is open.
The tree is alive.
The roots are set.

But the question is no longer whether life has begun...

It is whether that life is being formed, strengthened, and brought to maturity.

Because Christ did not only give life to His Body—

He gave **The Gifts Of Christ**
so that His Body would grow up into Him.

CHRIST GAVE PEOPLE TO THE BODY—NOT TO REPLACE HIM, BUT TO REVEAL HIS BUILDING PATTERN

SECTION 1. CHRIST GAVE PEOPLE TO THE BODY TO ESTABLISH GROWTH

These are not replacements for Christ, nor intermediaries that stand between Him and His people.

Core Scripture —

Ephesians 4:11–13 KJV
"And he gave some, apostles; and some, prophets; and some, evangelists; and some, pastors and teachers; For the perfecting of the saints, for the work of the ministry, for the edifying of the body of Christ: Till we all come in the unity of the faith, and of the knowledge of the Son of God, unto a perfect man, unto the measure of the stature of the fulness of Christ."

Christ did not leave His Body to grow by instinct alone. He ascended—and in ascending, He gave. Not systems first. Not structures first. People. Formed lives. Living patterns.

This is not a handover—it is a continuation.

The same Christ who walked with His disciples now builds through those who have been shaped by His love, carrying something of His nature into the lives of others.

The emphasis is not distance from Christ, but distribution of His life through the Body.

This reframes everything. These are not titles to be pursued, but functions to be supplied. The language of heaven is not "Who am I?" but "What is being built through me?"

A man may carry the language of an apostle, prophet, or teacher—but if no one is being strengthened, aligned, or formed, then the function has not yet taken root.

In the same way a beam is only proven by the load it carries, so these gifts are only seen in the growth they produce in others.

There is also a quiet correction here. These people are not standing between Christ and His people—they are standing with Christ for His people. They do not replace access to Him; they reinforce alignment with Him.

When they function rightly, they do not draw attention to themselves, but create clarity, stability, and direction so that others can walk more fully In Christ.

Their success is measured not by how many follow them, but by how many become steady, mature, and able to stand.

So the focus shifts—from identity to function, from recognition to responsibility, from platform to pattern.

Christ is still building His Body, and He does it both inwardly by His Spirit and outwardly through people who have learned to walk in His love.

These are not spiritual celebrities. They are living scaffolding—temporary supports that help establish something lasting in others until the structure can stand on its own.

1. THESE PEOPLE ARE GIFTS, NOT POSITIONS

They are given, not taken. Received, not claimed.

The wording is precise: *He gave*. That means they originate from Christ's initiative, not human ambition. No one promotes themselves into being a gift to the Body.

A gift is recognized by its supply, not its announcement.

Just as you don't argue with a beam about whether it is load-bearing—you see what it holds—so it is with these functions. The Body knows when it is being supported, strengthened, and built.

This removes the pressure to perform and replaces it with the responsibility to grow.

A person becomes useful to the Body not by declaring what they are, but by being formed in such a way that others are helped through their life.

The gift is not in the label—it is in the supply.

2. THE MEASURE OF THE GIFT IS THE GROWTH OF OTHERS

If nothing is being built, nothing is being given.

Paul anchors the purpose clearly: *for the perfecting of the saints… for the edifying of the body of Christ.*

The outcome is maturity. Unity. Clarity in knowing Christ.

This means the true evidence of these gifts is not activity, but transformation. People becoming more stable. More aligned. More able to walk in God's love In Christ.

This also guards against illusion. It is possible to have movement without growth, noise without formation, attention without transformation. But heaven measures differently.

Growth is quiet, steady, and visible over time—like a house rising beam by beam, or a tree thickening year by year. **Where these gifts are functioning, people do not just gather—they grow.**

3. FUNCTION FLOWS FROM FORMATION

You cannot give what has not been built into you.

A person cannot lead others into alignment with Christ if they themselves are not being aligned. This is why formation always precedes function.

The deeper the internal work of God's love, the more stable the external supply becomes. Without this, function becomes performance—and performance cannot carry weight.

This is where the earlier chapters matter. **Faith, virtue, knowledge, temperance, patience, godliness, brotherly kindness, and charity are not optional extras**—they are the internal structure that makes these outward gifts safe.

Without it the garden, the tools become dangerous. With it, they become life-giving.

4. CHRIST REMAINS THE HEAD— ALWAYS

These gifts never replace Him; they reveal Him.

The moment a gift begins to draw people to itself rather than to Christ, it has drifted from its purpose.

The healthiest expression of these functions makes Christ clearer, not more distant. It strengthens direct relationship, not dependency. It builds confidence in God's love, not reliance on a human personality.

This keeps the Body safe. The structure remains Christ-centered, not personality-driven. The flow remains from the Head, through the Body, to every part.

No one stands above the Body—only within it, under the same Head.

GUIDED DISCOVERY

1. **Where in your life have you seen someone genuinely help you grow in Christ—not by control, but by clarity, strength, or example?**

Think about moments where something "clicked" for you—not because someone impressed you, but because they helped you see more clearly. It may have been a conversation, a quiet example, or even a correction that brought alignment rather than pressure. Growth often comes through simple, steady influence rather than dramatic moments.

Now look again at that person or moment. What was actually being supplied? Was it direction, encouragement, truth, patience? Identifying the *function* helps you recognize how Christ builds through people, and it trains your eye to see these gifts operating beyond titles or positions.

2. In what ways could your own life begin to supply growth to others—not through position, but through formation?

Consider where God has already been working in you—areas where you have gained understanding, stability, or patience. These are not just for you; they are seeds of supply for others. Growth shared becomes growth multiplied. You don't need a platform to strengthen someone—you need a formed life.

Then ask honestly: what still needs strengthening in you so that your supply becomes more stable? This is not pressure —it is invitation. The more you are formed In Christ, the more naturally your life will begin to build others, often without you even trying.

3. How can you recognize the difference between someone gathering followers and someone forming people?

Look at the fruit over time. One draws attention to themselves, creates dependence, and keeps people circling around their voice. The other strengthens people, points them back to Christ, and quietly equips them to stand on their own. One builds a crowd; the other builds a life.

Now bring that closer to your own lens. What do you naturally respond to—and why? Awareness here protects you from being shaped by personality instead of truth. It also helps you become the kind of person who forms others well, because you begin to value growth over recognition, substance over spotlight.

If Christ gives people to establish growth, then the question naturally follows—*what kind of structure do these people form within the Body?* Not as a hierarchy of value, but as a sequence of support... where each part carries weight so the whole can stand.

SECTION 2. THE PURPOSE IS MATURITY, NOT ACTIVITY

Christ did not give people to His Body to keep it moving—He gave them to help it grow up.

Core Scripture

"And he gave some, apostles; and some, prophets; and some, evangelists; and some, pastors and teachers;
For the perfecting of the saints..." — Ephesians 4:11–12 (KJV)

The Body of Christ does not mature through activity alone—it matures through *right supply*. This is where many drift without realizing it. Movement increases, involvement grows, people stay busy... but something deeper remains under-formed. Why? Because maturity is not produced by motion—it is produced by what is being *built into* a life.

This is why Christ gave *people*.

Not titles. Not positions. Not platforms. But men and women shaped in such a way that their lives carry something others need.

The fivefold expressions—**apostles, prophets, evangelists, pastors, and teachers—are not badges of identity.**

They are functional supply lines into the Body, each carrying a different aspect of Christ's nature, each contributing to the *maturing of the whole.*

This section begins to re-establish their purpose.

Not as a hierarchy to climb, but as a structure that supports. Not as roles to admire, but as lives that *form others.*

The goal is not that people become more active in church life, but that they become more aligned with God's love **In Christ**—steady, grounded, and able to carry life well.

1 APOSTLES LAY WHAT OTHERS BUILD UPON

Apostles are sent ones—but not just sent to go, sent to *lay.* They carry the ability to establish foundations that others can safely build upon. Their work is not primarily visible in moments, but in what remains long after they have passed through.

They bring order, direction, and structure. They see how things fit together and how the Body should be aligned so that growth is not chaotic, but supported. Without this foundation, people may grow—but not necessarily in the right direction.

You cannot build forward on what has never been properly laid.

Apostolic supply gives the Body something solid to stand on so maturity has somewhere to *take root*.

2 PROPHETS KEEP THE BODY ALIGNED WITH THE HEART OF GOD

Prophets do not exist to impress—they exist to *align*. Their strength is not in prediction, but in perception. They help the Body stay connected to what is true, cutting through drift, distraction, and misalignment.

They remind people of God's heart. They bring clarity where things have become blurred. They strengthen what is right and expose what is out of place—not to tear down, but to restore proper direction.

Without this supply, the Body can stay active but slowly lose alignment.

Prophetic grace brings it back—again and again—into the flow of God's love.

3 EVANGELISTS AWAKEN LIFE AND DRAW PEOPLE IN

Evangelists carry a life that reaches outward. They are not just communicators—they are *connectors*. They help those outside the Body encounter the reality of God's love and begin the journey **In Christ**.

But their role does not end at introduction. They awaken something. They stir hearts. They bring people into the beginning of life with God, where everything is fresh, alive, and full of possibility.

Without evangelistic supply, the Body can become inward-focused.

Evangelists keep it breathing outward—reminding it that life is meant to be shared.

4. PASTORS CREATE SPACE WHERE LIFE CAN GROW SAFELY

Pastors do more than lead—they *care*.

They create environments where people are known, supported, and able to grow without fear. They watch over lives, not as controllers, but as protectors and nurturers.

Growth requires safety. Without it, people either withdraw or perform. Pastoral grace removes both. **Pastors allow people to be real, to heal, and to strengthen at a pace that is sustainable.**

This is where maturity becomes relational. Not just what a person knows, but how they are held within the Body. A healthy environment produces steady growth.

5 TEACHERS ESTABLISH TRUTH THAT MAKES GROWTH STABLE

Teachers bring clarity. They take what can feel abstract and make it understandable, usable, and dependable. They do not just share information—they establish *truth that can be lived on.*

Without truth, growth becomes unstable. People may feel inspired, but lack direction. Teaching anchors the soul. It gives language to what God is doing and helps people walk it out with confidence.

This is where maturity becomes consistent. **Not just experienced in moments, but understood and lived over time.**

Guided Discovery

1. Which of these expressions have shaped your life the most—and how?
Think back over your journey. Who has helped lay foundation in you? Who has brought clarity, alignment, care, or awakening? Maturity often comes quietly through people we didn't always recognize at the time.

2. Where might there be a lack of supply in your current environment?
Sometimes growth slows not because of resistance, but because of missing support. Recognizing what is lacking is not criticism—it is clarity. And clarity opens the door for God to provide.

3. How might Christ be using your life to bring maturity to others?
These are not distant roles—they are expressions of Christ that can begin to form in every believer over time. You may already be carrying something that helps others grow. The question is not what title you hold, but what *life* flows through you.

Now the structure begins to take shape.

Not a system of titles—but a living Body, supplied from every direction, growing into maturity together.

And from here, we move deeper into how this supply connects... and how the whole Body begins to function as one.

SECTION 3. WITHOUT FORMATION, THE BODY DRIFTS

A life can look alive on the outside while quietly losing its direction within.

Core Scripture (KJV)
"...that we henceforth be no more children, tossed to and fro, and carried about with every wind of doctrine..." — *Ephesians 4:14*

There is a kind of movement that feels like growth—but isn't.
It looks active, sounds spiritual, and can even gather momentum, yet underneath it lacks anchoring. Without formation, the Body does not stand still—it drifts.

Paul saw this early. Even in the first generation of believers, there were voices rising that sounded convincing but lacked substance. People were being pulled in different directions—not because they didn't love God, but because **they had not yet been formed in a way that could hold truth steady.**

And if we're honest, most of us have been there.
Pulled by a new idea... stirred by a new voice... certain for a moment, then unsure the next. Not rebellious—just unanchored. This is not failure; it is the natural outcome of growth without formation.

This is why Christ did not leave His Body without structure. Formation is not control—it is stability. It is **the quiet strength that allows a life to remain steady when everything around it shifts.**

1. DRIFT IS SUBTLE, NOT SUDDEN

Drift rarely announces itself. It doesn't arrive like a storm—it comes like a slow current.

A person can still attend, still speak the language, still appear engaged... yet internally, direction begins to loosen. What once felt clear becomes negotiable. What once felt anchored becomes optional.

This is what Paul was addressing. Not open rebellion—but quiet instability.

Where in your life have you felt this kind of subtle drift? It may not have looked like walking away, but more like losing clarity. A slow shift where what once felt firm became uncertain.

Recognizing this is not condemnation—it is awareness, and awareness is the first step back into alignment.

Not all voices are wrong—but not all are stable. Some stir emotion without building structure. Some excite without grounding. Learning to discern the difference is part of formation.

What would it look like to return to a place of steady footing?
Not by chasing another voice—but by reconnecting to what is true, tested, and life-giving. Stability begins when truth becomes something you stand on, not just something you hear.

2. TRUTH WITHOUT FORMATION IS HARD TO HOLD

Truth can be heard in a moment—but it is formed over time.

Without formation, truth becomes something we agree with... until something stronger pulls on us. This is why people can sincerely believe something one day and question it the next.

Formation gives truth weight. It moves it from the surface into the structure of a life.

This is the difference between inspiration and transformation.

What truths have you heard but struggled to hold onto? These are often the places where formation has not yet taken root. Not because the truth is weak—but because it hasn't yet been built into your life.

What would it take for that truth to become part of your structure?

Time, repetition, and lived experience. **Truth becomes stable when it is practiced, not just understood.**

Where have you seen truth become real through experience? These are your anchors. The places where you no longer question because you have lived it. This is formation at work.

3. EVEN IN PAUL'S TIME, NOT EVERY VOICE WAS SOUND

The early church was alive—but it wasn't perfect.

There were influences, personalities, and teachings that pulled people away from alignment. Paul didn't ignore it—he addressed it. Not with fear, but with clarity.

This matters, because it reminds us that confusion is not new.
And neither is the solution.

The answer was not isolation—it was proper formation through what Christ had already given.

It removes the illusion that something has gone wrong today. The need for discernment has always been part of the journey.

Growth requires recognizing that not all input builds stability. Some voices inspire—but others form.
It means choosing what builds long-term strength, even if it feels quieter or less exciting in the moment.

4. CHRIST GAVE STABLE BRANCHES FOR A REASON

A tree does not stabilize itself by intention—it stabilizes through structure.

Apostles, prophets, evangelists, pastors, and teachers are not titles to admire—they are supports to lean into. Not as hierarchy, but as **a sequence of support** that strengthens the whole.

These are the stabilizing branches in the Body.
Not controlling growth—but guiding it so it grows true.

You cannot move on from what has never been previously laid.

Sometimes we don't recognize them until we look back. **The voice that clarified, the person who steadied, the one who helped you understand**—these are not accidents.

5. FORMATION LEADS US BACK TO THE MESSAGE OF CHRIST

All true formation leads in one direction—not toward complexity, but toward clarity.

Jesus did not speak to confuse—He spoke to anchor.
To bring people back to what is true, simple, and life-giving.

Formation is not about knowing more—it is about becoming steady in what matters most.

This is where drift ends.
Stability doesn't begin with everything—it begins with something that is real and alive to you.
Not as a concept—but as a practice. What is lived becomes stable.

Not perfect—but steady. Not rigid—but grounded. This is the beginning of a formed life.

If drift reveals the need for formation...
then the next question becomes clear:

What does maturity actually look like when that formation begins to take hold?

Because the goal is not just to stop drifting—
but to become a life that stands.

SECTION 4. TRUTH AND LOVE FORM THE GROWTH ENVIRONMENT

Truth shows the way. Love makes it possible to walk it.

Core Scripture —

Ephesians 4:15 (KJV)
"But speaking the truth in love, may grow up into him in all things, which is the head, even Christ:"

Growth does not take place in pressure alone, nor in comfort alone.

A plant placed in harsh conditions will struggle to survive. A plant given only softness without structure will grow weak and unstable. In the same way, a life cannot mature through truth alone, nor through love alone. It requires both—working together as one environment.

This is where many have struggled in the Body. Some have experienced truth without love—sharp, correcting, but lacking care. Others have experienced love without truth—welcoming, but without direction. Both leave the believer limited. One hardens the heart. The other leaves it unformed. But when truth and love remain together, something different happens—growth begins to take root.

This is the atmosphere Christ designed for His Body. Not a place of control, and not a place of drift—but a place where truth gives direction and love makes that direction receivable.

This is where maturity becomes not only possible, but sustainable. This is where a life grows safely and strongly **In Christ**.

And just as a tree reveals its health through its fruit, so the Body reveals its condition through what it produces.

This section draws that connection clearly—between the structure Christ provides, the environment it creates, and the fruit that grows from it.

1 TRUTH SETS THE DIRECTION OF GROWTH

Truth is not harsh—it is dependable.

Without truth, there is no clear direction. A life may feel sincere, but sincerity without truth cannot produce stability. Truth defines what is real, what is right, and what leads to life. It is the fixed line that growth follows.

In Christ, truth is not merely information—it is alignment with the nature of God. It anchors the soul, steadies the mind, and gives clarity when everything else feels uncertain.

A life growing without truth may look active, but it will not remain stable. Eventually, it will drift. Truth keeps the growth pointed in the right direction.

Truth is the line the branch grows along.

2 LOVE CREATES THE ENVIRONMENT FOR GROWTH

Love is not weakness—it is support.

Truth may show the way, but without love, it becomes difficult to receive. Love creates safety. It allows correction to be heard without fear, and direction to be embraced without resistance.

This is why God's love is not optional—it is foundational. It is the environment where growth can happen without the fear of rejection or failure. Love makes room for process. It gives time for change. It supports the life while it is still forming.

A life surrounded by truth but lacking love will harden. A life surrounded by love but lacking truth will drift. But when love is present with truth, growth becomes both strong and steady.

Love is the soil the branch grows from.

3 THE FRUIT REVEALS THE ENVIRONMENT

Every tree is known by its fruit.

Growth is not measured by appearance, activity, or language—it is revealed in what a life produces. The fruit of the Spirit is not something we force; it is something that grows when the environment is right.

Where truth and love are working together, fruit begins to appear—**patience, kindness, faithfulness, gentleness.** Not as effort alone, but as evidence of a formed life.

This is where the reader is gently invited to look—not at performance, but at outcome. Not at intention, but at fruit.

And this applies to all—leaders and members alike. The fivefold ministry does not stand outside this measure. They are not only carriers of truth and love—they are to be living examples of the fruit that grows from it.

We do not examine titles. We examine fruit.

4 THE FIVEFOLD MINISTRY MUST BE ROOTED IN FRUIT

The branches that support growth must also produce it.

Apostles, prophets, evangelists, pastors, and teachers are not exempt from the environment—they are expressions of it. Their role is not only to guide growth, but to model it.

If truth is present but love is absent, their influence will harden those they lead. If love is present but truth is absent, their influence will lack direction. But when both are present, their lives become safe places for others to grow.

This brings clarity back to the reader. The gifts of Christ are not simply functions—they are living supports. And those supports must themselves be formed in truth and love.

Healthy branches produce healthy fruit.

5 GROWTH REQUIRES BOTH TO REMAIN TOGETHER

Separation weakens what unity strengthens. Truth and love are not competing forces—they are designed to remain together. When separated, both lose their effectiveness. Truth becomes rigid. Love becomes unstable. But together, they create strength.

This is the environment of a healthy Body—where truth is spoken, and love is felt. Where direction is clear, and hearts are supported. Where growth is not forced, but formed.

This is how a life matures—not through pressure alone, and not through comfort alone—but through a consistent environment where truth and love remain together.

This is how we grow up into Him in all things.

GUIDED DISCOVERY

1. Where in your life have you experienced truth without love, and what effect did it have on you?
Truth without love often leaves a mark. It may have brought clarity, but it likely also brought pressure, distance, or even resistance. Reflecting on this helps you recognize why love is not a weakness—it is the very thing that allows truth to take root without damaging the heart. This awareness begins to reshape how you both receive and give truth moving forward.

2. Where have you experienced love without truth, and how did that affect your growth?
Love without truth can feel safe in the moment, but over time it can leave you without direction. You may have felt accepted, but not strengthened. Supported, but not formed. Recognizing this helps you see why truth is necessary—not to control, but to guide. It brings clarity to the kind of environment your life truly needs to grow.

3. What fruit is currently visible in your life, and what does it reveal about your environment?
Fruit does not lie. It reflects what has been consistently present. Take a moment to consider what is growing in your life—patience or frustration, peace or anxiety, kindness or reaction. This is not for condemnation, but for clarity. When you see the fruit, you can begin to understand the environment—and from there, begin to align it more fully with truth and love **In Christ**.

BRIDGE TO SECTION 5

When truth and love are working together, growth begins—but growth was never meant to remain isolated.

A healthy environment does not produce a single strong branch. It produces a living tree.

And this is where the vision expands.

Because the goal of Christ is not just formed individuals—but a fully joined, fully supplied, living Body.

Which leads us into the next reality...

EVERY PART SUPPLYING CREATES A LIVING BODY

SECTION 5. EVERY PART SUPPLYING CREATES A LIVING BODY

Life flows when every part gives and receives.

Core Scripture —

Ephesians 4:16 (KJV)
"From whom the whole body fitly joined together and compacted by that which every joint supplieth... maketh increase of the body unto the edifying of itself in love."

The end goal is not a few strong individuals, but a fully joined and living Body. Growth was never designed to stop at personal maturity—it was always meant to flow outward into connection. What has been formed within the life now begins to move between lives.

This is where the picture shifts from branches to a whole tree. Not isolated limbs reaching in different directions, but a living organism—connected, supplied, and growing together. Every part matters here. Not just the visible parts, but the hidden ones.

Not just the strong, but the developing. Not just those who lead, but those who quietly support.

Christ did not design His Body to function through a few while the many observe. He designed it so that every part carries something of value. Something to give. Something to receive.

And when this exchange is active, the Body becomes alive— not just structured, but flowing.

This is where the environment of truth and love begins to move. What was once internal becomes relational. What was once forming now begins to supply.

1 CONNECTION IS THE DESIGN, NOT INDEPENDENCE

The Body only functions when it is joined.

Independence may feel strong, but it was never the design. A disconnected part cannot supply, and it cannot receive. It may still exist, but it cannot function as intended.

In Christ, connection is not optional—it is essential.

Each life is placed within the Body so that it can both contribute and be strengthened. This is not about control or dependence on people—it is about alignment within something greater than ourselves.

A branch cut off may look the same for a moment...
but life is no longer flowing. Connection is where life moves.

2 EVERY PART HAS A SUPPLY

No part is without purpose.

The Body does not grow because a few parts are strong—it grows because every part supplies something. Some supplies are visible. Others are quiet. Some lead from the front. Others strengthen from within.

But all are necessary.

This restores dignity to the reader. You are not waiting to become useful—you already carry something that contributes to the life of the Body. Your presence, your growth, your faithfulness, your love—all of it becomes supply when it is connected **In Christ**.

You are not extra. You are essential.

3 SUPPLY FLOWS THROUGH RELATIONSHIP

Life moves through connection, not isolation.

Supply is not transferred through position—it flows through relationship. It is in the daily interactions, the shared moments, the encouragement, the correction, the presence of one another that life begins to move.

This is where truth and love take on form. Not as ideas, but as lived experience between people.

A word spoken at the right time. A quiet act of kindness. A steady presence when someone is struggling.

These are not small things. They are the ways the Body builds itself.

Supply is not always loud—but it is always powerful.

4 WHEN EVERY PART SUPPLIES, THE BODY GROWS ITSELF

Growth becomes natural when supply is active.

The Body does not need to be forced into growth. When every part is connected and supplying, increase happens organically. Strength builds. Stability forms. Maturity spreads.

This is the wisdom of Christ's design.

Instead of relying on constant external input, the Body begins to edify itself. Life flows from within. Each part contributing. Each part strengthening the other.

This removes pressure from a few and places value on all.

The Body grows best when it grows together.

5. EVERY PART SUPPLYING CREATES A LIVING BODY

The end goal is not a few strong individuals, but a fully joined and living Body.

What Christ began by giving, what formation stabilized, and what truth and love nurtured—now comes alive through connection. Every part matters. Every supply counts. Every life contributes.

Maturity is not measured by how well a person stands alone, but by how well they are joined. Each part both gives and receives, strengthening the whole.

This is where the structure becomes alive—not just a framework of truth, but a functioning organism, growing together in God's love In Christ.

The fivefold supply is not a collection of titles—it is a flow of support. Each grace carries something the others do not, and together they create a Body that is stable, aligned, outward-reaching, safe, and grounded in truth.

SUMMARY

1. APOSTLES LAY WHAT OTHERS BUILD UPON

Apostles are sent ones—but not just sent to go, sent to lay. They establish what others can safely build upon. Their work is not measured in moments, but in what remains.

They bring order, direction, and structure. They see how things fit together so growth is not scattered, but supported. Without this supply, people may grow—but not necessarily in the right direction.

You cannot build forward on what has never been properly laid. Apostolic grace gives the Body something solid to stand on so maturity has somewhere to take root.

2. PROPHETS KEEP THE BODY ALIGNED WITH THE HEART OF GOD

Prophets do not exist to impress—they exist to align. Their strength is not in prediction, but in perception. They help the Body stay connected to what is true.

They bring clarity where things drift. They strengthen what is right and expose what is out of place—not to tear down, but to restore direction.

Without this supply, the Body can remain active while quietly losing alignment. Prophetic grace brings it back— again and again—into the flow of God's love.

3. EVANGELISTS AWAKEN LIFE AND KEEP THE BODY BREATHING OUTWARD

Evangelists carry a life that reaches beyond itself. They are not just communicators—they are connectors, drawing people into the reality of God's love.

They awaken hearts. They stir beginnings. They bring people into the first steps of life In Christ, where everything is alive with possibility.

Without this supply, the Body can turn inward. Evangelists keep it breathing outward—reminding it that life is meant to be shared, not stored.

4. PASTORS CREATE SPACE WHERE LIFE CAN GROW SAFELY

Pastors form environments where people are known, supported, and able to grow without fear. They care for lives —not as controllers, but as protectors and nurturers.

Growth requires safety. Without it, people either withdraw or perform. Pastoral grace removes both, allowing people to be real, to heal, and to strengthen steadily.

This is where maturity becomes relational—not just what a person knows, but how they are held within the Body.

5. TEACHERS ESTABLISH TRUTH THAT MAKES GROWTH STABLE

Teachers bring clarity to what can otherwise feel out of reach. They make truth understandable, usable, and dependable.

They do not just inform—they establish. They give language to what God is doing and help people walk it out with confidence.

Without this supply, growth becomes unstable. With it, maturity becomes consistent—lived, not just experienced.

Closing Anchor

When each part supplies what it has received, the Body is no longer a structure being built—it becomes a life being lived. Not isolated strength, but shared strength. Not scattered growth, but joined growth.

This is the living Body—formed, aligned, and moving together... In Christ.

GUIDED DISCOVERY

1. **Where are you currently connected—and where might you be functioning independently?**

Take a moment to look honestly at your connections. Not just attendance or proximity, but true relational connection. Are you known? Are you allowing others to speak into your life?

Independence can feel strong, but it often limits both your growth and your ability to supply others. Recognizing this opens the door to re-engage in the flow of the Body.

2. What supply do you already carry that others could benefit from?

You may be overlooking what you bring because it feels normal to you. But what is natural to you may be exactly what strengthens someone else.

Consider your encouragement, your consistency, your perspective, your care. These are not small things—they are part of the life flow of the Body. When you begin to see this, you step into your place with confidence, not pressure.

3. How can you intentionally give and receive supply this week?

Supply is not accidental—it is lived. This could be as simple as reaching out, listening, sharing truth with kindness, or allowing someone to support you where you need it. Growth happens when the flow becomes intentional.

Small steps taken in love create real movement over time.

CLOSING BRIDGE — THE LIVING BODY

What began as a structure has now become something more. Not just a framework... but a living, breathing Body.

Christ as the Head. Truth as the direction. Love as the environment. People as the supply. All working together.

This is not theory.
This is life **In Christ**.

And when every part finds its place...
the Body does not just stand—

it lives.

CHAPTER 6. THE OTHER GRACES OF THE BODY

The strength you don't see is often the life you feel most

Core Scripture
"Having then gifts differing according to the grace that is given to us..." — Romans 12:6 (KJV)

Not every grace stands in front—but every grace carries something essential.

There are parts of the Body that are seen, and there are parts that are felt. The visible may draw attention, but the hidden is what sustains life. Without it, things may still gather... but they no longer function as a living organism.

In the previous chapter, we explored gifts that establish, reveal, and demonstrate the life of God. Here, we step into the graces that **carry, support, and continue that life daily**.

These are not occasional expressions—they are **lifestyle supply lines**, quietly moving God's love through the Body In Christ.

These graces rarely come with titles. They are not built for platforms. But they show up—again and again—meeting needs, strengthening people, and holding things together. And without them, the strongest structure begins to strain.

1. SERVICE AND HELPS CARRY THE DAILY LOAD

Some graces don't announce themselves—they simply show up and lift what needs lifting.

Service (Romans 12) and **helps** (1 Corinthians 12) form the muscle and movement of the Body.

These are the people who see a need and step into it without waiting for permission, recognition, or structure. They don't ask, *"Is this my role?"* They ask, *"Does this need love?"*

This grace is deeply practical. It carries chairs, prepares meals, fixes problems, fills gaps, and quietly removes burdens from others.

What looks natural on the outside is often flowing from something deeply spiritual within—a heart aligned with God's love in action. Without it, the Body becomes heavy and dependent on a few. With it, everything becomes light, responsive, and alive.

2. EXHORTATION AND ENCOURAGEMENT STRENGTHEN THE HEART

Some graces don't lift the load—they lift the person carrying it.

Exhortation (Romans 12) is more than advice—it is the ability to speak life at the right moment. It steadies the discouraged, refocuses the distracted, and strengthens the weary. It says, *"You're not done. Keep going. There's more in you than you think."*

This grace carries timing. It knows when to speak, how to speak, and when to stay silent. It doesn't push people—it builds them.

Without it, truth can feel heavy. With it, truth becomes livable. This is how the Body avoids burnout—not by removing responsibility, but by strengthening one another in love.

3. GIVING AND STEWARDSHIP RELEASE SUPPLY

Some graces don't carry or speak—they release.

Giving (Romans 12) is not about amount—it is about flow.

It recognizes that what has been placed in our hands is not meant to stop with us, but to move through us. Time, energy, resources, opportunities—each becomes a channel when aligned with God's love.

This grace sees supply differently. It doesn't ask, *"How much do I have?"* but *"Where can this become life?"* True giving flows from freedom, not pressure—from love, not obligation. When active, the Body stops functioning like individuals and starts living like a connected organism. Stewardship protects that flow, ensuring what is given continues to multiply.

4. MERCY, HOSPITALITY, AND COMPASSION CREATE SAFE SPACE

Some graces don't build the structure—they make it safe to live inside.

Mercy (Romans 12) moves toward pain. **Hospitality** (1 Peter 4:9) creates room for belonging. Compassion carries both. Together, they form the relational covering of the Body—the reason someone stays instead of leaving, heals instead of hiding, and receives truth without fear.

This is where your foundation becomes visible: mercy, compassion, patience. These are not just values—they are operational graces. Without them, truth feels sharp. With them, truth becomes restorative.

This is the environment where people grow—not perfectly, but safely.

5. LEADERSHIP, ORDER, AND ADMINISTRATION HOLD THINGS TOGETHER

Some graces don't stand in front—they hold everything in place.

Leadership (Romans 12) and **administration** (1 Corinthians 12) provide clarity, direction, and structure so the Body does not drift. This is not about control—it is about alignment. These graces help answer: *Where are we going? How do we move together? What matters now?*

They organize without suffocating and guide without dominating. They serve the mission, not themselves. Without this grace, even strong people scatter. With it, the Body moves as one—each part functioning within a shared direction.

6. CREATIVE AND WORSHIPFUL EXPRESSIONS REVEAL THE HEART

Some graces don't explain—they express.

Music, creativity, craftsmanship, and **storytelling** are often overlooked, yet they carry something unique: they reveal what words cannot. Throughout scripture, expression has been used to reflect God's love and presence, opening hearts and drawing people into truth.

This is not decoration—it is communication at the level of the soul.

A song can reach where a sermon cannot. A story can unlock what logic cannot. These graces remind us that the Body is not only functional—it is beautiful.

7. INTERCESSION AND HIDDEN FAITHFULNESS SUSTAIN THE UNSEEN

Some graces are almost entirely invisible—but without them, everything weakens.

Intercession—standing in the gap, carrying others before God—is one of the deepest forms of love.

It often happens alone, unseen, and uncelebrated. Yet it shifts atmospheres, strengthens people, and prepares ground others will walk on.

Faithfulness lives here—quiet obedience, steady presence, showing up again and again. This is not dramatic, but it is powerful. Because in the Kingdom, what is hidden is never wasted.

BRIDGE — INTO SECTION 1

If there is one place where this becomes immediately visible, it is in the grace of service.

Because before anything is revealed...
before anything is recognized...

something has to be carried.

And often, the ones carrying it...are not the ones being seen.

SECTION 1 — SERVICE AND HELPS CARRY THE DAILY LOAD

Some of the strongest parts of the Body are the ones you rarely notice— until they're missing.

There are graces in the Body that don't arrive with a microphone.
They don't introduce themselves, and they don't need a platform to feel complete.

They simply show up... and things start working.

A chair gets carried.
A meal appears.
A burden quietly lifts off someone else's shoulders.

And most of the time, no one stops to ask who did it.

This is the grace of service.
This is the gift of helps.

It is not driven by recognition, and it is not sustained by applause.
It flows from something far deeper—a life that has aligned itself with God's love in action, where seeing a need naturally becomes meeting a need.

Not because it *has to*...
...but because it *wants to*.

1. SEEING WHAT OTHERS WALK PAST

This grace begins with sight—not natural sight, but a kind of awareness that notices what others overlook.

Where some see a room, they see what's needed in the room.

Where some see a person, they see what's weighing on that person.

It's not intrusive.
It's not controlling.
It's simply attentive.

And that attentiveness becomes the doorway to love in motion.

This is often where the Spirit quietly nudges—
"That... right there... that's yours to lift."

And when that moment is met with willingness, something powerful happens:

Love becomes visible.

2. MOVING WITHOUT WAITING FOR PERMISSION

Service does not stand still waiting to be assigned. It doesn't need a title to function, and it doesn't need a system to validate it.
It moves because it understands something many miss:

If the Body needs it... it belongs to the Body.

There is a freedom in this grace that breaks the cycle of hesitation. Not reckless independence—
but confident alignment.

It doesn't ask,
"Is this my role?"

It asks,
"Does this need love?"

And in that question, the whole structure begins to lighten.

3. STRENGTH THAT DOESN'T NEED TO BE SEEN

Helps is one of the strongest structural graces in the Body—
and one of the quietest.

It carries weight without announcing it.
It reinforces what others build without needing to stand in
front of it.

Like the internal framing of a house, you don't see it when
everything is finished...
but without it, nothing stands.

This is strength without spotlight.

**And because it is not fueled by visibility, it doesn't
collapse when no one notices.
It just keeps holding.**

4. THE MARTHA MOMENT — AND THE TWIST

At first glance, Martha looks like the perfect picture of this
gift.

She's moving.
Serving.
Carrying the load.

While others are sitting, she's making things happen. But
then comes the moment that turns the whole picture:

*"Martha, Martha, thou art careful and troubled
about many things:
But one thing is needful..."* — Luke 10:41–42 (KJV)

And here's the twist...

Martha wasn't wrong for serving.
She was misaligned in *how* she was serving.

Her service had quietly shifted from *flowing from love...*
to *striving for validation.*

From
"I love to"
to
"Why am I the only one?"

And in that shift, the very grace designed to bring life...
started carrying frustration instead.

5. SERVICE THAT FLOWS, NOT STRIVES

The correction Jesus gives is not a rebuke of service—it's a realignment of source. Service must flow from being anchored... not from trying to prove something. Because when service flows from God's love:

It stays light.
It stays joyful.
It stays sustainable.

But when it flows from comparison, pressure, or expectation:

It becomes heavy.
It becomes draining.
It eventually burns out.

The difference is not in the *action...*
It's in the *source.*

One is striving.
The other is flowing.

6. THE GIFT THAT KEEPS EVERYTHING MOVING

Without service and helps, the Body becomes slow, heavy, and dependent on a few. With it, everything changes.

Movement increases.
Burden decreases.
Connection strengthens.

What looks like "small" actions becomes the very thing that keeps the entire structure alive. This is not a background gift.

This is the gift that allows *all the others* to function.

BRIDGE TO SECTION 2

If service and helps carry the daily load, then something must guide how that load is carried. Because movement alone is not the goal.

Direction matters.
Alignment matters.
Maturity matters.

And this is where we begin to see the next layer of grace unfold...

Not just people who *do*—
but people who help others *grow*.

SECTION 2.
EXHORTATION AND ENCOURAGEMENT STRENGTHEN THE HEART

Some graces don't lift the load—they lift the person carrying it.

Core Scripture:
"He that exhorteth, on exhortation..." — *Romans 12:8 (KJV)*

There are moments in life where the weight doesn't need removing—it needs **strengthening**.

This is where **exhortation** steps in. Not as noise, not as pressure, but as a steady voice that reaches into the middle of a person's struggle and reminds them who they are *In Christ.*

Exhortation is not about having the right answer—it's about bringing the right **spirit** into the moment. It sees beyond fatigue, beyond confusion, beyond temporary failure, and calls something higher forward.

It doesn't deny reality... it **reframes it in the light of God's love**.

This is why the Body needs it so deeply. Truth alone can instruct, but encouragement gives a person the strength to **live what they know**.

Without it, people can carry knowledge and still feel heavy. With it, even difficult truth becomes something they can stand up inside.

1. EXHORTATION SPEAKS LIFE AT THE RIGHT MOMENT

Timing is everything with this grace.

It doesn't flood people with words—**it meets them *exactly where they are***. A single sentence, spoken at the right time, can shift a whole direction.

This is the voice that says:

- *"You're not done."*
- *"Get back up."*
- *"There's more in you than you think."*

Not as hype… but as truth spoken through love.

This grace listens first, discerns quietly, and then speaks with purpose. And because it is aligned with God's love, it lands not as pressure—but as **strength**.

2. EXHORTATION SEES WHAT OTHERS MISS

Where others see struggle, this grace sees **potential in motion**.

This is where our scriptural picture comes into focus through
Barnabas, known as the *Son of Encouragement*.

When others hesitated with Saul (Paul), Barnabas stepped forward.

He didn't ignore Saul's past—he saw beyond it.

He didn't just speak encouragement—he **created opportunity**.

This is exhortation at its highest level:

calling out what someone can become before they have fully become it.

It is not blind positivity—it is **spirit-led vision** anchored in God's love.

3. EXHORTATION STRENGTHENS WITHOUT CONTROLLING

This grace does not push—it **builds**.

It doesn't try to take over someone's journey. It stands beside them and strengthens their ability to walk it.

There's a difference between:

- Telling someone what to do
- And strengthening them so they can do it

Exhortation always chooses the second.

It respects process. It honors growth. It gives space for people to rise rather than forcing them to perform.

4. EXHORTATION KEEPS THE BODY FROM BURNOUT

Without encouragement, even the strongest people grow weary.

Responsibility without reinforcement leads to fatigue. Truth without warmth can slowly drain the heart.

But when exhortation is present:

- The weary are refreshed
- The discouraged are steadied
- The distracted are refocused

It doesn't remove responsibility—it **makes it sustainable**.

Without it, truth can feel heavy. With it, truth becomes livable.

This grace is the **breath between the bricks**—the unseen force that keeps the structure from becoming rigid and brittle.

5. EXHORTATION FLOWS FROM THE HEART OF GOD'S LOVE

At its core, this is not a personality trait—it is a **flow**.

Every true expression of encouragement carries the tone of heaven. It reflects the nature of God's love—patient, strengthening, and forward-moving.

The more a life is aligned *In Christ*, the more natural this becomes.

Not forced.
Not scripted.
Not motivational for the sake of it.

But real.

And when it flows, it changes environments.

It turns pressure into possibility.
It turns heaviness into movement.
It turns individuals into a strengthened, living Body.

GUIDED DISCOVERY

1. Where in your life do you feel the weight more than the strength right now?

Sometimes the issue is not the load—it's the lack of reinforcement around it. Take a moment to recognize where encouragement has been missing. This isn't about weakness—it's about identifying where God's love may want to meet you through others... or even through your own renewed perspective.

2. Who has spoken life into you at the right moment before?

Think back to a time when someone's words shifted something in you. What did they say? How did it land? This helps you recognize the pattern of exhortation—and how powerful simple, timely encouragement can be when it flows from truth and care.

3. Where could you become that voice for someone else this week?

Exhortation doesn't require a platform—it requires awareness. Look around. Someone near you is carrying something quietly. What would it look like to speak one honest, strengthening sentence into their situation? Not to fix them... but to lift them.

GIVING AND GENEROSITY RELEASE THE FLOW OF LOVE

SECTION 3. GIVING AND STEWARDSHIP RELEASE SUPPLY

What flows through your hands reveals what lives in your heart.

Core Scripture —

Romans 12:8 (KJV)
"...he that giveth, let him do it with simplicity..."

Some graces don't carry or speak—they release.

Giving is one of the purest expressions of God's love in motion. It does not begin with abundance, and it does not depend on surplus. It begins with recognition—that what has been placed in our hands was never meant to stop there.

This is not limited to finances, though it includes them. Giving moves through every part of life:

Time.
Energy.
Resources.
Opportunities.

It is the quiet awareness that something in your world could become life in someone else's.

And when this grace is alive, the question changes.

Not, *"How much do I have?"*
But, *"Where can this become life?"*

There is a simplicity to it. A freedom. A lack of strain. It flows without noise, without pressure, without the need to be seen. It simply recognizes a gap—and steps into it.

In the early church, there was a man who lived this way without needing to define it.

Barnabas didn't build a name around generosity—he simply allowed what was in his hands to become strength for others. Land was sold. Needs were met. People were lifted. And just as quietly, he stood beside those others were unsure of and made room for them to grow.

That same current still moves through the Body today—not drawing attention to itself, but leaving strength wherever it passes.

This is giving as a lifestyle.
Not a moment—but a movement.

We give because He already gave

1. GIVING SEES SUPPLY AS SOMETHING THAT MOVES

Giving begins with sight.

Not natural sight—but a deeper awareness that what you have carries potential beyond you.

It recognizes that supply is not ownership—it is assignment. What comes into your hand is entrusted for a moment, with the possibility of becoming life somewhere else.

This is why giving feels different when it is aligned with God's love. It is not forced. It is not calculated for recognition. It is simply responsive. A need appears, and something within you answers it.

This is the beginning of flow.

2. GIVING FLOWS FROM FREEDOM, NOT PRESSURE

True giving cannot be produced by demand.

Pressure may create moments of release, but it cannot sustain a lifestyle. Only freedom can do that. And freedom comes from trust—trust that your source is not what you hold, but the One you are connected to In Christ.

This is why simplicity matters. Giving becomes clean when it is free from inner negotiation. No performance. No reluctance. No hidden expectation.

Just willingness. And in that space, giving becomes light.

We give not because we have to but because we love to...

3. GIVING EXTENDS BEYOND FINANCES INTO LIFE ITSELF

Finances are only one expression of supply.

Some of the most powerful giving never passes through a bank account. It shows up as time given when it would have been easier to walk away. Energy invested when you are already stretched. Encouragement offered when someone is close to giving up.

Even opportunity itself can be given—opening a door for someone else to step through.

This is where giving becomes relational.

**Giving is no longer about *what leaves your hand...*
but about *what reaches another life.***

4. STEWARDSHIP DIRECTS WHAT GIVING RELEASES

Giving releases.
Stewardship directs.

Because not everything that is released is automatically multiplied. What is given must also be handled—wisely, faithfully, and with care—so that supply continues rather than leaks.

Stewardship asks:

Is this being placed where it can grow?
Is this strengthening what God is building?
Is this aligned with love, or just relieving pressure?

This is where the grace deepens.

It is no longer just about responding—it is about positioning.

When giving and stewardship work together, something stable begins to form.

5. A HEALTHY FLOW CREATES A LIVING BODY

When supply moves properly, the Body changes.

It stops functioning like isolated individuals...
and begins living like a connected organism.

Needs are met.
Strength is shared.
Weight is distributed.

No one part carries everything.
No one part is left empty.

This is the effect of unseen giving working beneath the surface—quietly holding the whole structure together.

Much like that early example we saw, where one man's simple decision to release what he had strengthened far more than a single moment. It helped establish a pattern—one where supply moved freely, and people grew because of it.

Giving is the Body, living as it was designed.

Guided Discovery

1. Where in your life do you already have something that could become life for someone else?

Look beyond finances. Consider your time, attention, skills, or experience. Often, the supply is already present—it simply hasn't been seen through the lens of purpose yet. When you recognize it, giving becomes natural.

2. What tends to interrupt your flow—fear, hesitation, or uncertainty about where to place it?

Sometimes the resistance isn't lack—it's internal. Fear of not having enough, uncertainty about timing, or even past experiences can slow the flow. Bringing this into the light helps restore movement.

3. Where could greater stewardship strengthen what you release?

Consider where your current output is going. Is it producing life? Is it aligned with God's love? Stewardship doesn't limit generosity—it focuses it, so that what you release continues to multiply beyond the moment.

Giving is not about losing something. It is about participating in how God's love moves.

And when it is joined with faithful stewardship, it becomes more than generosity—it becomes a living supply line within the Body of Christ.

As supply begins to move, something else becomes essential.

Because what is released must be carried, coordinated, and sustained in daily life.

This leads us into the next grace—

Where direction, structure, and faithful oversight ensure that what flows...continues to function.

SECTION 4. MERCY, HOSPITALITY, AND COMPASSION CREATE SAFE SPACE

Some graces don't build the structure —they make it safe to live inside.

Core Scripture:

Romans 12:8 — *"...he that sheweth mercy, with cheerfulness."*

Anchor Scripture: 1 Peter 4:9 — *"Use hospitality one to another without grudging."*

Not everything that builds the Body is visible in its structure. Some things are felt long before they are understood.

A life can be well-formed—clear in truth, grounded in direction, active in purpose—and still feel difficult to enter. Not because anything is wrong... but because something is missing. Something unspoken. Something that allows a person to *exhale*. This is where mercy, hospitality, and compassion quietly step in.

They do not compete with truth.
They prepare the heart to receive it.

They do not remove responsibility.
They make growth *approachable*.

They do not draw attention to themselves...
but without them, people slowly drift to the edges.

This is the relational covering of the Body. And when it is
present, something subtle but powerful happens: People
stop bracing... and start opening.

It is rarely loud.
Often barely noticed in the moment.

But like the quiet life of **Dorcas (Tabitha)**, its impact is
revealed not in what it claims... but in what remains in the
lives of others.

1 MERCY MOVES TOWARD, NOT AWAY

Mercy does not stand at a distance and evaluate—it steps
closer and understands.

It sees the struggle, the inconsistency, the weakness... and
instead of withdrawing, it leans in. Not to excuse, but to
restore. Not to overlook truth, but to carry it in a way that
can be received.

There is a strength in mercy that is often misunderstood. It
is not softness—**it is controlled strength.** The ability to
respond with care when reaction would be easier.

Mercy says:
"I see where you are... and I'm not leaving you there."

This is how people begin to come out of hiding. Because
they sense that they are not being measured...
they are being *met.*

And when mercy flows consistently, the environment begins
to shift.

Not into compromise...
but into *restoration*.

2 HOSPITALITY CREATES ROOM FOR BELONGING

Hospitality is more than opening a door—it is opening *space*.

Space in conversation.
Space in time.
Space in relationship.

It allows people to arrive without pressure to perform. To sit, to listen, to find their footing without being rushed into expectation.

True hospitality does not say, "Fit in."
It says, "There is room for you here."

And this goes far beyond physical settings. It shows up in how we listen. How we respond.
How we make room for people to grow at different speeds.

Hospitality removes the quiet tension that says, *"I don't know if I belong here."* And replaces it with something far more powerful:

"You're welcome here... while you grow."

This is how connection forms—not by force, but by freedom.

3 COMPASSION CARRIES WHAT OTHERS CANNOT

Compassion feels... but it does not stop there. It carries.

It steps into the weight someone else is under and helps hold it—not permanently, not instead of them—but *with* them, for a time. This is where love becomes tangible.

A meal prepared.
A need noticed.
A moment of care that arrives without being asked for.

These things may appear small on the surface... but they speak deeply into the human heart:

"You are seen."
"You matter."
"You are not alone."

Compassion does not always announce itself. Often, it is remembered long after the moment has passed. Like something quietly made...
and given at just the right time.

The kind of life that leaves evidence behind—not in words, but in people... much like those who once stood holding the garments Dorcas had made, each one telling a story without her needing to say a thing.

4 SAFE SPACE ALLOWS TRUTH TO HEAL, NOT HARM

Truth is essential—but the environment it enters determines how it is received.

Without mercy, truth can feel sharp.
Without hospitality, it can feel distant.
Without compassion, it can feel heavy.

But when these graces are present, truth changes its effect.

It still corrects.
It still aligns.
It still calls forward.

But it no longer pushes people away in the process. Instead of triggering defense... it invites response. Instead of producing shame... it opens the door to change.

This is the difference between being *right*...
and being *restorative*.

And this is where real growth begins to take hold.

Not forced.
Not fragile.

But rooted in an environment that can sustain it.

5 THE BODY BECOMES A PLACE PEOPLE CAN LIVE

A Body can be active, structured, and even effective...
but still not feel like a place to remain. These graces change that.

They turn movement into *home*.
They turn connection into *care*.
They turn truth into something people can actually *live inside*.

Not through noise or recognition...
but through quiet, consistent expressions of love— the kind that rarely stands in front...
yet would be deeply missed if it were gone.

This is where the earlier foundation becomes visible:

Mercy.
Compassion.
Patience.

Not just as values...
but as *operational graces*.

And when they are present, something deeper begins to form.

Not just a gathering...
but a people.

Not just a system...
but a living environment.

Not just individuals functioning...
but a Body that feels safe enough to grow *together*.

Quietly...
consistently...
like a life that leaves traces of care behind it wherever it goes.

GUIDED DISCOVERY

1. Where in your life do you naturally move toward people instead of away from them?

There are moments where your first instinct is not to withdraw, but to lean in. Pay attention to those spaces—they reveal how mercy is already working through you. Growth is not about forcing something new, but recognizing what is already alive and giving it room to strengthen.

2. In what environments have you felt most safe to be yourself—and why?

Think about what made those places different. Was it how people listened? How they responded? How they allowed space? These are not accidental—they are the result of these graces at work. What you have experienced, you are now able to extend.

3. Where could you create more room for others to belong this week?

This does not require a grand gesture. It may be a conversation, a moment of patience, or a simple act of care. Small spaces, consistently opened, become environments where people begin to settle and grow.

What mercy starts...
hospitality holds...
compassion carries.

And together, they create something the whole Body depends on:

A place where people don't just arrive...
they *remain*.

...because someone, somewhere in the Body,
has made it safe for them to do so.

BRIDGE TO SECTION 5

When people feel safe, something begins to unlock.

They stop holding back...
and start bringing what has been placed within them.

Because a safe environment does not just protect people—
it *releases* them.

And this is where the Body begins to shift again...

From being a place that receives...
to a people that *supplies*.

SECTION 5. LEADERSHIP, ORDER, AND ADMINISTRATION HOLD THINGS TOGETHER

Some graces don't stand in front— they hold everything in place.

Core Scripture:

"He that ruleth, with diligence..." — Romans 12:8

There is a kind of strength in the Body that is not always seen, but is always felt. It doesn't draw attention to itself, yet without it, everything begins to loosen, drift, and eventually fracture.

This is the grace of **leadership** and **administration**— quietly holding alignment so life can continue to flow.

Leadership, in its true form, is not about standing above others—it is about standing *responsible* for the direction things are moving.

Administration is not about control—it is about clarity. Together, they create a framework where people are not guessing their place, but growing into it.

And beneath this grace, there is often a quiet kind of preparation...
the kind that doesn't announce itself.

Like **Nehemiah** who once walked the broken walls of a city at night— not speaking yet, not directing yet...
just seeing, measuring, understanding what would be required to rebuild.

That kind of leadership doesn't rush.
It prepares so that when others step in, the work can *hold*.

1. DIRECTION GIVES MOVEMENT MEANING

Movement alone is not progress. Without direction, energy gets spent but nothing gets built.

Leadership answers the question: *Where are we going?*
It brings clarity to the path so effort becomes intentional.

Without direction, people:

- Work hard but feel lost
- Serve faithfully but without connection
- Drift into their own lanes without realizing it

But when direction is clear, something shifts.
Effort aligns. Movement gathers. Purpose becomes shared.

It often begins quietly—
with someone seeing what others haven't yet seen...
and carrying that vision carefully until it's time to speak.

2. STRUCTURE CREATES STRENGTH, NOT RESTRICTION

Structure often gets mistaken for control—but true structure is what allows life to *hold its shape.*

Administration answers the question: *How do we move together?*

It organizes:

- People into places where they function best
- Resources so they are used wisely
- Timing so things don't collide or collapse

Without structure, even strong people struggle.
Not because they lack heart—but because there is nothing stable to build on.

But when structure is healthy:

- People feel secure
- Roles become clear
- Growth becomes sustainable

Like placing families along a wall— each one strengthening the section in front of them...
not randomly, but intentionally...
so the whole structure stands.

3. ALIGNMENT PROTECTS UNITY

Unity is not automatic. It must be held.

Leadership and administration together answer: *How do we stay together while moving forward?*

Because without alignment:

- Vision fragments
- Effort divides
- Small misunderstandings grow into large separations

Alignment doesn't force sameness—it holds direction.

It allows:

- Different gifts to function without competing
- Different personalities to move without clashing
- Different roles to support, not pull apart

There is a wisdom in knowing where each person belongs—not by title... but by placement.

And when that happens, unity stops being fragile...
and starts becoming structural.

4. ORDER CREATES PEACE IN MOTION

Where there is no order, there is unnecessary strain.

Order answers: *What matters most right now?*

It brings:

- Priority into confusion
- Focus into distraction
- Calm into pressure

Without order:

- Everything feels urgent
- Energy gets pulled in too many directions
- Burnout becomes common

But with order:

- People know where to give their strength
- Effort becomes effective
- Peace settles into the process

It's the difference between reacting…
and rebuilding.

5. DILIGENCE KEEPS EVERYTHING FROM DRIFTING

Things don't usually fall apart suddenly—they drift slowly.

Leadership and administration answer: *How do we stay steady over time?*

This is where diligence comes in.

Not bursts of effort—but consistent attention:

- Checking alignment
- Adjusting where needed
- Strengthening weak points before they fail

Without diligence:

- Small gaps become large cracks
- Misalignment grows unnoticed
- The structure weakens quietly

But with it:

- Stability increases over time
- Trust builds
- The whole Body becomes dependable

It's the quiet refusal to come down from the work—
even when distraction calls...
even when pressure rises...
even when it would be easier to leave it half finished.

GUIDED DISCOVERY

1. Where in your life do you feel movement... but not clear direction?

Sometimes we are active, but not aligned. Recognizing this is not failure—it is awareness. Direction doesn't require starting over, just adjusting forward. What would shift if you paused long enough to ask where this is actually heading?

2. What areas of your life feel unstructured or scattered right now?

This isn't about control—it's about support. Where things feel heavy or chaotic, structure may be missing. What small adjustment could bring clarity or order back into that space?

3. Where might you be called to help hold things together for others?

Not everyone is called to the front—but many are called to strengthen what others stand on. This may already be happening quietly in your life. Where are you already bringing stability, even if no one has named it yet?

There is a grace that lifts...
a grace that speaks...
a grace that gives...
a grace that comforts...

And there is a grace that *holds it all together*.

Not loud.
Not central.
But essential.

Like **Nehemiah**—
who didn't build the wall alone...
but made sure it could be built *together*.

Without this grace, things drift.
With it, the Body moves as one.

———

Bridge to Chapter Close

And when these graces are in place—
service, encouragement, giving, mercy... and now leadership
and order—

Something powerful becomes visible: Not just a group of
people... but a functioning Body.

Every part different.
Every part needed.
Every part supplying.

And somewhere in the background...
someone is still making sure the structure holds...

...and someone else is still quietly making room for others to
belong.

SECTION 6. CREATIVE AND WORSHIPFUL EXPRESSIONS REVEAL THE HEART

Some graces don't explain—they express.

Core Scripture:
"I will praise thee, O Lord, with my whole heart; I will shew forth all thy marvellous works." — Psalm 9:1 (KJV)

Music, creativity, craftsmanship, storytelling, and **artistic expression** are often overlooked as "spiritual gifts," yet they carry something unique:

They reveal what words cannot.

There is a quiet thread running through scripture—moments where sound, poetry, and expression open what pressure never could.

A king finds peace, not through counsel, but through a harp—played by King David, a shepherd-turned-psalmist whose songs carried both heaven's joy and the weight of a human heart.

A nation finds its voice, not just through law, but through song. And generations later, those same words still reach into places untouched by explanation.

Not loud.
Not forced.
But steady... carrying something deeper than sound.

Throughout scripture, we see songs, instruments, poetry, and design used to reflect God's love and presence. These expressions open the heart, soften resistance, and draw people into truth through experience rather than explanation.

This is not decoration.
This is communication at the level of the soul.

A song can reach where a sermon cannot.
A story can unlock what logic cannot.
A crafted space can create peace before a word is spoken.

And somewhere in the background of it all... the sound of a harp still lingers.

1. EXPRESSION CARRIES WHAT EXPLANATION CANNOT

There are moments where truth is clear... but not yet received.

Not because it is wrong—
but because the heart is not open.

This is where creative grace steps in.

It doesn't argue.
It doesn't push.

It *invites*.

A melody can bypass resistance.
A story can slip past defenses.

A moment of beauty can quiet the noise long enough for truth to land.

This is why these graces matter.

They don't replace truth—
they prepare the ground for it.

And often, without a single word, something inside a person shifts...

Not because they were convinced—
but because they were *reached.*

2. WORSHIP CREATES AN ENVIRONMENT WHERE GOD'S LOVE IS FELT

There is a difference between knowing something is true...
and *feeling* it.

Worship bridges that gap.

It creates an atmosphere where the heart becomes aware of what has always been present. Not forced. Not manufactured. Just... revealed.

There is a quiet pattern in scripture—moments where sound becomes space.

Where tension eases.
Where heaviness lifts.
Where clarity returns.

Not through instruction...
but through presence.

And in those moments, something real happens:

The soul settles.
The spirit becomes attentive.
And God's love is no longer just understood...

It is *experienced*.

3. CREATIVITY REFLECTS THE NATURE OF THE CREATOR

We were not only made to function.

We were made to *create*.

To shape.
To design.
To bring something into form that did not exist before.

This is not accidental—it is reflective.

Creation itself speaks of a God who did not build a world of necessity alone...
but of beauty, variation, and expression.

And when this grace is active in the Body, something powerful happens: Spaces begin to feel different. Moments carry weight. Environments become intentional. Not because they are impressive—but because they are aligned.

A simple table set with care.
A room prepared with thought.
A piece of art, a line of poetry, a melody carried gently...

All of it becomes a quiet witness:

**God's love is not only true—
it is *beautiful*.**

4. HONEST EXPRESSION KEEPS THE HEART REAL

One of the greatest strengths of this grace...
is its honesty.

Creative expression does not require perfection.
It requires truth.

Joy can be sung.
Grief can be written.
Repentance can be poured out.

Nothing needs to be hidden. And this is where something deeper begins to flow: When the heart is allowed to express itself truthfully, it becomes *reachable* again.

Not hardened.
Not guarded.

Open.

There is a reason the songs of scripture carry both celebration and brokenness... Because real connection is not found in polished words— but in honest ones. And behind many of those expressions...
the same quiet pattern continues—

A life that brings everything before God,
not as performance...
but as relationship.

5. BEAUTY MAKES THE BODY LIVABLE

Structure is necessary.
Truth is essential.
Function is vital.

But without beauty... the Body can feel cold.

These graces don't hold the structure together—
they make people want to stay inside it.

They soften edges.
They warm spaces.
They create moments where people can breathe.

And this matters more than it seems. Because people don't
just grow where things are correct...
they grow where they feel safe enough to remain.

This is the quiet work of creative and worshipful expression:

Not drawing attention to itself—
but shaping the environment where life can flourish.

6. WHEN EXPRESSION FLOWS FROM GOD'S LOVE, IT BECOMES MINISTRY

Not all creativity carries life. But when it flows from God's
love... it becomes something more than expression.

It becomes *ministry*.

Not because of platform.
Not because of audience.

But because of source.

When a song flows from love, it carries peace.
When a story flows from love, it carries truth.
When something is created from that place, it carries
presence.

And people may not always be able to explain what they felt... But they will know they were touched by something real.

GUIDED DISCOVERY

1. Where does expression already exist in your life— and what is it carrying?

Take a moment to notice what naturally flows from you. It may not look like a stage or a spotlight. It could be the way you set a space, the way you speak, the way you create, the way you respond in quiet moments. These are not random— they are revealing something.

Ask yourself honestly: *Is what I express creating life, peace, and openness in others?* When expression flows from God's love, it carries more than creativity—it carries presence.

This is not about becoming someone else... it is about recognizing what is already moving through you and allowing it to align more deeply In Christ.

2. What happens in you when truth is expressed creatively instead of explained?

Think about moments where something reached you—not through instruction, but through experience. A song, a story, a moment of beauty that stayed with you. Why did it land?

Creative expression has a way of bypassing resistance and meeting the heart directly.

This question turns that awareness inward: *How might God's love want to flow through me in a way that reaches others the same way?*

Sometimes the most powerful ministry is not what you say—
it is what people feel when truth is expressed through you.

3. Is your expression flowing from pressure... or from relationship?

There is a difference between creating to be seen... and
expressing because something real is happening inside. One
drains. The other overflows.

Take a moment to check the source. Are you trying to
produce something... or are you responding to something
God is already doing within you?

When expression flows from relationship, it carries honesty,
peace, and depth. It doesn't strive—it *resonates*. And that
resonance is often what opens hearts far beyond what effort
ever could.

These graces remind us that the Body is not only
functional... it is beautiful. Not only structured...
but expressive. Not only built...
but alive.

And beneath it all—steady, consistent, and often
unnoticed... the sound of worship continues.

Not to be seen.
Not to be praised.

But to keep the heart open...
so everything else God is building can be received.

SECTION 7.
INTERCESSION AND HIDDEN FAITHFULNESS SUSTAIN THE UNSEEN

Some love is never seen on the platform, but it holds the platform up.

Core Scripture:
"And Moses returned unto the LORD, and said, Oh, this people have sinned a great sin... Yet now, if thou wilt forgive their sin—; and if not, blot me, I pray thee, out of thy book which thou hast written."
Exodus 32:31–32

Some graces are almost entirely invisible, but without them, everything weakens.

Intercession is one of those graces. It does not always stand in front of people. It often stands before God on behalf of people.

It carries names, burdens, weaknesses, failures, families, leaders, communities, and nations into the secret place where no applause is heard and no one else may ever know what was carried.

Moses understood this hidden place. He stood before Pharaoh in public, but some of his deepest work happened away from the crowd, standing between God and the people when they were weak, afraid, rebellious, or lost.

He carried them when they could not carry themselves. He pleaded when they had no words. He remained faithful when the people he served did not always understand the cost.

This is where the Body is supported from the inside out.

1. INTERCESSION STANDS IN THE GAP

Intercession is not simply praying about people. It is standing with love between need and mercy.

It sees the gap and steps into it.

Moses did this again and again. When Israel failed, he did not simply condemn them and walk away. He went before the Lord. He carried the weight of their condition into the presence of God. That does not mean he excused sin, softened truth, or avoided correction. It means his first movement was not abandonment.

It was love.

This grace is often hidden because its work happens where only God can see.

A person may be strengthened by a prayer they never heard. A family may be held together by intercession they never knew was happening.

A leader may find courage because someone, somewhere, was standing in the gap.

In the Kingdom, unseen does not mean unused.

2. HIDDEN FAITHFULNESS KEEPS SHOWING UP

Faithfulness is not always dramatic.

Sometimes it is simply showing up again.

Again with prayer.
Again with patience.
Again with obedience.
Again with love.

Moses' faithfulness was not tidy. It was tested by delay, complaint, pressure, disappointment, and people who sometimes wanted to go back to the very bondage God had delivered them from.

Yet he kept returning to the Lord. He kept listening.

He kept leading.

He kept carrying what had been placed in his hands.

This is one of the quiet strengths of the Body of Christ.

Not everyone is called to speak loudly. Not everyone is called to lead visibly. But some are called to remain steady in hidden places, where consistency becomes a form of spiritual strength.

Faithfulness may not look powerful in the moment.

But over time, it becomes a pillar.

3. PRIVATE PRAYER PREPARES PUBLIC GROUND

Much of what looks sudden in public has been prepared slowly in private.

The breakthrough may be visible.
The prayer was hidden.

The healing may be celebrated.
The intercession was quiet.

The moment may look instant.
The ground was watered for years.

Moses' public leadership was sustained by private encounter. He went up the mountain. He entered the tent. He met with God away from the noise of the camp. What he carried back to the people was formed in the unseen place.

This matters because the Body can become too impressed with what is visible.

But the visible branches are often alive because hidden roots are still drinking.

Intercessors, faithful servants, quiet prayer-carriers, and hidden worshippers may never be known by the crowd, but heaven knows their names.

And heaven keeps better records than people do.

4. HIDDEN LOVE DOES NOT NEED TO BE SEEN TO BE REAL

One of the hardest parts of hidden faithfulness is that it may not be recognized.

No one may thank you.
No one may understand the burden.
No one may see the tears.
No one may know how many times you stood before God for someone else.

But love that needs recognition to keep going is still learning freedom.

Moses did not intercede because Israel deserved it. He interceded because love had made him responsible before God. That is a holy thing. Not control. Not ownership. Not ego dressed in spiritual language.

Just love carrying what love has been given.

In Christ, hidden faithfulness becomes worship. The quiet prayer, the steady obedience, the private tears, the unseen sacrifice—none of it is wasted.

The Father sees in secret.

And what the Father sees, the Father values.

5. THE BODY IS STRENGTHENED BY WHAT IT CANNOT SEE

A healthy Body is not sustained only by visible ministry. It is sustained by hidden supply.

The person praying before sunrise.
The grandmother carrying her family before God.
The quiet believer asking the Father to strengthen the weary.
The faithful servant who keeps showing up when no one claps.
The intercessor who senses a burden and responds with love.

These graces may not organize the room, preach the sermon, lead the song, or carry the microphone. But they help hold the atmosphere in which those things can live.

Moses reminds us that someone must go before God for the people. Someone must carry the burden when others are too weak, too distracted, or too wounded to carry it themselves. Someone must remain faithful in the hidden place.

In the Kingdom, what is hidden is never wasted.

Guided Discovery

1. Where in your life might God be inviting you to stand in the gap for someone else?

This may not begin with a dramatic burden. It may begin with a name that keeps coming to mind, a situation that keeps stirring your heart, or a quiet awareness that someone needs strengthening.

Intercession often starts simply. You notice. You care. You carry that person before the Father in love. And in that hidden place, God's love begins to move through you without needing anyone else to see it.

2. What hidden faithfulness have you been tempted to undervalue because no one notices it?

Sometimes the most important obedience feels ordinary. Showing up. Praying again. Serving again. Remaining steady when nothing seems to change.

But heaven does not measure faithfulness by applause. It measures love by truth, endurance, and obedience. What feels small to the soul may be deeply significant in the Spirit.

3. How would the Body grow stronger if hidden faithfulness was honored as much as visible gifting?

We would stop measuring value by visibility. We would begin to see that the Body is held together not only by those who speak, lead, build, or create, but also by those who quietly sustain the unseen.

This would make room for a deeper kind of honor. The intercessor, the faithful servant, the quiet encourager, and the hidden prayer-carrier would no longer feel like background figures. They would be recognized as living supply within the Body of Christ.

Bridge to Chapter 7

And this brings us to the responsibility that follows every gift.

Whether a grace is visible or hidden, dramatic or quiet, public or private, it has still been given by God. It is not meant to be buried, ignored, compared, or used for self-importance. It is meant to be stewarded.

The gifts of Christ are not decorations on a spiritual shelf. They are living graces placed within people for the building of the Body.

So now we turn from recognizing the gifts...
to using what has been given.

Because love that has been received
must eventually become love that is lived

CHAPTER 7. THE GIFTS ARE GIVEN TO BE USED

Bearing, Pruning, and Faithful Cultivation

Core Scripture
"Every branch in me that beareth fruit, he purgeth it, that it may bring forth more fruit." — John 15:2 (KJV)

Introduction

The foundation has been laid.

We began with the Spirit—the unseen support that holds everything together. From there, we formed the vessel, understanding the body as the structure through which life is lived.

We then stepped into the soul—the interpreter, the steersman, the place where meaning is formed and direction is chosen.

From there, relationships built the living fabric, and stewardship shaped how value flows through our hands.

Then we lifted our eyes to Christ and His Body—seeing that we are not meant to live this life alone, but as part of something living, connected, and purposeful.

Now we arrive at the response.

Because everything that has been built up to this point leads to one simple question:

What will you do with what you've been given?

This chapter shifts from structure to cultivation. Not theory—but practice. Not potential—but participation.

Like a well-built home with land around it, what surrounds the structure now matters. The driveway begins to form through repeated use. The trees begin to grow—or they don't. What is planted either becomes fruitful... or remains unused potential.

This is the gardener's chapter.

Here we learn that gifts are not just received—they are **tended**.
They are used, grown, stewarded, refined, and expressed over time.

Because in the Kingdom, nothing living is meant to stay still.

SECTION 1. WHAT IS PLANTED MUST BE USED OR IT WITHERS

What is given must move. A gift left unused does not remain in its original strength—it slowly fades into potential that was never realized. Like a tree never exposed to wind or season, it may exist, but it does not mature. Use is the beginning of growth.

This is where hesitation is broken. You don't start with mastery—you start with movement. As what has been placed in your life begins to flow, clarity forms, strength builds, and fruit begins its early stages.

Life responds to use.

SECTION 2. GROWTH REQUIRES CULTIVATION, NOT COMPARISON

Each life grows differently, and comparison disrupts that process. When attention shifts to others, what has been entrusted to you is neglected. Growth becomes strained, uneven, and often discouraged.

Cultivation brings focus back to responsibility. What has God placed in your care? When attention returns to watering, strengthening, and tending your own life, growth becomes steady again. Healthy fruit forms where consistent care is present.

SECTION 3. STEWARDSHIP PROTECTS THE FLOW OF LIFE

What flows into your hands carries purpose. Gifts, time, energy, and resources are not random—they are entrusted. Stewardship ensures that this flow remains clean, directed, and effective.

Here, maturity begins to show. Not in what someone has, but in how they handle it. When stewardship is present, life is not wasted or scattered. It becomes dependable, and that dependability strengthens everything connected to it.

SECTION 4. PRUNING IS NOT LOSS —IT IS PREPARATION FOR MORE

There are seasons where things are cut back—not because they were wrong, but because they are no longer aligned. Pruning removes what drains life so that what remains can grow stronger.

Though it may feel like loss, it is actually refinement. Focus sharpens. Direction clears. Strength concentrates. What remains is no longer divided—it is prepared to bear more fruit with greater purpose.

SECTION 5. FAITHFULNESS OVER TIME PRODUCES A HARVEST

Fruit forms slowly. It is the result of consistency, not intensity. A life that continues to show up, align, and respond in love will eventually carry visible evidence of growth.

Harvest is not forced—it is revealed. And when it comes, it is not just for the one who grew it. It becomes supply for others. This is the cycle of life in the Body: what was given to you becomes life through you.

SECTION 6. WHO IS THE SOURCE OF ALL THIS LIFE... AND HOW DO WE STAY CONNECTED TO HIM?

All growth, all fruit, all supply traces back to one source.

Without connection to Him, even the strongest branch cannot sustain life. This closing section brings everything back to where it began—not with effort, but with relationship. Not with striving, but with abiding.

Here we return to the core truth:
we do not produce life—we remain connected to the One who does.

And in that connection, everything we have built, formed, and cultivated finds its true strength, its true purpose, and its unending supply.

SECTION 1. WHAT IS PLANTED MUST BE USED OR IT WITHERS

What is given must move, or it begins to fade.

Core Scripture:
"For unto every one that hath shall be given... but from him that hath not shall be taken away even that which he hath." — Matthew 25:29 (KJV)

What is placed in your life is not meant to sit—it is meant to flow. A gift does not remain in its original strength when left unused. It does not stay "safe." It slowly drifts into something weaker... quieter... less certain... until what once felt alive begins to feel distant.

This is not punishment—it is design.

Just as a tree strengthens under wind, deepens through seasons, and bears fruit through continual exchange with its environment, so it is with what God has planted in you. Without movement, there is no development. Without expression, there is no maturity. What is alive must move to remain alive.

This is where many hesitate—not because nothing has been given, but because what has been given feels small, unclear, or untested.

The expectation of clarity before movement becomes the very thing that prevents it. But growth does not begin with clarity—it begins with use.

You don't start with mastery.
You start with movement.

As you begin to use what is in your hand—however simple it may seem—something begins to shift. Understanding forms. Strength develops. Confidence grows—not in theory, but through lived experience. What once felt uncertain begins to take shape.

Life responds to use.

This is where stewardship quietly begins—not in abundance, but in willingness.

1. RECOGNIZING WHERE YOU ARE HOLDING BACK

Many are not lacking—they are hesitating.

There are places in your life where something has already been placed in your hands. A capacity. A sensitivity. A way of helping, speaking, building, giving, or seeing. And yet, instead of moving with it, you've held it... weighed it... questioned it... or compared it.

Sometimes it feels too small to matter.
Sometimes it feels too exposed to risk.
Sometimes it feels like it needs more time.

But often, it is already enough to begin.

Holding back doesn't preserve a gift—it pauses its growth. What feels like "waiting for the right moment" can quietly become a pattern of delay. And over time, delay begins to feel like normal.

But the truth is simple:

If it's in your hand... it's ready to move.

2. SEEING IT IN MOTION — THE PARABLE OF THE TALENTS

Jesus told a story of a master who entrusted his servants with resources before leaving on a journey (Matthew 25:14–30). Each was given something—not equally, but intentionally.

Two of them moved immediately.
They used what they were given.
They traded, worked, and engaged.

The third did something different.

He buried what he was given.

Not out of rebellion... but out of fear.
Not out of laziness... but out of hesitation.

He preserved it—but he never used it.

And when the master returned, the difference was clear. The ones who used what they were given had grown. What they carried had multiplied. But the one who buried his gift had nothing new to show—only what had been given at the start.

This is the principle:

Use creates increase.
Hesitation creates stagnation.

The issue was not what was given—
it was what was done with it.

3. LOCATING YOUR CURRENT SEASON

So where does this land for you?

Are you in a place where something has already been stirring—but you've been waiting for clarity before stepping forward?

Are you holding something that feels small... wondering if it really matters?

Or have you already begun moving—but feel unsure if it's "enough"?

Growth seasons don't always feel dramatic. Often, they feel simple. Repetitive. Quiet. Like showing up again... doing the same thing again... offering what you have again.

This is how roots form.

You don't need to have the full picture.
You just need to respond to what's already in your hand.

Because movement reveals what thinking never will.

4. THE PRINCIPLE REMAINS — USE BRINGS LIFE

The pattern does not change.

What is used grows.
What is withheld weakens.

Not because it was taken...
but because it was never released.

This is how life works in the Body.

When what has been placed in each part begins to flow,
something larger than the individual begins to form. Supply
increases. Strength connects. Growth becomes shared, not
isolated.

But it begins here—personally.

With you choosing to move.

Not perfectly.
Not completely.
Just faithfully.

Because the moment something begins to flow...
it begins to grow.

5. GUIDED DISCOVERY — STARTING WHERE YOU ARE

**1. What is something already in your life that you
sense could be used more intentionally?**

There is often something present—simple, familiar, easy to
overlook. It may not feel like a "gift," but it carries the
potential to become one through use. Recognizing it is the
first step toward movement.

**2. Where have you been waiting for clarity instead
of taking a small step forward?**

Clarity often follows movement, not the other way around.
Identifying where hesitation has replaced action helps break
the cycle and opens the door to growth.

**3. What is one simple way you could begin using
what you already have this week?**

Not a big step—just a real one. Something practical. Something doable. Because growth does not begin with intensity—it begins with consistency.

Bridge to Section 2

Once movement begins, something else becomes just as important...

Not just that we use what has been given—
but *how* we use it.

Because growth is not only about activity—
it is about direction.

And this is where we begin to learn:

What needs to be strengthened...
and what needs to be pruned.

WHAT GROWS MUST BE SHAPED OR IT BECOMES WILD

SECTION 2. GROWTH REQUIRES CULTIVATION, NOT COMPARISON

What you tend will grow—what you compare will weaken.

Core Scripture:
"But they measuring themselves by themselves, and comparing themselves among themselves, are not wise." — 2 Corinthians 10:12 (KJV)

Every tree grows differently.

Some rise quickly.
Some deepen slowly.
Some spread wide.
Others grow upward with quiet strength.

None of them are wrong—because each one was designed with purpose.

Comparison disrupts this design. It shifts your attention away from what has been placed in your care and redirects it toward what was never entrusted to you. Instead of tending your own ground, you begin measuring your growth against someone else's shape, pace, or fruit.

And in that moment, something subtle happens:

You stop cultivating... and start evaluating.

But growth does not respond to comparison.
It responds to care.

Cultivation brings everything back into focus. What has been placed in your life? What needs watering? What needs strengthening? What needs protection? Growth is not automatic—it responds to attention, consistency, and intention over time.

When you return to what is yours to tend, something settles. Pressure lifts. Clarity returns. And what once felt scattered begins to grow in a steady, personal way.

This is how maturity forms—not by measuring...
but by cultivating.

1. RECOGNIZING WHERE COMPARISON HAS CREPT IN

Comparison rarely announces itself—it quietly redirects your focus.

It shows up when you begin questioning your pace because someone else seems further ahead. When what you carry starts to feel smaller because someone else's expression appears stronger. When your attention drifts from stewardship... to measurement.

And once comparison takes root, it does two things:

It either discourages you—
or distorts you.

Discouragement says, "I'm not enough."
Distortion says, "I need to be like them."

Both pull you away from truth.

Because what has been given to you was never meant to look like what was given to someone else. And the moment you start measuring your growth by another branch, you lose sight of your own.

But awareness breaks the pattern.

When you see it—you can release it.
And return to what is actually yours to tend.

2. SEEING IT IN MOTION — PETER AND JOHN WALK DIFFERENT PATHS

After His resurrection, Jesus spoke with Peter about what lay ahead for him (John 21:18–22). It was personal. Specific. A path uniquely shaped for Peter's life.

But Peter did something very human.

He looked over at John... and asked,
"Lord, and what shall this man do?"

Jesus' response was simple—and sharp in its clarity:

"What is that to thee? follow thou me."

In other words:

Peter—your path is yours.
John's path is his.

Comparison had entered the moment. Not out of rebellion—but out of curiosity. Yet even that small shift was enough to redirect focus away from responsibility.

Jesus brought it straight back.

Follow me.

This is the pattern:

Your growth is not measured against another's calling.
It is shaped by your response to what God has placed before you.

3. LOCATING YOUR GROUND TO TEND

So where does this meet you?

Are you looking sideways more than forward?

Has someone else's growth caused you to question your own?

Or have you been trying to shape your life around what you see working for others... instead of what is actually in your hands?

Cultivation begins with clarity:

What has been placed in your care? Not in theory. Not in potential. But right now.

It may be small.
It may feel ordinary.
It may seem unfinished.

But it is yours.

And when you begin tending what is yours—watering it, strengthening it, protecting it—growth becomes steady. Not rushed. Not forced. But real.

The soil responds to attention...

4. THE PRINCIPLE REMAINS — CULTIVATION PRODUCES STRENGTH

The pattern holds true:

What you tend… grows.
What you neglect… weakens.
What you compare… distracts.

Growth is not found in watching—it is found in working with what has been given.

And over time, something begins to form:

Roots deepen.
Structure strengthens.
Fruit develops—not because it was chased… but because it was cultivated.

This is where peace returns to the process.

You are no longer trying to become someone else.
You are becoming fully aligned with what has been placed in you.

And that is where real strength lives.

GUIDED DISCOVERY

1. Where in your life have you been comparing your growth to someone else?

Take a moment to notice where your attention has shifted outward. Comparison often hides in subtle thoughts, but once seen, it loses its hold and allows you to refocus on what is yours.

2. What has already been placed in your care that needs more intentional cultivation?

Look at what is present—not what is missing. Growth begins by tending what already exists, even if it feels small or incomplete.

3. What is one practical way you can "water" or strengthen this area this week?

Simple, consistent action creates real growth. Choose one step—something tangible—that moves you from awareness into cultivation.

Bridge to Section 3

As cultivation begins, something else becomes clear...

Growth is not just about tending what is there—
it is also about allowing what is *not needed* to be removed.

Because healthy growth requires more than care...

It requires pruning.

WHAT IS FRUITFUL MUST BE PRUNED FOR MORE FRUIT

SECTION 3.
STEWARDSHIP PROTECTS THE FLOW OF LIFE

What flows to you must be handled faithfully, or it loses its purpose.

Core Scripture:
"Moreover it is required in stewards, that a man be found faithful." — 1 Corinthians 4:2 (KJV)

Gifts are not possessions—they are trusts.

What comes into your hands—time, energy, resources, influence, opportunity—is not random. It is entrusted. Not to be controlled, but to be carried with care, wisdom, and intention. Stewardship is the quiet responsibility of protecting the purpose of what has been given.

Without stewardship, flow becomes scattered.

Time slips.
Energy drains.
Resources drift without direction.

But when stewardship is present, something changes. There is clarity in how things are handled. There is intention behind decisions. There is care in what is allowed to remain —and what is not.

This is where maturity begins to show.

Not in how much someone has...
but in how faithfully they handle what they've been given.

A well-stewarded life becomes steady. Dependable. Grounded. And that dependability strengthens everything connected to it. Because in the Body, flow is not sustained by abundance alone—it is sustained by faithfulness.

Stewardship protects the flow of life.

1. RECOGNIZING WHERE FLOW IS BEING LOST

Not all loss is obvious.

**Sometimes loss is not what is taken—
but what is slowly leaking.**

Time given without intention.
Energy spent without direction.
Opportunities missed through distraction or delay.

It can feel subtle. Normal, even. But over time, lack of stewardship begins to show—not in one moment, but across many small ones. What could have grown... didn't. What could have multiplied... scattered.

And the root is often not inability— but inattention.

Stewardship begins with awareness.

Where is flow being lost?
Where are things slipping through your hands—not because they weren't given, but because they weren't guarded?

Because what is not protected...
will not remain purposeful.

2. SEEING IT IN MOTION — JOSEPH AND FAITHFUL STEWARDSHIP

Joseph's life (Genesis 39–41) was marked by changing environments—but consistent stewardship.

In Potiphar's house, he was entrusted with responsibility—and he handled it faithfully.
In the prison, with nothing visible to gain—he still stewarded what was placed in front of him.
When he stood before Pharaoh, he didn't just interpret a dream—he presented a plan.

Store in the years of plenty.
Prepare for the years of famine.

Joseph understood something deeper than opportunity—he understood stewardship.

He didn't control the flow...
but he protected its purpose.

And because of that, when increase came, it didn't overwhelm him—it multiplied through him.

This is the pattern:

Faithfulness in small places prepares you for greater flow. And stewardship determines whether increase becomes life... or waste.

3. LOCATING WHAT HAS BEEN ENTRUSTED TO YOU

So where does this land?

What is currently flowing into your life?

Not what you hope for— but what is already present.

Your time.
Your energy.
Your relationships.
Your responsibilities.
Your opportunities.

Stewardship begins here—not in the future, but in the present.

Are these things being handled intentionally... or reactively?

Are they being directed... or simply used up?

Because what you do with what is *now* in your hands determines what can be trusted to you next.

You don't need more to begin stewarding well.
You need awareness... and intention.

Because faithful handling today...
creates capacity for tomorrow.

4. THE PRINCIPLE REMAINS — FAITHFULNESS SUSTAINS FLOW

The pattern is consistent:

What is stewarded well... remains purposeful.
What is neglected... becomes scattered.
What is handled faithfully... becomes trustworthy.

This is how flow is protected.

Not through control...
but through care.

Over time, this builds something deeper than success—it builds dependability. And dependability strengthens the Body, because others can lean on what is steady.

This is where growth matures into responsibility.

Where what flows through your life...
is not just used—but multiplied with intention.

Because when stewardship is present...
life continues to flow clean.

GUIDED DISCOVERY — STEWARDING WHAT YOU HOLD

1. Where in your life do you sense things are being used... but not intentionally stewarded?

Look for areas where flow exists but lacks direction. These are often the places where small adjustments can create significant change.

2. What has already been entrusted to you that needs greater care or attention?
Stewardship begins by recognizing what is already present. Not what is missing—but what is currently in your hands.

3. What is one practical step you can take this week to steward this area more faithfully?
Choose something simple and measurable. Stewardship grows through consistent, intentional action—not pressure or perfection.

Bridge to Section 4

As stewardship strengthens, something begins to emerge…

Not just movement.
Not just growth.
Not just order.

But fruit.

Because when what is given is used…
and what is growing is cultivated…
and what is flowing is stewarded…

Something begins to appear that was not there before.

FRUIT IS THE EVIDENCE OF A LIFE WELL TENDED

SECTION 4. PRUNING IS NOT LOSS—IT IS PREPARATION FOR MORE

What is cut back is not rejected—it is being refined for greater fruit.

Core Scripture:
"Every branch that beareth fruit, he purgeth it, that it may bring forth more fruit." — John 15:2 (KJV)

Every life that begins to bear fruit will eventually face pruning.

Not because something is wrong...
but because something is working.

This is where the journey shifts. What once felt like growth through addition now begins to include reduction. Certain things are cut back. Some opportunities fall away. Certain directions no longer remain. And at first, it can feel confusing—even discouraging.

Because it looks like loss.

But it is not loss—it is preparation.

Pruning removes what drains life so that what remains can grow stronger. It refines focus. It strengthens direction. It clears space for deeper, more effective growth. What is trimmed is not always bad—it is simply no longer aligned with where growth is going.

This is why pruning is one of the hardest parts of the journey.

It requires trust.

Because you are not just growing...
you are being shaped.

And in the Kingdom, pruning is not punishment—it is a sign of investment. It means growth is being prepared for its next level. What remains after pruning is not weaker—it is more focused, more capable, and positioned for greater fruit.

1. RECOGNIZING THE FEELING OF REDUCTION

Pruning often feels like something is being taken away.

An opportunity that once felt right begins to close.
A direction that once held momentum begins to slow.
An area you invested in no longer carries the same life.

And the natural response is to question:

"Did I get it wrong?"
"Did I lose something?"
"Should I hold on tighter?"

But pruning does not feel like growth—
it feels like reduction.

And this is where many resist the process. They try to hold onto what is being released. They attempt to revive what is being trimmed. Not realizing that what they are trying to preserve is the very thing that is limiting what could come next.

But when you recognize pruning for what it is, something shifts.

You stop resisting...
and begin trusting.

2. SEEING IT IN MOTION — THE VINE AND THE VINE DRESSER

Jesus paints the picture clearly in John 15.

He is the vine.
We are the branches.
And the Father is the vine dresser.

The one who tends.
The one who sees.
The one who knows what must remain... and what must be removed.

And here is the key:

The branches that don't bear fruit are the ones that get pruned.

Because fruit reveals potential—and potential invites refinement.

The vine dresser is not reacting randomly. He is working intentionally. Every cut is precise. Every removal has purpose. Not to diminish the branch—but to increase its capacity.

This is the pattern:

Pruning is not about what you lost—
it is about what brings focus and what you are being prepared to carry.

3. LOCATING WHERE PRUNING MAY BE HAPPENING

So where does this meet you?

Is there something in your life that once carried momentum... but now feels like it is being reduced?

Is there a direction that seems to be closing... even though it once felt right?

Or are there areas where your energy is being pulled back... forcing you to simplify?

These moments are not always setbacks. They are often adjustments.

Pruning brings clarity by removing excess. It narrows focus. It redirects energy. It strengthens what remains by no longer allowing life to be divided across too many directions.

And while it may feel uncomfortable, it is often one of the clearest signs that growth is being refined—not stopped.

Because what remains after pruning...
is what matters most.

4. THE PRINCIPLE REMAINS — PRUNING PRODUCES GREATER FRUIT

The pattern holds:

What is left untouched can become overgrown.
What is overgrown becomes weakened.
What is pruned becomes strengthened.

Pruning is not about reduction for its own sake—it is about multiplication through focus.

When excess is removed, life is no longer divided. Strength gathers. Energy concentrates. Growth becomes intentional and effective.

This is where fruit increases—not by doing more...
but by becoming more aligned.

And over time, what once felt like loss is revealed as gain. Because what remains is no longer competing for life—it is now fully supported by it.

This is the wisdom of pruning: Less... becomes more.

GUIDED DISCOVERY

1. Is there something in your life that feels like it is being reduced or taken away?

Take a moment to look again—not through loss, but through alignment. What may feel like removal could actually be preparation.

2. Where might you be holding onto something that no longer carries the same life?

Pruning often requires release. Identifying where you are resisting change helps open the door to growth.

3. What would it look like to trust this process instead of trying to control it?

Trust does not mean passivity—it means alignment. Consider one way you can cooperate with what is shifting instead of resisting it.

Once pruning has done its work...

Something begins to appear that cannot be manufactured—only revealed.

Not effort.
Not activity.
Not intention alone.... But fruit.

FRUIT REVEALS WHAT HAS BEEN TRULY FORMED

SECTION 5.
FAITHFULNESS OVER TIME PRODUCES A HARVEST

What is done consistently in love will eventually become visible in fruit.

Core Scripture:
"And let us not be weary in well doing: for in due season we shall reap, if we faint not." — Galatians 6:9 (KJV)

Fruit does not appear overnight.

It forms slowly. Quietly. Often without recognition. There are long stretches where nothing seems to change on the surface, yet beneath it all, something steady is taking place. Roots are deepening. Structure is strengthening. Life is building in ways that cannot yet be seen.

This is where many lose heart.

Not because growth isn't happening—
but because it isn't visible.

We live in moments, but growth happens over time. And when the process feels slow, the temptation is to look for intensity—to push harder, do more, or try to accelerate what was never meant to be rushed.

But the Kingdom does not respond to intensity—
it responds to faithfulness.

Faithfulness is not dramatic. It is consistent. It shows up again… and again… and again. It keeps aligning, keeps responding, keeps tending—even when there is no immediate reward.

And over time, something begins to change.

Not suddenly…
but surely.

Because harvest is not something you force—
it is something you arrive at.

And when it comes, it carries more than personal reward. It becomes supply. What was once given to you now flows through you. Strength becomes support. Growth becomes provision. Life multiplies outward.

This is the rhythm of the Kingdom:

What is planted… grows.
What is grown… matures.
What matures… produces.
And what is produced… feeds others.

1. RECOGNIZING THE TEMPTATION TO QUIT EARLY

The greatest challenge in growth is not starting—
it is continuing.

There are moments when the effort feels unnoticed. When the results feel delayed. When what you are doing seems small compared to what you hoped for. And in those moments, the thought begins to surface:

"Is this really working?"

This is where many step away—not because they failed, but because they stopped too soon.

Because harvest lives on the other side of consistency.

Not occasional effort.
Not bursts of motivation.
But steady, faithful movement over time.

The danger is not that nothing is happening—
it's that you don't see what *is* happening.

And if you quit in that space...
you walk away from what was already forming.

2. SEEING IT IN MOTION — THE SOWER AND THE SEED

Jesus described the Kingdom like a man who scatters seed on the ground (Mark 4:26–29).

He plants... and then something interesting happens.

He goes to sleep.
He rises.
Day after day.

And the seed grows—
he knows not how.

First the blade.
Then the ear.
Then the full grain.

There is a process unfolding that does not depend on constant interference—but on faithful participation. The sower does his part. The soil does its work. Time carries the rest.

And eventually…
harvest comes.

Not forced.
Not rushed.
But right on time.

This is the pattern:

Growth happens in ways you cannot always see…
but faithfulness keeps you connected to the outcome.

3. LOCATING YOUR CURRENT RHYTHM

So where does this meet you?

Are you in a season where you've been showing up—but not seeing much return yet?

Are you feeling the weight of repetition… wondering if it's making a difference?

Or have you been starting and stopping—never quite staying long enough to see what could form?

Faithfulness is not about doing everything—it is about staying with what matters.

Where is your ground?
What has been placed in your care?
What have you already begun?

Because harvest is tied to continuity.

You don't need to do more.
You need to remain.

To keep showing up.
To keep aligning.
To keep responding in love.

Because what feels like repetition...
is actually formation.

4. THE PRINCIPLE REMAINS — TIME REVEALS WHAT IS TRUE

The pattern does not fail:

What is planted faithfully... grows steadily.
What is grown steadily... matures naturally.
What matures naturally... produces fruit.

Time is not the enemy of growth—
it is the environment of it.

And over time, what was once invisible becomes visible. What felt uncertain becomes established. What seemed small becomes significant—not through sudden change, but through sustained faithfulness.

This is where trust deepens.

Because you begin to see that nothing done in alignment with God's love is wasted. Every act of faithfulness contributes to something larger than the moment it was done in.

And when the harvest comes...

It carries evidence.

Not of effort alone—
but of endurance.

GUIDED DISCOVERY

1. Where in your life have you been tempted to stop because you haven't yet seen results?

Look honestly at the places where discouragement may be pulling you away from something that is still forming beneath the surface.

2. What is one area where you know you need to remain consistent rather than intense?
Growth responds to steady presence, not pressure. Identify where consistency would make the greatest difference.

3. What would it look like for you to "stay the course" this week?
Not adding more—but continuing what matters. Choose one thing to remain faithful in, regardless of how it feels.

Bridge to Section 6

And as harvest begins to appear...

One question rises above all the others:

Where did this life come from...
and how do we remain connected to it?

Because behind every seed...
every season...
every harvest...

There is a source.

THE SOURCE OF LIFE AND THE SECRET OF REMAINING

SECTION 6. WHO IS THE SOURCE OF ALL THIS LIFE... AND HOW DO WE STAY CONNECTED TO HIM?

Life does not come from us—it flows through us when we remain connected to Him.

Core Scripture:
"I am the vine, ye are the branches... he that abideth in me, and I in him, the same bringeth forth much fruit: for without me ye can do nothing." — John 15:5 (KJV)

All growth traces back to one source.

Every seed that formed.
Every root that deepened.
Every branch that strengthened.
Every fruit that appeared.

None of it began with us.

And none of it can continue without Him.

This is where everything settles. Not in effort... but in relationship. Not in striving... but in abiding. Because the life we have been cultivating was never self-generated—it has always been sustained by connection.

Without that connection, even the strongest branch cannot hold life. It may look stable for a time. It may carry the memory of fruit. But slowly, quietly, life begins to fade—not because the branch failed, but because the source was no longer flowing.

But when connection remains...

Everything else finds its place.

Growth becomes natural.
Stewardship becomes clear.
Pruning becomes understandable.
Fruit becomes sustainable.

Because the life is not coming from us—
it is flowing through us.

This is the core truth:

We do not produce life.
We remain connected to the One who does.

And in that connection, everything we have built, formed, and cultivated finds its true strength, its true purpose, and its unending supply.

1. RECOGNIZING WHEN CONNECTION HAS WEAKENED

Disconnection rarely feels dramatic—it feels gradual.

A slowing.
A dryness.
A subtle shift from flow... to effort.

What once felt alive begins to feel heavy. What once flowed naturally now requires pushing. Not because the work has changed—but because the source connection has weakened.

And the instinct in that moment is often to try harder.

Do more.
Fix more.
Push through.

But the issue is not effort—
it is connection.

Because no amount of effort can replace what only
relationship provides.

And when you recognize this, everything begins to simplify.

You don't need to force life back into the branch...
you return to the vine.

2. SEEING IT IN MOTION — MARY AT THE FEET OF JESUS

In Luke 10:38–42, two responses to Jesus are shown in the same space.

Martha is active. Moving. Serving. Carrying responsibility.
Mary is still. Present. Sitting at His feet.

Both are near Him—
but only one is fully connected.

Martha becomes overwhelmed—not because she is doing wrong things, but because she is carrying them without resting in the relationship. Mary chooses something different—not inactivity, but priority.

Connection before activity.

Jesus calls it "the good part."

Because everything that flows outward must first be grounded inward.

This is the pattern:

Life is not sustained by what we do for Him—
but by how we remain with Him.

3. LOCATING YOUR POINT OF CONNECTION

So where does this meet you?

Are you still moving... but feeling less life in what you're doing?

Are you carrying responsibility... but sensing a quiet heaviness underneath it?

Or have you slowly shifted from being with Him... to working for Him?

Connection is not complicated—but it is intentional.

It is found in returning.
In pausing.
In realigning your attention back to Him.

Not as a task—
but as relationship.

Because connection is not something you achieve—
it is something you remain in.

And when that connection is restored, something changes:

What felt heavy becomes light.
What felt forced begins to flow again.

Because the source is no longer distant—
it is present.

4. THE PRINCIPLE REMAINS —
ABIDING SUSTAINS EVERYTHING

The pattern is unchanging:

Disconnected branches cannot sustain life.
Connected branches cannot help but bear fruit.

This is the foundation underneath everything we have built
in this chapter.

Use matters.
Cultivation matters.
Stewardship matters.
Pruning matters.
Faithfulness matters.

But none of it functions apart from connection.

Because the life behind it all is not human effort—
it is divine flow.

And abiding keeps that flow open.

Not occasionally.
Not when needed.
But continuously.

This is where peace settles into the process.

You are not trying to produce something for God—
you are living connected to Him.

And from that place...
everything else follows.

5. GUIDED DISCOVERY — RETURNING TO THE SOURCE

1. Where in your life do you sense you've been relying more on effort than connection?

Look gently. Not with pressure—but with honesty. Awareness is the first step back into alignment.

2. What helps you personally reconnect with Him in a real and present way?

Not routine for its own sake—but relationship. Identify what brings you back into awareness of His presence.

3. What is one simple way you can prioritize connection this week?

Keep it real. Keep it consistent. Because connection grows through presence, not performance.

Bridge — Closing the Chapter

And here, the whole picture comes together...

What is planted must be used. What grows must be cultivated. What flows must be stewarded. What is fruitful must be pruned. What is tended faithfully will produce a harvest.

But above it all— Everything depends on the Source.

Because the gifts were never the goal...
They were always the expression of a life connected to Him.

And when that connection remains...

The life never runs dry...

CHAPTER 8. THE GIVER, THE HEAD, AND THE FLOW

Everything begins with Him, flows through Him, and returns to Him.

Core Scripture:
"For of him, and through him, and to him, are all things: to whom be glory for ever. Amen." —
Romans 11:36 (KJV)

This was never about gifts.

Not at the core.

Not at the beginning...
and not at the end.

It has always been about life.

The life that comes from God.
The life that flows through Christ.
The life that finds expression in His Body.

Everything you have walked through in this book—every structure, every grace, every function, every movement—has been pointing to one reality:

Life is not something we create.
It is something we receive... and release.

In the beginning, the ground was prepared.

You saw where life grows from.
Not from outward strength—but from inward alignment.
Not from performance—but from foundation.

Then the root was revealed through fruit.

Because what is unseen will always become visible.
And what is visible will always reveal what is true.

The foundational graces formed the base.

Mercy.
Compassion.
Patience.
Loving-kindness.
Truth.
Forgiveness.
Justice.

Not as ideals...
but as living expressions of God's nature forming within a life.

Then the structure rose.

Gifts were set in place.
Not as titles...
but as functions.

Not to elevate individuals...
but to build the Body.

Then came the flow of growth.

Christ gave people.
Not to replace Him...
but to reflect Him.

Not to gather followers...
but to form maturity.

And through that, the Body began to stabilize—
not tossed, not scattered, but grounded and growing
together.

Then your vision widened.

You saw the other graces.

The quiet ones.
The unseen ones.
The ones that carry, strengthen, supply, and sustain.

Service.
Encouragement.
Giving.
Leadership.
Mercy.
Intercession.
Creativity.

Not spotlight gifts...
but life-giving ones.

The hidden current that keeps everything alive.

Then the shift came.

From understanding...
to responsibility.

What is given must be used.

What grows must be cultivated.

What flows must be stewarded.

What is fruitful must be pruned.

What is tended faithfully will produce a harvest.

And through it all, one truth remained:

Nothing grows by accident.
Everything responds to life.

And now we arrive here.

Not at the end...
but at the center.

Because everything you have seen—
every pattern, every principle, every process—

depends on one thing:

Connection.

Christ is not just the giver of gifts.

He is the Head of the Body.

Not distant.
Not symbolic.
But living.

Active.
Present.
Flowing.

And the Body does not function apart from Him.

It does not grow apart from Him.
It does not sustain itself apart from Him.

Because the life is not in the structure. The life is in the connection. This is where everything becomes simple again.

You do not have to manufacture life.
You do not have to force growth.
You do not have to carry what was never yours to produce.

You remain.

Connected.

Aligned.

Responsive.

And from that place, everything begins to flow. Not in theory...but in reality.

You begin to use what is in your hands—naturally.

You begin to cultivate what is growing—intentionally.

You begin to steward what is flowing—with clarity.

You allow what needs pruning—to fall away.

You remain faithful—over time.

And fruit appears.

Not forced.

Not borrowed.

Not imitated... But real.

This is the rhythm of a life In Christ:

Planted... and used.
Used... and grown.
Grown... and stewarded.
Stewarded... and refined.
Refined... and fruitful.
Fruitful... and shared.

And through it all—

Connected.

Because the goal was never the gift. The goal was always the flow.

And now the question is not just:

"What have I been given?"

The question now becomes:

"What is flowing through me?"

Because what flows through you... becomes life for someone else.

Strength for someone else.
Clarity for someone else.
Hope for someone else.

This is the Body.

Not individuals trying to succeed—
but a connected life supplying itself in love.

So this is not where you close the book. This is where you now walk it.

Not by just trying to remember everything—
but by staying connected to the One who holds it all
together.

Stay close.

Stay responsive.

Stay in the flow. **In Gods Love In Christ**

Because the Source has not run dry…. And it never will.

To Him be the glory… Amen…

Continue the journey...

1. Discover God's Love — *The Book of Christ*

2. Learn to Live In Christ — *The Doctrine of Christ*

3. Grow in the Body — *The Body of Christ*

4. Walk in the Gifts — *The Gifts of Christ*

For more resources, teachings, and related works, visit bodyofchrist.online

www.ingramcontent.com/pod-product-compliance
Lightning Source LLC
Chambersburg PA
CBHW032248070726
47590CB00017B/3128